What They *Really* Said series

MAO

What They *Really* Said series

Other available titles in this series :

What Darwin *Really* Said, by *Benjamin Farrington*

What Freud *Really* Said, by *David Stafford-Clark*

What Shaw *Really* Said, by *Ruth Adam*

What Jung *Really* Said, by *E. A. Bennet*

What Marx *Really* Said, by *H. B. Acton*

What St Paul *Really* Said, by *J. W. C. Wand*

PHILIPPE DEVILLERS

MAO

Translated by
Tony White

Schocken Books · New York

Published in the United States of America in 1969
by Schocken Books Inc., 67 Park Avenue, New York, N.Y. 10016

First published in the German language in 1967
under the title *Was Mao Wirklich Sagte*, by
Verlag Fritz Molden, Vienna

Contents

Foreword

China, the Cultural Revolution, Mao Tse-tung's thought . . .
The international Communist movement split down the middle
between Moscow and Peking; Asia, Africa and Latin America
awakened, receiving quotations and other writings from President Mao by the ton . . . Each day, thousands of voices from
the East chant: "Chairman Mao said . . ."

What exactly did Chairman Mao say? In the fifty years since
he began to make speeches, write and be published, he has
tackled many of the essential problems of our age. His writings
known to the West have increased so enormously in volume that
it is now becoming difficult to see them as a whole, in perspective
or even in outline. The same problem seems to have arisen in
China too, because it has been found necessary to publish a work
of quotations, the famous but very abstract *Little Red Book*.

Is it, however, possible to delve into Mao Tse-tung's thought
by reading a series of extracts thus isolated from works which are
in themselves an integral part of his life? It seems that this
question can be answered only in the negative. Hence the present
work.

What is known as "the Chinese example" has gained too
much importance today for anyone to cling on to clichés,

"maxims" and hearsay, or to stop looking for what in Mao Tse-tung's works really concerns China, naturally, but also the contemporary world. These works, it must be said from the start, do in fact have profound value as textbooks : Mao's experiences in China, first from 1927 to 1937, then from 1945 to the present day, are being repeated elsewhere, in South-East Asia, in Latin America, in Central Africa, perhaps in the Middle East too. The lessons of history must not be forgotten or ignored by those waging a struggle that is sometimes so similar.

It would be genuinely impossible to understand and present Mao's thought objectively without seeing his character in relation to his entire historical and personal evolution. What he has said, is saying today, and will say tomorrow about the United States, the U.S.S.R., Vietnam, socialism and culture, has neither meaning nor justification (and is therefore not comprehensible) except in so far as it relates to the experiences of China and himself over nearly sixty years. If he takes issue with the United States, it is because the United States helped Chiang Kai-shek, and it must therefore also be known why Mao is fighting Chiang Kai-shek. If he takes sides in Vietnam, it is because Vietnam borders China and because he sees the United States carrying out almost exactly the same policy there as she did in China from 1945 to 1950, or in another form in Korea from 1945 to 1960. If he takes issue with the U.S.S.R. – in fact only seriously since 1958 – it is because it seemed to him that Nikita Khrushchev had become the *de facto* ally of the United States, and that "Khrushchevism" or " goulash Communism" seemed to be stifling the Soviet Union's revolutionary vocation, its will to resist American expansionism.

But the "anti-imperialist dimension" is itself only *one* aspect – although a basic one – of Mao Tse-tung's thought. What is vital, because it is the very basis of all his works, is to know *why* Mao wants a new China, and why he does not think it possible except as a result of a long Revolution, in which armed struggle is to play a primary role. This is to move from the Chinese context, in which Mao worked, into the universal.

In Mao Tse-tung's vast – more than 2,500 pages – but sometimes so arid works, it was absolutely essential from the start, to preserve everything which, while explaining China, also had universal value, and which, in going beyond the present day, acquired permanent significance.

In such a light, China's modern history emerges as a kind of allegory, in which the names of Yüan Shih-k'ai or Chiang Kai-shek, for instance, become symbols. They must from now on unquestionably be taken as such. Throughout this history, Tradition is pitted against Progress, Oppression against Rebellion, the Landlords against the Peasants, Reaction against Revolution, the Chinese People against Foreign Imperialism. Where the Chinese see "Chiang Kai-shek", other peoples read in "Farouk", "Nury Said", "Batista", "Ngo Dinh Diem", "General Ky", etc. The West will better understand why Mao is so widely read in the Three Continents and how lessons are learned from him.

Must we therefore become obsessed, as they are across the Atlantic, with the Marxist character of Mao's thought? History provides many examples of revolutions of the type which he began and pursued. In his day, Voltaire gave a brief account of a more or less comparable revolution in Europe, as described in the following passage :

Sweden was rent by civil wars . . . About the year 1520, this unhappy kingdom was horribly harassed by two tyrants: the one was Christian II, king of Denmark, a monster whose character was entirely composed of vices without the least ingredient of virtue; the other an archbishop of Upsal, and primate of the kingdom, as barbarous as the former . . .

Gustavus Vasa, a young man sprung from the ancient kings of the country, arose from the forests of Dalecarlia where he had long lain concealed and came to deliver his country from bondage . . . Brave with circumspection, and mild and gentle in a fierce and cruel age, he was as virtuous as it is possible for the leader of a party to be.

Gustavus Vasa had been the hostage of Christian and had been kept a prisoner . . . Having found a means to escape from prison, he had dressed himself in the habit of a peasant, and in that disguise had wandered about in the mountains and woods of Dalecarlia, where he was reduced to the necessity of working in the copper mines, at once to procure a livelihood and to conceal himself from his enemies. Buried as he was in these subterranean caverns, he had the boldness to form the design of dethroning the tyrant. With this view he revealed himself to the peasants, who regarded him as one of those superior beings, to whom the common herd of mankind are naturally inclined to submit. These savage boors he soon improved into hardy and warlike soldiers. He attacked Christian and the archbishop, beat them in several encounters, banished them both from Sweden, and at last was justly chosen by the states king of the country, of which he had been the deliverer.

Hardly was he established on the throne, when he undertook an enterprise still more difficult than his conquests. The real tyrants of the state were the bishops who, having engrossed into their own hands almost all the riches of Sweden, employed their ill-got wealth in oppressing the subjects, and in making war upon the king. This power was all the more formidable as, in the opinion of the ignorant populace, it was held to be sacred. Gustavus punished the Catholic religion for the crimes of its ministers; and in less than two years, introduced Lutheranism into Sweden, rather by the arts of his policy than by the influence of authority. Having thus conquered the kingdom, as he himself was wont to say, from the Danes and the clergy, he reigned a happy and absolute monarch to the age of seventy and then died full of glory, leaving his family and his religion in quiet possession of the throne* . . .

Voltaire could say of the 20th century as well as the 16th, of the Chinese revolution today as well as of the Swedish revolution of yesterday: "A new event gave a sudden turn to the state of affairs in the North." Ideologies change: conversion to Lutheranism, Proletarian Cultural Revolution, but does the essence of things change so greatly?

The Chinese revolution is known as and considers itself Marxist. China believes that it has become the principal centre of world revolution. Peking claims that Mao Tse-tung's thought

*Voltaire, *History of Charles XII*, Book I (trans. Smollett), pp. 6–8.

is the most perfect expression of Marxism-Leninism *in our time,* the Marxism-Leninism best adapted to the concrete problems facing the peoples of the world in the next few decades.

Mao is holding out the Chinese experience to them : how the Chinese people liberated themselves from domination by the landlords and big bourgeoisie linked with foreign interests; how power was seized; how it is defended against a return offensive by capitalism, whether in town or countryside, or against "revisionism" and *embourgeoisement.* Finally, how China, after liberating herself, viewed the problem of the "liberation of proletarian peoples".

The various conflicts which characterized the epoch of imperialism, when Lenin and Stalin analysed them, are according to Peking, now transposed and in a sense unified on a world level. Class struggle has been complicated by national antagonisms.

What human groups should today be called "feudalism", "aristocracy", "bourgeoisie" or "proletariat"? Certainly, each (country) has its proletarians, its feudalists, its bourgeois, but is it not worth considering that numerically the vast majority of the world proletariat is yellow, brown or black, and that the "bourgeoisie" and the people who enjoy a higher level of existence are nearly all white? A White power, the United States, with 6 per cent of the earth's population, owns more than 40 per cent of the world's wealth, and according to many American observers, tends to regard herself as the world's police force.

For this reason, the problem of "social revolution" does not arise as it did in Marx's time. When Chinese propaganda states that Mao's thought is Marxism-Leninism adapted to our time, surely this is because Peking regards the working class in industrial countries as partly *"embourgeoisée"* and therefore no longer a driving force on a world scale? To Peking, the revolutionary centres of Europe are or soon will be extinct. With the development of the third sector, leisure, "affluence" in a word, economic demands have stolen a march on political problems.

Today's revolutionary class is, according to China, the

peasantry, the masses of poor peasants spread across vast spaces in the three continents of the farming "South". The new Marxism-Leninism is aimed at them, no longer at the "white collar workers" of the industrial North. But the "North" is anxious to know what is thought on the other side of the river.

This is why we are presenting, in their historical context, two or three hundred pages of Mao's writings, chosen, selected from over two thousand. Mao Tse-tung's thought has been relieved of a host of parentheses, of references to characters practically unknown in the West, and also of countless names of places and localities. It has, in a sense, been reduced to essentials. As Mao himself advocates, "the chaff has been thrown away and the grain preserved".

In reading these texts, one wonders if Maoists today, so ineffectively applying President Mao's thought, have in fact read the latter's works. This is China's affair. However, for all non-Chinese, "Mao's thought" can be stimulating.

We believe that, by making Mao's works available to the largest possible readership and by cutting away the myth which surrounds one of the most important figures of our time, we are rendering a service to the Western world.

23 November 1967.

*   *   *   *

To anyone who wants to know it or make a selection from it, Mao Tse-tung's work raises special problems. Firstly, it has never been collected, still less published, in its entirety. Probably no more than two-thirds of it are known outside China. The *Selected Works* make up only about half of it. Secondly, when the *Selected Works* were published, Mao revised and corrected many texts.

Since the aim of the present study is to present the reader with a significant, however limited selection of Mao Tse-tung's thought *as it is being currently disseminated,* such considerations have not affected this book. The texts which have been chosen come, with very few exceptions, from those which have recently been published in English – and other languages – in Peking.

We feel that these are the ones which China and its leaders regard as "valid", to the exclusion of "original versions" which now have a historical rather than an ideological value.

To make for easier reading, we have done our best to limit the number of Chinese words and proper names as far as possible. For those which have been kept (usually fairly well known), the spelling adopted is that which Peking (Foreign Language Press, Peking Review, etc. . . .) has been using in all recent publications in English.

We should like to express our thanks to Mr. Stuart Schram, to whom we owe so much in our understanding of Mao's life, for allowing us to reproduce several old texts of Mao's which he himself translated from the Chinese; also to Penguin Books Ltd., for permission to reproduce extracts from his book *Mao Tse-tung* and the Pall Mall Press Ltd. for extracts from his book *The Political Thought of Mao Tse-tung*.

Major dates in Mao Tse-tung's life

1893   *26 December.* Mao Tse-tung born in Shaoshan, in Hunan.

1913–1918   Mao studies at the Normal School in Changsha, in Hunan.

1918   *Autumn.* Mao arrives in Peking, where he meets Li Ta-chao and is introduced to Marxism.

1920   Mao starts a Communist group in Hunan.

1921   *1 July.* Mao attends the First Congress of the Chinese Communist Party in Shanghai.

1924–1927   Collaboration between the Communists and the Kuomintang.

1925   Mao begins to organize the movement in Hunan.

1927   *12 April.* Chiang Kai-shek turns on the Communists in Shanghai. Beginning of anti-Communist repression in China. Mao organizes the Autumn Harvest Uprising in Hunan. Beginning of armed struggle in the Tsingkiang Mountains.

1929   Mao Tse-tung and Chu Teh set up a provincial government in Kiangsi.

1931   *November.* Proclamation of the Chinese Soviet Republic in Kiangsi. Mao elected Chairman.

1934   *October*. Beginning of the Long March.

1935   *January*. In Tsunyi (Kweichow), Mao Tse-tung takes over effective leadership of the Chinese Communist Party.

        October. The Long March over, the Red Army and the Communist Party Central Committee are established in the North-West.

1936   Interviews with Edgar Snow, who makes Mao known outside China (*Red Star Over China*) and also in China.

1937   *7 July*. Beginning of the war with Japan. Mao writes *On Practice* and *On Contradiction,* marries Lan-p'ing (Chiang Ch'ing), his present wife.

1938   Military writings (*Problems of Strategy in Guerilla War Against Japan*, *On Protracted War*, etc.).

1942   *February*. Rectification movement within the ranks of the Party.

1945   *August*. Capitulation of Japan. Mao sees Chiang Kai-shek for the first time since 1926. Negotiations in Chungking. Agreement (not effected), rift, renewal of civil war (spring 1946).

1949   *January*. Capture of Peking. *October*. Mao proclaims the Chinese People's Republic and takes over its leadership.

        16 December 1949–February 1950. Mao's first journey outside China : on 14 February 1950 he signs the Sino-Soviet treaty of alliance in Moscow.

1950–1953   Korean War against the U.S.A. (armistice in July 1953).

1955   Beginning of the socialization of agriculture.

1957   *27 February*. Mao's speech *On the Correct Handling of Contradictions Among the People*. Mao in Moscow for the Conference of 64 Communist Parties.

1958   *August*. Mao launches People's Communes and opposes soviet attempts to negotiate with the U.S.A.

1959   *April.* Mao hands over the chairmanship of the Republic to Liu Shao-ch'i. *October.* Mao disapproves of the U.S.S.R.'s search for agreement with the U.S.A. which would endorse the recognition of "two Chinas".

1960   *November.* Mao's third journey to Moscow (Conference of 81).

1962   *September.* Mao reminds the Tenth Session of the Eighth Central Committee that "the class struggle must never be forgotten".

1963   *June.* The Chinese Communist Party, at odds with "Khrushchevism", formulates its "proposals along the general line of the international Communist movement".

1966   *August.* Mao Tse-tung reappears in Peking, and relying on Lin Piao and the Army, takes over the leadership of the "Great Proletarian Cultural Revolution".

K'unlun (poem)*

Towering aloft
   above the earth,
Great K'unlun,
   you have witnessed
   all that was fairest
   in the human world.
As they fly across the sky
   the three million dragons
   of white jade
Freeze you with piercing cold.
In the days of summer
   your melting torrents
Fill streams and rivers
   till they overflow,

*K'unlun is a mountain in Sinkiang. It is also the name of the chain of mountains stretching from Pamir to South-West China by way of the borders of Sinkiang and Tibet. In a note to this poem, Mao Tse-tung wrote: "The Ancients said: 'When the three million jade dragons are at grips, their torn scales fly "through the sky" ': thus they evoked the whirling snow. I borrowed this image to describe the snow-covered mountains." (English translation by Michael Bullock and Jérôme Ch'én, reproduced by permission of the Oxford University Press.)

Changing men
  into fish and turtles.
What man can pass judgment
  on all the good and evil
You have done
  these thousand autumns?
But today
  I say to you, K'unlun,
You don't need your great height,
  you don't need all that snow!
If I could lean on the sky
  I would draw my sword
And cut you in three pieces.
One I would send to Europe,
One to America,
And one we would keep in China.
Thus would a great peace
  reign through the world,
For all the world
  would share your warmth and cold.

I Nationalism and Marxism

At the beginning of the 20th century, China's position was critical. The Middle Kingdom, the oldest and most densely populated state in the world, was about to crumble beneath the combined assault of the great White powers joined by Japan.

She had been facing up to this assault for some years. Conscious how very important the Chinese market was for their rapidly expanding industries, the West had tried to gain access to it by force. The first, England, acquired an enclave in Hong Kong, opened up five ports, and was given an indemnity and consular and commercial privileges by the Treaty of Nanking, 29 August 1842. The United States wasted no time in claiming the same advantages at the Treaty of 3 July 1844 and France followed suit, also obtaining the so-called right of "evangelization" by the Treaty of Whampoa on 24 October 1844. During the Second Opium War, 1858–60, during which their troops took Peking and sacked the Summer Palace, England and France also extorted other concessions – the opening up of new ports, including Tientsin, the surrender of Kowloon, and control over the Customs administration. It was now Russia's turn to intervene. In return for her neutrality, she acquired* (1) the maritime province south of the River Amur where she built Vladivostok. She then turned her attention to Turkestan and Mongolia, while England and the United States extended their influence to Shanghai, and thence to the Yangtze basin. France, which had just subdued Annam, attacked Formosa in 1885 and insinuated her agents into Yünnan.

Back in 1874, Japan had tried to seize Formosa. In 1894, as the result of a dispute with China over Korea, she attacked China, seized Formosa and acquired its concession by the Treaty of Shimonoseki in March 1895. At this point Germany entered the lists: in 1898 she acquired the enclave of Chiao-chow in Shantung which provoked the Boxer Rising.

In the next few years, Germany, Russia, England and France acquired rights for building railways and prospecting for mines in various areas of China. They recognized each other's "spheres of influence" on a map of the country, and Peking was also forced to cede them new territories "on lease" (Port Arthur, Dairen, Wei-hai-wei, etc.). The United States, making full use of the "open door" principle, benefited effortlessly from all the economic concessions granted to the other powers. Was this really, as an European diplomat suggested, the "dismemberment of China"?

This impressive run of defeats finally roused an important section of the Chinese intelligentsia against the Manchu dynasty which had governed the destiny of China for two and a half centuries.

Since the 1870s, there had been serious talk, in the imperial Chinese administration, of the possibilities of adopting Western techniques in order to make a stand, to resist assault (2). Foreigners had been allowed to establish factories and workshops in China in the open ports. Some, while agreeing to acquire weapons and techniques, were afraid that Chinese civilization would collapse under the effects of "modernization". Now, it was essential for them to preserve that civilization (in their view superior to all others) and the social structure which then

*Treaty of 1858 and 1860: the figures between brackets refer to the bibliographical notes at the end of the book.

reflected it. But others argued that Western dynamism threatened to sweep everything away : areas of Chinese influence, such as Burma and Annam, had already succumbed. It was China's independence, her survival as a state and a nation which were at stake.

While Sun Yat-sen, a Cantonese, began to mobilize guerillas to overthrow the Manchu dynasty from outside, in certain intellectual circles in the North there was a growing conviction that far-reaching political reforms were needed. The leading figures in this reformist movement were two scholars, K'ang Yu-wei and Liang Ch'i-ch'ao. But would not such reforms and the resulting "Occidentalization" challenge the regime itself? Would not the Manchu dynasty and aristocracy, and the structure on which they relied, be threatened by the emergence of a modern political regime of a Western type in which the Han (Chinese) majority would inevitably play a dominant role? Convinced of this, the Manchu clan put up furious resistance against the modernization of China, resistance which neutralized the political reforms in 1898 and the 1900 Boxer Rising.

The latter gave the Powers a fresh opportunity to impose humiliating conditions on China by the 1901 protocol, but it aggravated their rivalry. England sent an expedition to Tibet. In February 1904, Russia, who had contrived a privileged position in Manchuria, suddenly found herself attacked by Japan, encouraged by England. Japan's victory, ratified by the 1905 Treaty of Portsmouth enabled her to destroy the Russian position in South Manchuria, lay hands on the Russian railway in that area, seize Port Arthur and Dairen, and finally establish her protectorate over Korea.

Childhood, adolescence and youth

At the time when Japan, having defeated Russia, was entering Manchuria and Korea, Mao Tse-tung was studying the Classics and History in a primary school in Central China. He was twelve.

He was born on 26 December 1893 in Shaoshan, a village in

the province of Hunan in Central China. It lay among wooded hills, in a rather narrow valley, with terraced rice-fields and meadows. The family lived in a low, fairly large house, with tiled and thatched roofs (3).

His parents were of peasant stock. His father, Mao Jen-sheng, originally a poor peasant, had been a soldier for several years before returning to his village. He had gradually managed to save enough to buy some land and had finally owned 22 *mou* (three and a half acres) on which they raised 84 piculs (11,500 lbs) of rice. As the family consumed only 35 piculs, they were left with a surplus of 49 which they sold. Having thus become a rich peasant and a grain merchant, he lived in comparative ease. But he was harsh and demanding (4).

Mao's mother, Wen Chi-mei, was a good, gentle and charitable woman. A fervent Buddhist but wholly illiterate, she taught religion to her three children (5).

At about the age of seven or eight, round about 1900, Mao Tse-tung first went to the village primary school where he remained until he was thirteen and where it seems that he rubbed shoulders mainly with the sons of big landlords and rich peasants. There he read classical books (Confucius, etc.), learnt Chinese history, steeped himself in patriotism and a deep consciousness of China's greatness and acquired a great admiration for certain great emperors, such as Ch'in Shih Huang-ti and Han Wu-ti. But he was especially fond, he confessed, of stories and novels, such as the *Romance of the Three Kingdoms* and *Water Margin,* portraying bandits or heroic rebels helping the poor and punishing the rich, wicked and unjust. He learnt long passages of them off by heart and even today can quote from their characters. Mao recognized that he had been very influenced in his conception of the world by these novels. He also read a collection of biographies of world heroes such as Napoleon, Peter the Great, Gladstone, Montesquieu, Rousseau and Lincoln, which merely increased his admiration for determination, energy and moral and physical courage.

Arguments between father and son were common. Later

Mao said that there were two parties in the house, the "Ruling Power" (his father) and the "Opposition" (he, his mother and his brother). But there was a harsh, severe master at the school. One day, at the age of ten, unable to stand it any longer, Mao ran away and threatened to kill himself. Cowed, his father and the master tempered their ways. "The result of my act of protest," said Mao, "impressed me very much. It was a successful 'strike' " (6).

On leaving primary school, Mao worked for a while with his parents on their farm. But in 1909 he left the village and went to Changsha, capital of the province, to pursue his studies and thus be able to help his father more effectively. Revolt was brewing in the town, provoked by famine and the attitude of the big landlords. Secret societies had been very active, but an uprising had failed.

It was in Changsha, though much later, that Mao read his first paper, a nationalist and revolutionary newspaper which described the April 1911 Canton uprising against the Manchu dynasty. It was at this point too, according to Mao, that he first heard of Sun Yat-sen and of the *T'ung Meng Hui,* the revolutionary nationalist organization which Sun Yat-sen had founded in 1905 and which was to be the nucleus of the Kuomintang. Until then, among political figures of the time, Mao had particularly admired, over a number of years, K'ang Yu-wei and Liang Ch'i-ch'ao (7).

China was then on the eve of its first democratic revolution, in 1911, and Mao felt strong enough to take an active part in it. He wrote an article, which he pinned, like a notice, on the wall of the school. It was, he said, his first expression of a political view: in it he suggested recalling Sun Yat-sen from Japan and making him President, with K'ang Yu-wei as Prime Minister and Liang Ch'i-ch'ao as Foreign Minister.

In autumn 1911 the revolution triumphed. After the Wuchang uprising on 10 October 1911, official date of the revolution, Changsha was captured by the rebels, and a provincial revolutionary government set up with members of secret societies. Schoolboys and students were harangued and incited to support the movement and Mao decided to join the revolutionary army. He spent six months in it.

But Sun Yat-sen, summoned to Peking after the success of the great autumn movement, did not yet have an adequate political basis with which to take over effective control of the country. In February 1912, while the Manchu dynasty was fading and the Empire was giving way to the Republic, he in fact abdicated in favour of the man trusted by the Court and Conservative circles, Yüan Shih-k'ai. In Hunan, the big landlords and "militarists" gained control of affairs. In the ensuing months and years, Yüan Shih-k'ai placed governors, mainly army men, that he trusted, in charge of provinces, and with them formed what was known as the Peiyang Party. It was made up chiefly of northern clans.

Back in Changsha, Mao-Tse-tung reapplied himself earnestly to his studies, devouring a large number of Western works in translation : Adam Smith, Darwin, Stuart Mill, Spencer, Rousseau and Montesquieu, thus discovering the politico-philosophical culture of countries of which until then he had known only their political and military "heroes". Some masters, who had studied in Japan, also opened his mind to the way in which the resources of Western technique could be used to the benefit of the Asiatic peoples (8).

However, the shock-waves of the revolution and rivalries between Chinese clans invited fresh foreign pressure, new threats to the independence of China. On 18 January 1915, Japan, taking advantage of the self-effacement of the West as a result of the war in Europe, presented "twenty-one demands" to Peking, acceptance of which would have in fact led to China being placed under Japanese protectorate. Yüan Shih-k'ai's weak response aroused a fresh upsurge of nationalism chiefly in the towns, especially among the intelligentsia and mercantile bourgeoisie.

Influenced by intellectuals convinced that China would not be able to resist the foreigners and even survive as a people, nation and state, unless she went over, like Japan, to the Western school, a movement then arose which vigorously recommended a cultural revolution. The two leading spirits of this movement were Hu Shih and Ch'en Tu-hsiu, and in 1915 they founded a magazine, *Hsin Ching-nien (New Youth)* which had a decisive influence on the intellectual orientation of modern China. In its first number, Ch'en Tu-hsiu issued an "appeal to youth", drawing its attention to the need to learn from the West in order to save China. The latter, object of foreign aggression, could only resist, said Ch'en, if she changed, as a society, in such a way as to produce a dynamism comparable with that which inspired the West. The first condition was to break the fetters binding individual initiative. A bold reformer, Ch'en advocated a radical Westernization of China based on democracy, science and personal freedom, but also on military as well as civil organization. In his view, the American and British love of economic activity, German organization, the French and German scientific spirit were examples from which China should seek inspiration (9).

Mao Tse-tung was deeply influenced by these appeals and from 1915, when the magazine began, Hu Shih and Ch'en Tu-hsiu replaced K'ang Yu-wei and Liang Ch'i-ch'ao as the inspiration of his dreams and his actions (10). The *New Youth* magazine spread to the provinces. Thanks to it and to Changsha, Mao was able to relate what he was reading and what he had read to the national problem of altering Chinese society. Like Ch'en, and for personal reasons, he believed in the need to renew Chinese society, start a "cultural revolution", put an end to "feudalism", and restore the military virtues, individual initiative and conscious action; one of his dominant traits clearly emerges : the cult of the will (11).

But his knowledge of Chinese literature also enabled him to identify this Western idea with certain purely Chinese currents of thought. In other words, he incorporated, integrated Western concepts and schemes into his mental processes which still remained basically Chinese. Very soon, Mao Tse-tung launched a student movement, the "Society for the Study of New Men", inspired mainly by topics discussed in *New Youth*.

In April 1917, Mao Tse-tung wrote a long article for *New*

Youth, "A Study of Physical Education", which appeared in the magazine under a pseudonym. Sprinkled with references to the Chinese classics, the text reveals both character and a way of thought and is, from beginning to end, a plea for physical education as a means of developing courage, will and knowledge. Here is a short extract from it (12) :

The power of the sentiments is also extremely great. The ancients endeavoured to discipline them with reason . . . But reason proceeds from the heart, and the heart resides in the body. We often observe that the weak are enslaved by their sentiments and are incapable of mastering them. Those whose senses are imperfect or whose limbs are defective are often enslaved by excessive passion, and reason is incapable of saving them. Hence it may be called an invariable law that when the body is perfect and healthy, the feelings are also correct . . .

Physical education not only harmonizes the emotions, it also strengthens the will. The great utility of physical education lies precisely in this. The principal aim of physical education is military heroism. Such objects of military heroism as courage, dauntlessness, audacity and perseverance are matters of will . . . To wash our feet in ice water makes us acquire courage and dauntlessness as well as audacity. In general, any form of exercise, if pursued continuously, will help to train us in perseverance . . . The will is the antecedent of a man's career.

Those whose bodies are small and frail are flippant in their behaviour. Those whose skin is flabby and soft are dull in will. Thus does the body influence the mind. The purpose of physical education is to strengthen the muscles and bones; as a result knowledge is enhanced, the sentiments are harmonized, and the will is strengthened. The muscles and bones belong to our body; knowledge, sentiments and will belong to our heart. When both the body and the heart are at ease, one may speak of perfect harmony. Hence physical education is nothing else but the nourishing of our lives and the gladdening of our hearts.

During the winter of 1917–18, Mao Tse-tung began to take interest in social change. But it was in the name of the rights of the individual that he took issue with "the three relations"

(Confucian) which, he said, "make up, with religion, capitalists and autocracy, the three evil spirits of the Empire". This was, according to Stuart Schram, the first time that a reference to capitalists and even to any social category was to be found in Mao's thought (13).

Meanwhile, China was a prey to anarchy. Since Yüan Shih-k'ai, wooed by the Anglo-Americans, had tried to restore the monarchy to his advantage, the South had risen up and the Republic had been proclaimed in Canton in May 1916. On the death of Yüan Shih-k'ai on 6 June 1916, military elements had seized power in Peking, but the country was now entering on a period of civil war which was to last *more than thirty-three years*. The men appointed by Yüan in the provinces retreated into provincial fiefs from which they could defy the central power and the revolution. In the North, the Centre and the West, the "warlords" promoted their region to an autonomous state, collected taxes and maintained an army, acting as genuine little local monarchs or bloodthirsty satraps. The Peking government, though no longer exercising real authority, remained the only one recognized by the foreign Powers. But each of the Great Powers had her *"protégé"* among the "warlords", Japan in Manchuria, England in the Yangtze valley . . .

In spring 1918, when Mao Tse-tung received his diploma from the Normal School in Changsha, the breach was practically complete, politically at least, between the North, where Japanese and Anglo-American influences prevailed, and the South, where Sun Yat-sen and the Kuomintang endeavoured to inject life into the Republican regime. It was at this point that China began to feel the effects of the Russian Revolution and that Marxism, as a political doctrine, began to find its way into China.

The "4 May Movement" and the founding of the Chinese Communist Party.

In spring 1918, Mao was, at twenty-four, as he himself admitted, still an "idealist" (14). Liberalism, democratic reformism, a rather utopian socialism, anti-militarism and nationalism, even chauvinism co-existed within him. But events made him evolve more rapidly.

In autumn 1918, accompanying some Hunanese students who were off to learn a little French before leaving for France, Mao Tse-tung went to Peking for the first time. Thanks to one of his former professors, he was given an obscure post as library assistant at the University there and made the acquaintance of the man who was trying to reconcile Marxism-Leninism with Chinese nationalism, Li Ta-chao, the librarian of Peking University, then aged twenty-nine.

Li Ta-chao had already worked for some time on *New Youth*, the magazine of literary and cultural revival. But he had only been on the editorial staff since September 1918. He was primarily a nationalist, deeply affected by the humiliations and defeats inflicted on China by foreigners. Yet in spite of his nationalism, his mind was not closed to Western thought. Thus he admired Condorcet and believed in the virtues of parliamentary democracy. But shortly before Mao's arrival in Peking, in October, Li had published an article in *New Youth* entitled "The Victory of Bolshevism" in which he had shown his enthusiasm for the Russian Revolution which, he said, "gives the cue for twentieth century world revolution". The victory of Bolshevism, Li asserted, was that "of the spirit of all mankind", and of the people of all countries over militarism and autocracy. The call for the liberation of peoples oppressed by imperialism also influenced Li's mind and he found excellent justification for Chinese nationalism in Leninist theories of imperialism.

During the winter of 1918–19, "under Li Ta-chao", Mao Tse-tung, in company with other young men, began to study, at first with curiosity, then with passionate interest, the Russian experiment. What Li developed among his "disciples" was not quite Marxism, but more a form of "populism", such as Russia had known thirty years earlier. In an article entitled "Youth and the Villages", Li for instance praised the moral superiority of the countryside to the town and claimed: "Our China is a rural nation and her peasants comprise the majority of the labouring class. If they are not liberated, then the whole of the nation will not be liberated (15)." Li went further: he held for instance that the vast majority of the Chinese nation, with the exception of a tiny handful of exploiters, was made up of workers who had to be made aware of their solidarity against the feudalists, militarists and capitalists. What was more, such groups of "exploiters" generally turned out to have links with foreign interests. At this stage Li formulated the idea that China as a whole was a "proletarian nation" and that she could not avoid playing an important part in the great world revolution for which the Russians had given the cue. Thus, with Li Ta-chao, Chinese nationalism found a place in the "world anti-imperialist movement", an ally in Soviet Russia, and an example of organization and strategy in Leninism. This was not exactly Marxism, merely a presentiment that Marxism—or Communism—could be the most effective means of modernizing Chinese society. Li Ta-chao seems to have had a very profound influence on Mao Tse-tung. This is why it was necessary to expound the various basic ideas that Mao apparently derived from him.

In spring 1919, Mao left Peking. After accompanying some of his comrades who were going to Shanghai to board ship for France, he returned to Hunan, to Changsha, where he almost immediately became involved in the agitation which had gripped the province after the 4 May events in Peking.

Once again it was nationalism that was the principal spur to the revolution. Since the crisis of the "twenty-one demands" in 1915, anti-Japanese feeling in China had grown very widespread. Public opinion was enraged at the sight of the Japanese taking over, because of the Great War, from the Germans in Shantung (Chiao-chow and Tsing-tao), as it had been hoped that China, having taken part in the war, would have restored to her the ex-German areas at the peace treaty. Now in spring 1919, the Western Allies, meeting in Paris for the peace conference, refused to consider the Chinese point of view, decided to accede to Japan's demands and allocated her the rights previously held by Germany in Shantung. The Peking Government, under Anglo-American pressure, was about to agree to sign the peace treaty when, on 4 May 1919, the students in Peking, expressing the indignation of Chinese public opinion, made a violent demonstration against the "imperialists" and the Peking Government which, they said, was betraying China's interests. This action was immediately echoed in the provinces where by 3 June a vast national revolutionary movement had sprung up, aimed at the "imperialist" powers and their "Chinese lackeys". The intellectual circles also launched a new offensive for a cultural revival in numerous areas.

It was at this point that Soviet Russia, through the voice of L. Karakhan, People's Commissar for Foreign Affairs, announced that she was ready to give up all special privileges obtained in China through Tsarism, and that she would apply, in her relations with China, the principles of equality which governed her relations with other nations. In this way she won the sympathy of Chinese nationalism, whose energies were directed, after July 1919, for a long period, against Japan, Great Britain and the United States. Soviet Russia emerged as new China's only friend.

In the weeks that followed his return to Changsha, Mao Tse-tung was prodigiously active, organizing movements against the provincial "warlord", managing several periodicals which were banned one after another, and writing numerous articles on the situation. The most important was unquestionably that which appeared in the magazine *The Hunan Critic* in July and August 1919 entitled: "The Great Union of Popular Masses". It is interesting from many points of view (16):

Aristocrats, capitalists and other powerful men in society have carried their oppression to the limit . . . and consequently the decadence of the state, the sufferings of humanity, and the darkness of society have all reached an extreme. To be sure, among the methods of improvement and reform, education, industrialization, strenuous efforts, the destruction (of that which is bad and outmoded), and construction are all good, but there is a method more fundamental than these, which is that of the great union of the popular masses.

If we study history, we find that all movements that have occurred in the course of history, of whatever type they may be, have all without exception resulted from the union of a certain number of people. A greater movement naturally requires a greater union . . .

When the great union of the popular masses of France opposed the great union of the adherents of the monarchy, and the victory of "political reform" had been attained, many countries followed the French example and undertook all sorts of "political reforms". After last year's struggle in Russia, which pitted the great union of the popular masses against the great union of the aristocracy and the great union of the capitalists and led to the victory of "social reform", many countries – Hungary, Austria, Czechoslovakia, Germany – have followed Russia's example and have undertaken all sorts of social reforms. Although this victory is not complete . . . it may certainly become so and one can also imagine that it will spread throughout the world.

Why is the great union of popular masses so terribly effective? Because the popular masses in any given country are much more numerous than the aristocracy, the capitalists and the other holders of power in society . . .

We should know that our brothers in other lands have often employed this method in pursuing their interests. We must arise and imitate them, we must achieve our great union . . . As soon as we arise and let out a shout, the traitors will get up and tremble and flee for their lives . . .

If we wish to achieve a great union to resist the powerful men whom we face and who harm their fellow men, and in order to pursue our own interests, we must necessarily have many small unions to serve as its foundation . . .

Mao went on to advocate unions of peasants, workers, students and women, and he continued :

It is not that basically we have no strength. The source of our impotence lies in our lack of practice. For thousands of years, the Chinese people of several hundred millions have all led a life of slaves. Only one person – "the emperor" – was not a slave . . .

B

Our Chinese peoples possess great intrinsic energy. The more profound the opression, the greater the resistance to it; that which has accumulated a long time will surely burst forth quickly. The great union of Chinese peoples must be achieved. Gentlemen! We must all exert ourselves, we must all advance with the utmost strength. Our golden age, our age of brilliance and splendour, lies ahead!

The article caused a great stir, was discussed as far away as Peking where similar ideas were evolving too. Li Ta-chao had created a "Marxist Study Group" in the capital, and under its influence the movement for a cultural revival was heading towards nationalism as well as towards Marxism, and its Leninist interpretation, in which the movement of *national* liberation of oppressed peoples played a key role. Chinese translations of the basic Marxist texts were beginning to appear in Peking and Shanghai. On the other hand, Ch'en Tu-hsiu, who was the Dean of the Faculty of Letters and had received a six months prison sentence for supporting the 4 May Movement, had also turned to Marxism during his term of imprisonment and had been able to do a lot of reading. On being released in December 1919 he went to Shanghai.

It was also during the winter of 1919–20 that Mao Tse-tung first embraced Marxism. On a second visit to Peking during which he read the *Communist Party Manifesto* for the first time, he became "converted", and the journey which he made to Shanghai to discuss the question with Ch'en Tu-hsiu, completed his conversion. Mao later told Edgar Snow that he was deeply impressed by Ch'en's profession of faith, at this critical moment in his existence (17). It was also at the beginning of 1920, that Voitinsky (18), the first delegate from the Third International, arrived in Peking and then Shanghai, in search of a Chinese party or group prepared to "play along". In May 1920, a "society for the study of Marxist theory", a Communist cell, was formed in Shanghai. Peking had its own in September, Changsha in October. This was halfway to the formation of a Chinese Communist Party. But at this point, it must be emphasized that the men banding together to form this Communist Party were far from being tools of the Russians. They were men who had already acquired eminent positions in the Chinese intellectual movement, who were known for their patriotism and their integrity, and who thanks to *New Youth* and other writings, had part of the Chinese youth as their audience. In 1920, these men were convinced of the value of Marxist ideas and the Soviet example for a solution of China's national problems. Marxism-Leninism became an essential weapon and tool in what they regarded as the vital task: regaining China's independence and restoring her dignity and integrity, by modernizing the whole of society and by eliminating all that was out-dated, rotten or simply intolerable. Only at this price, they thought, could China fight with some chance of success against imperialism and avoid foreign domination.

Mao Tse-tung returned to Changsha in June 1920. He was now well-known. But from now on his activities became "Marxist". He organized trade unions. The article which he published (19) in November 1920, for the first anniversary of the Workers Association, was the first that was truly Marxist. In it Mao referred only to workers – not a word about the peasantry – and evoked the guiding role of the working class. His beginner's zeal made him rather lose sight of Chinese realities.

After a series of debates, at the beginning of July 1921, twelve persons met in Shanghai, in difficult circumstances (20) and announced the creation of the Chinese Communist Party. It was the first Party Congress. Mao was among the twelve but neither Li Ta-chao nor Ch'en Tu-hsiu were able to attend the congress. The Party, according to the adopted programme, intended to overthrow the capitalist classes and to establish the dictatorship of the proletariat in order to abolish classes one day. It did not intend to collaborate either with the bourgeoisie —even the national bourgeoisie—or with the peasantry. The Party then consisted, throughout the whole of China, of seventy members.

By thus adopting the theoretical principles of Marxism in the most absolute and indeed the most sectarian way, the

Chinese Communists embarrassed the Russians. The latter believed it necessary at this juncture to begin the liberation of colonial or semi-colonial peoples as a first step, admittedly a major one, in the struggle against imperialism. In a country like China where the working proletariat was very small in numbers, the principal force was the national bourgeoisie, which was required as an ally. In January 1922, at the First Congress of the Toilers of the Far East in Moscow, Zinoviev (21) advised the Chinese delegates not to distrust or ignore the bourgeois nationalists and begged them to make common cause with them.

While Mao Tse-tung, along with two other Hunanese, Li Li-san and Liu Shao-ch'i, was organizing a series of strikes in his province, the Chinese Communist Party, at its Second Congress in May 1922 decided to abandon the "sectarian" policy which it had adopted in 1921 and to adopt a policy of alliance with the nationalists. Mao did not take part in this Congress.

But what nationalists? China was still a prey to anarchy. Military cliques continued to share the country and to argue over vital areas: Chang Tso-lin in Manchuria, Wu P'ei-fu in Peking, etc. In Canton, Sun Yat-sen also had to deal with the "militarists", but as spokesman for the nationalists, he had the sympathy of the Kremlin. However Sun Yat-sen was still unwilling to form a united front with the Communists whom he distrusted. He finally agreed, in 1922, to the principle of their personal adherence to the Kuomintang. From then on, collaboration between the Communists and the Kuomintang became possible, and when the Nine Power Treaty in Washington on 6 February 1922 had confirmed the permanence of Anglo-American ambitions, and the massacre of the railway strikers by Wu P'ei-fu had shown that the proletariat could not fight alone against the armed forces of the "warlords", Communists like Li Ta-chao and Mao Tse-tung embraced the policy of collaboration with the Kuomintang, in order to pursue the national revolution together and to achieve the unity of China.

2 Social Classes and Evolution in China

It was China's national destiny, in the face of foreign intervention, which now dominated the activities of the new generation, to which Mao Tse-tung belonged. Mao had been the
Party's organization secretary for Hunan since 1922, and still
ignoring the peasants, he brought his efforts to bear on the
syndicalist organization of students and workers, which he still
saw as the one and only incarnation of the proletariat.

But persistent anarchy had by now forced Sun Yat-sen to
take some major decisions. Ignored or attacked by the English
and Americans, and convinced that without good troops he
was totally powerless against the "warlords" who controlled all
the power, he turned to Moscow.

In late 1922, after Adolf Joffe, a Soviet envoy who had come
to China to negotiate an agreement for his government, had
been shown the door in Peking, he met Sun Yat-sen in Shanghai.
On 26 January 1923, the two men signed a joint declaration
defining a basis for collaboration between the Soviet Union and
the Kuomintang. In it, the Russians affirmed their wish to help
China to achieve her national unity and to obtain the fullest
national independence (1).

The effect of this *rapprochement* was to define the attitude of the Chinese Communists. Their Third Congress, held in Canton in June 1923, recognized that the Kuomintang was the central force in the national revolution in China and that it had to assume its leadership. The Congress decided that the Communist Party would co-operate with the Kuomintang, and would form an "united front" with it against the militarists of the North. At this Third Congress, Mao was elected a member of the Party's Central Committee; afterwards he settled in Shanghai and worked there in collaboration with the local organization of the Kuomintang.

Meanwhile tension with the Anglo-Americans only increased. Under foreign pressure, the Peking authorities granted new fiscal and customs facilities to Anglo-American firms, and the Chinese bourgeoisie, the merchants at their head, reacted vigorously. Mao Tse-tung then wrote two significant articles, "The Peking *Coup d'Etat* and the Merchants", published in July 1923, and "The Cigarette Tax", published in August 1923, from which the following two passages are highly significant :

. . . The merchants who remained silent for three years, now speak in awesome tones.

The present political problem in China is none other than the problem of a national revolution. To use the strength of the people to overthrow the militarists and foreign imperialism, which are in collusion to accomplish their treasonable acts, is the historic mission of the Chinese people. This revolution is the task of the people as a whole. The merchants, workers, peasants, students and teachers should all come forward to take on the responsibility for a portion of the revolutionary work; but because of historical necessity and current tendencies, the work for which the merchants should be responsible in the national revolution is both more urgent and important than the work that the rest of the people should take upon themselves.

Mao then showed that the merchants were anxious to take part in a national revolution which would put a regime in power that could defend them against foreign competition and protect the national industry. He added :

The positions of the merchants on the one hand, and the foreign powers and the militarists on the other, are truly incompatible . . .
They must know that foreign powers and the militarists are the common enemies of all the merchants, as well as of the whole nation. Moreover, the advantages obtained after a successful revolution will be common advantages . . . It is essential to unite and struggle to overthrow the common enemy and to ensure the common advantage . . . The broader the organization of merchants, the greater will be their influence, the greater will be their ability to lead the people of the whole country, and the more rapid the success of the revolution ! . . .
Everyone must believe that the only way to save both himself and the nation is through the national revolution . . . To open a new era through revolutionary method and to build a new nation – such is the historic mission of the Chinese people We must not forget it ! (2)

In the second article, Mao denounced, in plain terms, the inertia of the authorities in respect of England, America, and Japan :

The "Council of Ministers" of the Chinese Government is really both accommodating and agreeable. If one of our foreign masters farts, it is a lovely perfume. If our foreign masters want to export cotton, the Council of Ministers thereupon abolishes the prohibition of the export of cotton; if our foreign masters want to bring in cigarettes, the Council of Ministers thereupon "instructs the several provinces to stop levying taxes on cigarettes". Again, I ask my 400 million brothers to ponder a little : Isn't it true that the Chinese Government is the counting-house for our foreign masters? (3)

In September 1923, the government of Canton came into open conflict with the English and Americans over receipts from the Kwangtung Customs. The crisis, a violent one, provoked new anti-imperialist demonstrations. Sun Yat-sen concluded that there was no alternative except to rely heavily on the Soviet Union.

In August, Sun, anxious to know why and how the Russians obtained their successes, sent his right-hand man, Chiang Kai-shek, to Moscow. Chiang saw Trotsky and Chicherin, but was especially impressed by the discipline of the Soviet Army. In October, a Soviet adviser, Borodin, arrived in Canton, to undertake, at Sun's request, a complete reorganization of the Kuomintang, which was transformed into a highly efficient organization on the Soviet pattern. The Kuomintang then tried to acquire a people's, even a peasant and worker basis.

In January 1924, it held its first National Congress in Canton, attended by Mao Tse-tung and Li Ta-chao. The Congress adopted new statutes for the Kuomintang, a political manifesto announcing the alliance with Russia, the alliance with the Communist Party, and its determination to achieve the national revolution on the basis of the Three Principles of the People. Mao Tse-tung was elected an alternate member of the Central Executive Committee of the Kuomintang. The Congress over, he went back to Shanghai where he worked both in the Communist Party Central Committee and in the Executive Bureau of the Kuomintang in Shanghai.

In 1924, in spite of mutual suspicion, collaboration between the Communists and the Kuomintang improved. The Communist Party had to give up its separate organizations of workers and reintegrate them with those of the Kuomintang. But elsewhere it had its place in the institutions. The Russians, determined to help Sun Yat-sen obtain a modern army, supplied instructors and advisers. With their assistance the Whampoa Military Academy was created and opened in May 1924 with Chiang Kai-shek as military chief, and Chou En-lai, a member of the French cell of the Communist Party, as political chief. Kuomintang and Communists later trained their military cadres there.

In 1923, the International had stated that the peasantry was Asia's "central problem" and in October 1923, the *Krestintern,* the peasant international, had been set up. At that time, the Chinese Communists had not yet paid much attention to the peasantry, and even Ch'en Tu-hsiu, secretary-general of the Communist Party in August 1923, had decided that the Chinese peasants did not want Communism. On the Kuomintang side, however, there was not the same scepticism, and in 1924 the Kuomintang established an Institute for training cadres of the Peasant Movement in Canton. In 1925 Borodin said that the success of the Chinese revolution depended wholly on the organization given to the peasants and the solution brought to the agrarian problem.

Feeling more secure, Sun Yat-sen now made a last attempt to avoid a clash with the North, but he fell ill and died in Peking on 12 March 1925. He left a will of which various beneficiaries have since tried to be executors*.

Mao Tse-tung, falling ill in Shanghai, went home to Hunan for a rest. He had not seen his native village since his Changsha days, and as he himself admitted, had lost contact with the countryside and had no inkling of the importance of the class struggle there. This "return to the land" was a turning-point in his life.

In fact, after the incident of 30 May 1925†, the Hunan peasantry began to rouse itself. Mao left his family house and

*In this will, Sun Yat-sen pointed out that he had devoted forty years of his life to revolutionary activity "whose aim is to win independence and equality for China". He added: To achieve "this aim, it is however essential to awaken the whole nation and to bind it into a single solid entity", "to join with countries which treat us on an equal footing".

†In May 1925, huge strikes, organized by the Communists, broke out in certain Japanese textile factories in Ching-tao and Shanghai. The "warlords" set about breaking them. On 30 May 1925, several thousand persons demonstrated in the foreign concessions in Shanghai in support of the strikers and for the return of the concessions to China. The police, under British control, opened fire, killing and wounding many demonstrators, mainly students. The incident had considerable impact in China where demonstrations and strikes, aimed chiefly at the English, increased: a general strike in Shanghai, and another in Hong Kong, lasting some months.

devoted himself to rural organization. In a few months he formed some twenty "peasant associations" and attracted the hatred and anger of the landlords in the province who demanded his arrest. Mao had to leave the area and retired to Canton in November 1925.

There he took over effective leadership of the Propaganda Department of the Kuomintang Central Executive Committee, and it was in this capacity that in early 1926 he presented a "report on propaganda", at the Second Congress of the Kuomintang; its mood was reflected in the following resolution:

The success of a party depends necessarily on the fact that it has a centre of gravity. The centre of gravity of the Kuomintang is hidden among the countless masses of the exploited peasantry. The Propaganda Department must ceaselessly draw the attention of party members to this point, and direct them to rely more on this centre of gravity (4).

At the same time, Mao Tse-tung became the chief editor of the weekly newspaper of the political department of the Kuomintang and was given the job of holding classes at the Peasant Movement Training Institute. Thus he was taking on growing responsibilities in the organization of the Kuomintang and the Communist Party. He had become one of the men in China who already had a world-wide view of the forces at work, concrete experience of political struggle, and a fairly clear idea of the strategy necessary to achieve the national revolution, and of the various interests that it would challenge. It was on the basis of this experience that, early in 1926, Mao Tse-tung wrote his famous essay, "Analysis of the Classes in Chinese Society", of which these are the key passages (5):

Who are our enemies? Who are our friends? This is a question of the first importance for the revolution. The basic reason why all previous revolutionary struggles in China achieved so little was their failure to unite with real friends in order to attack real enemies. A revolutionary party is the guide of the masses, and no revolution ever succeeds when the revolutionary party leads them astray. To ensure that we will definitely achieve success in our revolution and will not lead the masses astray, we must pay attention to uniting with our real friends in order to attack our real enemies. To distinguish real friends from real enemies, we must make a general analysis of the economic status of the various classes in Chinese society and of their respective attitudes towards the revolution.

What is the condition of each of the classes in Chinese society?

The landlord class and the comprador class. In economically backward and semi-colonial China the landlord class and the comprador class are wholly appendages of the international bourgeoisie, depending upon imperialism for their survival and growth. These classes represent the most backward and most reactionary relations of production in China and hinder the development of her productive forces. Their existence is utterly incompatible with the aims of the Chinese revolution. The big landlord and big comprador classes in particular always side with imperialism and constitute an extreme counter-revolutionary group. Their political representatives are the *Etatistes* and the right-wing of the Kuomintang.

The middle bourgeoisie: This class represents the capitalist relations of production in China in town and country. The middle bourgeoisie, by which is meant chiefly the national bourgeoisie, is inconsistent in its attitude towards the Chinese revolution: they feel the need for revolution and favour the revolutionary movement against imperialism and the warlords when they are smarting under the blows of foreign capital and the oppression of the warlords, but they become suspicious of the revolution when they sense that, with the militant participation of the proletariat at home and the active support of the international proletariat abroad, the revolution is threatening the hope of their class to attain the status of a big bourgeoisie. Politically, they stand for the establishment of a state under the rule of a single class, the national bourgeoisie. A self-styled true disciple of Tai Chi-tao wrote in the *Chen Pao,* Peking, "Raise your left fist to knock down the imperialists and your right to knock down the Communists." These words depict the dilemma and anxiety of this class. It is against interpreting the Kuomintang's Principle of the People's Livelihood according to the theory of class struggle, and it opposes the Kuomintang's alliance with Russia and the admission of Communists and left-wingers. But its attempt to establish a state under the rule of the national bourgeoisie is quite impracticable, because the present world situation is such that the two major forces, revolution and counter-revolution, are locked in final struggle. Each has hoisted a huge banner: one is the red banner of revolution held aloft by the Third International as the rallying point for all the oppressed classes of the world, the other is the white banner of counter-revolution held aloft by the League of Nations as the rallying point for all the counter-revolutionaries of the world. The intermediate classes are bound to disintegrate quickly, some sections turning left to join the revolution, others turning right to join the counter-revolution; there is no room for them to remain "independent". Therefore the idea cherished by China's middle bourgeoisie of an "independent" revolution in which it would play the primary rôle is a mere illusion.

The petty bourgeoisie. Included in this category are the owner-peasants, the master handicraftsmen, the lower levels of the intellectuals—students, primary and secondary school teachers, lower government functionaries, office clerks, small lawyers—and the small traders. Both because of its size and class charac-ter, this class deserves very close attention. The owner-peasants and the master handicraftsmen are both engaged in small-scale production. Although all strata of this class have the same petty-bourgeois economic status, they fall into three different sections. The first section consists of those who have some surplus money or grain, that is, those who, by manual or mental labour, earn more each year than they consume for their own support. Such people very much want to get rich and are devout worshippers of Marshal Chao*; while they have no illusions about amassing great fortunes, they invariably desire to climb up into the middle bourgeoisie. Their mouths water copiously when they see the respect in which those small moneybags are held. People of this sort are timid, afraid of government officials, and also a little afraid of the revolution. Since they are quite close to the middle bourgeoisie in economic status, they have a lot of faith in its propaganda and are suspicious of the revolution. This section is a minority among the petty bourgeoisie and constitutes its right-

*Marshal Chao is Chao Kung-ming, God of Wealth in Chinese folklore.

wing. The second section consists of those who in the main are economically self-supporting. They are quite different from the people in the first section; they also want to get rich, but Marshal Chao never lets them. In recent years, moreover, suffering from the oppression and exploitation of the imperialists, the warlords, the feudal landlords and the big comprador-bourgeoisie, they have become aware that the world is no longer what it was. They feel they cannot earn enough to live on by just putting in as much work as before. To make both ends meet they have to work longer hours, get up earlier, leave off later, and be doubly careful at their work. They become rather abusive, denouncing the foreigners as "foreign devils", the warlords as "robber generals" and the local tyrants and evil gentry as "the heartless rich". As for the movement against the imperialists and warlords, they merely doubt whether it can succeed (on the ground that the foreigners and the warlords seem so powerful), hesitate to join it and prefer to be neutral, but they never oppose the revolution. This section is very numerous, making up about one-half of the petty bourgeoisie. The third section consists of those whose standard of living is falling. Many in this section, who originally belonged to better-off families, are undergoing a gradual change from a position of being barely able to manage to one of living in more and more reduced circumstances. When they come to settle their accounts at the end of each year, they are shocked, exclaiming, "What? Another deficit!" As such people have seen better days and are now going downhill with every passing year, their debts mounting and their life becoming more and more miserable, they "shudder at the thought of the future". They are in great mental distress because there is such a contrast between their past and their present. Such people are quite important for the revolutionary movement; they form a mass of no small proportions and are the left-wing of the petty bourgeoisie. In normal times these three sections of the petty bourgeoisie differ in their attitude to the revolution. But in times of war, that is, when the tide of the revolution runs high and the dawn of victory is in sight, not only will the left-wing of the petty bourgeoisie join the revolution, but the middle section too may join, and even right-wingers, swept forward by the great revolutionary tide of the proletariat and of the left-wing of the petty bourgeoisie, will have to go along with the revolution. We can see from the experience of the 30 May Movement of 1925 and the peasant movement in various places that this conclusion is correct.

The semi-proletariat. What is here called the semi-proletariat consists of five categories : (i) the overwhelming majority of the semi-owner peasants, (ii) the poor peasants, (iii) the small handicraftsmen, (iv) the shop assistants, and (v) the pedlars. The overwhelming majority of the semi-owner peasants together with the poor peasants constitute a very large part of the rural masses. The peasant problem is essentially their problem. The semi-owner peasants, the poor peasants and the small handicraftsmen are engaged in production on a still smaller scale than the owner-peasants and the master handicraftsmen. Although both the overwhelming majority of the semi-owner peasants and the poor peasants belong to the semi-proletariat, they may be further divided into three smaller categories, upper, middle and lower; according to their economic condition. The semi-owner peasants are worse off than the owner-peasants because every year they are short of about half the food they need, and have to make up this deficit by renting land from others, selling part of their labour, or engaging in petty trading. In late spring and early summer when the crop is still in the blade and the old stock is consumed, they borrow at exorbitant rates of interest and buy grain at high prices; their plight is naturally harder than that of the owner-peasants who need no help from others, but they are better off than the poor peasants. For the poor peasants own no land, and receive only half the harvest or even less for their year's toil, while the semi-owner peasants, though receiving only half or less than half the harvest of land rented from others, can keep the entire crop from the land they own. The semi-owner peasants are therefore more revolutionary than the owner-peasants, but less revolutionary than the poor peasants. The poor peasants are tenant-peasants who are exploited by the landlords. They may again be divided into two categories according to their economic status. One category has comparatively adequate farm implements and some funds. Such peasants may retain half the product of their year's toil. To make up their deficit they cultivate side-crops, catch fish or shrimps, raise poultry or pigs, or sell part of their labour, and thus eke out a living, hoping in the midst of hardship and destitution to tide over the year. Thus their life is harder than that of the semi-owner peasants, but they are better off than the other category of poor peasants. They are more revolutionary than the semi-owner peasants, but less revolutionary than the other category of poor peasants. As for the latter, they have neither adequate farm implements nor funds nor enough manure, their crops are poor, and, with little left after paying rent, they have even greater need to sell part of their labour. In hard times they piteously beg help from relatives and friends, borrowing a few *tou* or *sheng* of grain to last them a few days, and their debts pile up like loads on the backs of oxen. They are the worst off among the peasants and are highly receptive to revolutionary propaganda. The small handicrafts-men are called semi-proletarians because, though they own some simple means of production and moreover are self-employed, they too are often forced to sell part of their labour and are somewhat similar to the poor peasants in economic status. They feel the constant pinch of poverty and dread of unemployment, because of heavy family burdens and the gap between their earnings and the cost of living; in this respect too they largely resemble the poor peasants. The shop assistants are employees of shops and stores, supporting their families on meagre pay and getting an increase perhaps only once in several years while prices rise every year. If by chance you get into intimate con-versation with them, they invariably pour out their endless grievances. Roughly the same in status as the poor peasants and the small handicraftsmen, they are highly receptive to revolu-tionary propaganda. The pedlars, whether they carry their wares around on a pole or set up stalls along the street, have tiny funds and very small earnings, and do not make enough to feed and clothe themselves. Their status is roughly the same as that of the poor peasants, and like the poor peasants they need a revolution to change the existing state of affairs.

The proletariat. The modern industrial proletariat numbers about two million. It is not large because China is economically backward. These two million industrial workers are mainly em-ployed in five industries – railways, mining, maritime transport, textiles and ship-building – and a great number are enslaved in enterprises owned by foreign capitalists. Though not very numerous, the industrial proletariat represents China's new pro-ductive forces, is the most progressive class in modern China and has become the leading force in the revolutionary movement. We can see the important position of the industrial proletariat in the Chinese revolution from the strength it has displayed in the strikes of the last four years, such as the seamen's strikes, the railway strike, the strikes in the Kailan and Tsiaotso coal mines, the Shameen (Canton) strike and the general strikes in Shanghai and Hongkong after the 30 May Incident. The first reason why the industrial workers hold this position is their concentration. No other section of the people is so concentrated. The second reason is their low economic status. They have been deprived of all means of production, have nothing left but their hands, have no hope of ever becoming rich and, moreover, are subjected to the most ruthless treatment by the imperialists, the warlords and the bourgeoisie. That is why they are particularly good fighters. The coolies in the cities are also a force meriting attention. They are mostly dockers and rickshawmen, and among them, too, are sewage carters and street cleaners. Possessing nothing but their hands, they are similar in economic status to the industrial workers but are less concentrated and play a less important rôle in production. There is as yet little modern capitalist farming in China. By rural proletariat we mean farm labourers hired by the year, the month or the day. Having neither land, farm implements nor funds, they can live only by selling their labour. Of all the workers they work the longest hours, for the lowest wages, under the worst conditions, and with the least security of employment. They are the most hard-pressed people in the villages, and their position in the peasant movement is as important as that of the poor peasants.

Apart from all these, there is the fairly large *lumpenproletariat*, made up of peasants who have lost their land and handicraftsmen who cannot get work. They lead the most precarious existence of all. In every part of the country they have their secret societies, which were originally their mutual aid organizations for political and economic struggle, for instance, the Triad Society in Fukien and Kwangtung, the Society of Brothers in Hunan, Hupeh, Kweichow and Szechuan, the Big Sword Society in Anhwei, Honan and Shantung, the Rational Life Society in Chihli and the three north-eastern provinces, and the Green Band in Shanghai and elsewhere. One of China's difficult problems is how to handle these people. Brave fighters but apt to be destructive, they can become a revolutionary force if given proper guidance.

To sum up, it can be seen that our enemies are all those in league with imperialism – *the warlords, the bureaucrats, the comprador class, the big landlord class and the reactionary section of the intelligentia attached to them. The leading force in our revolution is the industrial proletariat. Our closest friends are the entire semi-proletariat and petty bourgeoisie.* As for the vacillating middle bourgeoisie, their right-wing may become our enemy and their left-wing may become our friend – but we must be constantly on our guard and not let them create confusion within our ranks. . . .

This attempt at an "analysis of the classes" in China, in which Mao underlined the primary importance of the peasantry and the great numerical weakness of the working class, received a cold welcome within the Communist Party. The secretary-general, Ch'en Tu-hsiu, was even opposed to its publication in the Party's central organ.

In fact, a crucial point had already been reached in the collaboration between the Kuomintang and the Communists. The majority of the latter, concerned at the increasing strength of the Right within the Kuomintang, wanted to withdraw from this party. They had been dissuaded by representatives of the International, who had insisted that the collaboration should go on.

Mao Tse-tung, returning to Canton in November 1925 with clear ideas of the political importance of the peasantry and searching for an appropriate framework in which to put these ideas into practice, had noticed that the Kuomintang was showing more interest in what was going on in the countryside than was the Central Committee of the Communist Party.

The Peasant Movement Training Institute, where Mao was holding his classes, provided him with excellent opportunities for action. A considerable proportion (40 per cent) of Hunanese, recruited by the provincial organization of the Communist Party – no doubt on Mao's initiative – had followed the Fifth Session in autumn 1925. We saw elsewhere the orientation which he had given to the Kuomintang Central Executive Committee Propaganda Department (resolution on peasantry). Mao's independence of mind in respect of the Communist Party and his concern for national unity became clear in 1926.

Until now, the Russians had backed Chiang Kai-shek and the Kuomintang to the hilt against the warlords of the North and East. Sun Yat-sen, who long before his death had intended to launch a military expedition to overthrow the military cliques of the North and to establish a unified national government, had accepted Soviet aid largely because he thought that it was the only way to obtain the military resources necessary to such an operation.

Now, in late March 1926, the Politburo of the Soviet Communist Party, meeting in Moscow, discussed and adopted a report presented by Trotsky on the Far East situation. The Soviets, alarmed by incidents on the Chinese Eastern Railway, and in order to ensure the security of the U.S.S.R., felt it more expedient to recognize the *de facto* autonomy of Chang Tso-lin, the pro-Japanese warlord in Manchuria; to negotiate an arrangement with the Peking clique (Wu P'ei-fu) and to move towards a recognition of the Canton revolutionary government as the *de-facto* government of southern China, in order to "balance" Chang Tso-lin; in effect this was to accept the dismemberment of China. Consequently, Stalin came out against Chiang Kai-shek's military plans, especially the Northern Expedition, the offensive in the direction of Hankow, Shanghai, etc.

On 20 March, a few days before these deliberations, Chiang had made a "*coup d'état*" in Canton and ordered the arrest of the Chinese Communists and the "house arrest" of the Soviet advisers. From now on Chiang held strong cards for negotiating with the Kremlin and obtaining its consent to the Northern Expedition. Mao was, to all intents and appearances, in agreement with this view of things. On 30 March 1926, ten days after the "*coup d'état*", Mao was in fact taking part in a meeting of the Committee on the Peasant Movement (Kuomintang) and proposed a motion summarized in the minutes as follows:

Inasmuch as there is a close link between politics and the movement of the popular masses, and in view of the peasant movement now going on in many provinces, we should devote careful attention to the peasant movement in the provinces . . . which will be crossed by the Northern Expedition in the future (6).

This was a demonstration of independence, not only in respect of the Chinese Communist Party but also in respect of Moscow. It was also prescience that the Northern Expedition would considerably stimulate the peasant revolution. It was perhaps something else too : Mao, aware of the weakness of the Communist Party in the towns, and no doubt foreseeing that the Kuomintang might well turn on its allies, probably thought it useful to form rural cadres in order to be ready, when the day came, for the guerilla struggle, which is what he told a friend in spring 1926. The Institute was in any case a means of providing himself with a political base independent of the Kuomintang.

Shortly afterwards, Chiang Kai-shek "made peace" with the Soviets, freed the advisers and received, in return for continuing the collaboration with Moscow and the Communists, support from the Kremlin for the Northern Expedition and a decrease in the number of Communists in the ruling bodies. Thus Mao had to give up his functions in the Propaganda Department, but kept the Peasant Movement Training Institute where from 3 May to 5 October 1926 he took charge of the sixth session.

He still shared a certain vision of the national revolution with Chiang Kai-shek. Early in May 1926, at the Labour and Peasant Congress of the Kuomintang, Chiang affirmed "The armed workers and peasants play a more important rôle in the revolution than in the army", which was certainly closer to Mao Tse-tung's ideas than the intervention of Liu Shao-ch'i who, advancing the theories of the Communist Party, declared that the workers must "take the peasants by the hand" and "lead them forward". And it is understandable that Mao was able, at this juncture, sometimes to feel more at ease within the Kuomintang, where he also met several Communists of his opinions, than within his own party.

He had not however fallen out with his party. The latter, keeping its distance from the Kuomintang, decided to set up, under the aegis of the Central Committee, a "peasant department", and put Mao Tse-tung in charge of it. However, this was done on the quiet, because Stalin had given orders to maintain close collaboration with the Kuomintang.

Launched in June 1926, the Northern Expedition went ahead successfully. In August, Hunan fell into the hands of the "revolutionary" army – Changsha was occupied on 12 August – and peasant revolutionary enthusiasm was on the increase everywhere. In November, Nanchung was captured and Chiang Kaishek established his high command there. In Changsha he had declared:

Only after the overthrow of imperialism can China obtain freedom . . . In the present world revolution, there is the Third International, which can be called the general staff of the revolution . . . If we want our revolution to succeed, we must unite with Russia to overthrow imperialism . . . If Russia aids the Chinese revolution, does that mean she wants to oblige China to apply Communism? No, she wants us to carry out the national revolution . . . I am persuaded that the Communists who have joined our party do not, at the present time, want to apply Communism, but want rather to carry out the national revolution . . . The Chinese revolution is part of the world revolution. We want to unite the partisans of the world revolution to overthrow imperialism (7).

Everything indicates that, at the time, Mao Tse-tung fully shared this point of view.

3 The Revolutionary Potential of the Peasantry

At the end of October 1926, when the session of the Peasant Movement Training Institute in Canton was over, it seems that Mao Tse-tung went to Shanghai to take up his post as head of the "Peasant Department" of the Communist Party. But he did not remain there long. It is thought that, in November, he made contact with the peasant movements in the provinces nearest to Shanghai (Kiangsu and Chekiang), but in December he took part in the First Peasant Congress at Changsha in the province of Hunan. It was then that he made his famous investigation in five *hsien* (districts) of the province, including Changsha, and wrote his report* from which long extracts must be quoted to give an exact idea of its content.

This report is a key document in China's contemporary history. Hunan was at that time the centre of the peasant movement in China. Mao did not "discover" the formidable revolutionary potential of the Chinese peasantry there, as has been claimed. He already knew it from the stay which he had

*"Report on an Investigation of the Peasant Movement in Hunan", March 1927.

made in the province a year earlier. Lenin, M. N. Roy and Borodin had already drawn attention to it. But until now Mao had felt that the peasants lacked organization. In Hunan this time, he noted on the contrary that, roused and "left to themselves", they had set up a most effective but purely peasant organization, and that at this stage, they were getting along well without the urban proletariat and the Communists. What ought the Marxists to do, what could they do about such a situation?

The importance of the peasant problem

During my recent visit to Hunan I made a first-hand investigation of conditions in the five counties of Hsiangtan, Hsianghsiang, Hengshan, Liling and Changsha. In the thirty-two days from 4 January to 5 February, I called together fact-finding conferences in villages and county towns, which were attended by experienced peasants and by comrades working in the peasant movement, and I listened attentively to their reports and collected a great deal of material. Many of the hows and whys of the peasant movement were the exact opposite of what the gentry in Hankow and Changsha are saying. I saw and heard of many strange things of which I had hitherto been unaware. I believe the same is true of many other places, too. All talk directed against the peasant movement must be speedily set right. All the wrong measures taken by the revolutionary authorities concerning the peasant movement must be speedily changed. Only thus can the future of the revolution be benefited. For the present upsurge of the peasant movement is a colossal event. In a very short time, in China's central, southern and northern provinces, several hundred million peasants will rise like a mighty storm, like a hurricane, a force so swift and violent that no power, however great, will be able to hold it back. They will smash all the trammels that bind them and rush forward along the road to liberation. They will sweep all the imperialists, warlords, corrupt officials, local tyrants and evil gentry into their graves. Every revolutionary party and every revolutionary comrade will be put to the test, to be accepted or rejected as they decide. There are three alternatives. To march at their head and lead them? To trail behind them, gesticulating and criticizing?

Or to stand in their way and oppose them? Every Chinese is free to choose, but events will force you to make the choice quickly.

Get organized!

The development of the peasant movement in Hunan may be divided roughly into two periods with respect to the counties in the province's central and southern parts where the movement has already made much headway. The first, from January to September last year, was one of organization. In this period, January to June was a time of underground activity, and July to September, when the revolutionary army was driving out Chao Heng-ti, one of open activity. During this period, the membership of the peasant associations did not exceed 300,000–400,000, the masses directly under their leadership numbered little more than a million, there was as yet hardly any struggle in the rural areas, and consequently there was very little criticism of the associations in other circles. Since its members served as guides, scouts and carriers of the Northern Expeditionary Army, even some of the officers had a good word to say for the peasant associations. The second period, from last October to January of this year, was one of revolutionary action. The membership of the associations jumped to two million and the masses directly under their leadership increased to ten million. Since the peasants generally enter only one name for the whole family on joining a peasant association, a membership of two million means a mass following of about ten million. Almost half the peasants in Hunan are now organized . . . Nearly all the peasants have combined in the peasant associations or have come under their leadership. It was on the strength of their extensive organization that the peasants went into action and within four months brought about a great revolution in the countryside, a revolution without parallel in history.

Down with the local tyrants and evil gentry!
All power to the peasant associations!

The main targets of attack by the peasants are the local tyrants, the evil gentry and the lawless landlords, but in passing they also hit out against patriarchal ideas and institutions, against the corrupt officials in the cities and against bad practices and customs in the rural areas. In force and momentum the attack is tempestuous; those who bow before it survive and those who resist perish. As a result, the privileges which the feudal landlords enjoyed for thousands of years are being shattered to pieces. Every bit of the dignity and prestige built up by the landlords is being swept into the dust. With the collapse of the power of the landlords, the peasant associations have now become the sole organs of authority and the popular slogan "All power to the peasant associations" has become a reality. Even trifles such as a quarrel between husband and wife are brought to the peasant association. Nothing can be settled unless someone from the peasant association is present. The association actually dictates all rural affairs, and, quite literally, "whatever it says, goes". Those who are outside the associations can only speak well of them and cannot say anything against them. The local tyrants, evil gentry and lawless landlords have been deprived of all right to speak, and none of them dares even to mutter in dissent. In the face of the peasant associations' power and pressure, the top local tyrants and evil gentry have fled to Shanghai, those of the second rank to Hankow, those of the third to Changsha and those of the fourth to the county towns, while the fifth rank and the still lesser fry surrender to the peasant associations in the villages.

"Here's ten yuan. Please let me join the peasant association," one of the smaller of the evil gentry will say.

"Ugh! Who wants your filthy money?" the peasants reply.

Many middle and small landlords and rich peasants and even some middle peasants, who were all formerly opposed to the peasants associations, are now vainly seeking admission. Visiting various places, I often came across such people who pleaded with me: "Mr. Committeeman from the provincial capital, please be my sponsor!" . . . In short, what was looked down upon four months ago as a "gang of peasants" has now become a most honourable institution. Those who formerly prostrated themselves before the power of the gentry now bow before the power of the peasants. No matter what their identity, all admit that the world since last October is a different one.

"It's terrible!" or "It's fine!"

The peasants' revolt disturbed the gentry's sweet dreams. When the news from the countryside reached the cities, it caused immediate uproar among the gentry. Soon after my arrival in Changsha, I met all sorts of people and picked up a good deal of gossip. From the middle social strata upwards to the Kuomintang right-wingers, there was not a single person who did not sum up the whole business in the phrase, "It's terrible!" Under the impact of the views of the "It's terrible!" school then flooding the city, even quite revolutionary-minded people became downhearted as they pictured the events in the countryside in their mind's eye; and they were unable to deny the word "terrible". Even quite progressive people said, "Though terrible, it is inevitable in a revolution." In short, nobody could altogether deny the word "terrible". But, as already mentioned, the fact is that the great peasant masses have risen to fulfil their historic mission and that the forces of rural democracy have risen to overthrow the forces of rural feudalism. The patriarchal-feudal class of local tyrants, evil gentry and lawless landlords has formed the basis of autocratic government for thousands of years and is the cornerstone of imperialism, warlordism and corrupt officialdom. To overthrow these feudal forces is the real objective of the national revolution. In a few months the peasants have accomplished what Dr. Sun Yat-sen wanted, but failed, to accomplish in the forty years he devoted to the national revolution. This is a marvellous feat never before achieved, not just in forty, but in thousands of years. It's fine. It is not "terrible" at all. It is anything but "terrible". "It's terrible!" is obviously a theory for combating the rise of the peasants in the interests of the landlords; it is obviously a theory of the landlord class for preserving the old order of feudalism and obstructing the establishment of the new order of democracy, it is obviously a counter-revolutionary theory. No revolutionary comrade should echo this nonsense. If your revolutionary viewpoint is firmly established and if you have been to the villages and looked around, you will undoubtedly feel thrilled as never before. Countless thousands of the enslaved – the peasants – are striking down the enemies who battened on their flesh. What the peasants are doing is absolutely right; what they are doing is fine! "It's fine!" is the theory of the peasants and of all other revolutionaries. Every revolutionary comrade should know that the national revolution requires a great change in the countryside. The Revolution of 1911 did not bring about this change, hence its failure. This change is now taking place, and it is an important factor for the completion of the revolution. Every revolutionary comrade must support it, or he will be taking the stand of counter-revolution.

The question of "Going too far"

Then there is another section of people who say, "Yes, peasant associations are necessary, but they are going rather too far." This is the opinion of the middle-of-the-roaders. But what is the actual situation? True, the peasants are in a sense "unruly" in the countryside. Supreme in authority, the peasant association allows the landlord no say and sweeps away his prestige. This amounts to striking the landlord down to the dust and keeping him there. The peasants threaten, "We will put you in the other register!" They fine the local tyrants and evil gentry, they demand contributions from them, and they smash their sedan-chairs. People swarm into the houses of local tyrants and evil gentry who are against the peasant association, slaughter their pigs and consume their grain. They even loll for a minute or two on the ivory-inlaid beds belonging to the young ladies in the households of the local tyrants and evil gentry. At the slightest provocation they make arrests, crown the arrested with tall paper-hats, and parade them through the villages, saying, "You dirty landlords, now you know who we are!" Doing whatever they like and turning everything upside down, they have created a kind of terror in the countryside. This is what some people call "going too far", or "exceeding the proper limits in righting a wrong", or "really too much". Such talk may seem plausible, but in fact it is wrong. First, the local tyrants, evil gentry and lawless landlords have themselves driven the peasants to this. For ages they have used their power to tyrannize over the peasants and trample them underfoot; that is why the peasants have reacted so strongly. The most violent revolts and the most serious disorders have invariably occurred in places where the local tyrants, evil gentry and lawless landlords perpetrated the worst outrages. The peasants are clear-sighted. Who is bad and who is not, who is the worst and who is not quite so vicious, who deserves severe punishment and who deserves to be let off lightly – the peasants keep clear accounts, and very seldom has the punishment exceeded the crime.

Secondly, a revolution is not a dinner party, or writing an essay, or painting a picture, or doing embroidery; it cannot be so refined, so leisurely and gentle, so temperate, kind, courteous, restrained and magnanimous. A revolution is an insurrection, an act of violence by which one class overthrows another. A rural revolution is a revolution by which the peasantry overthrows the power of the feudal landlord class. Without using the greatest force, the peasant cannot possibly overthrow the deep-rooted authority of the landlords which has lasted for thousands of years. The rural areas need a mighty revolutionary upsurge, for it alone can arouse the people in their millions to become a powerful force. All the actions mentioned here which have been labelled as "going too far" flow from the power of the peasants, which has been called forth by the mighty revolutionary upsurge in the countryside.

It was highly necessary for such things to be done in the second period of the peasant movement, the period of revolutionary action. In this period it was necessary to establish the absolute authority of the peasants. It was necessary to forbid malicious criticism of the peasant associations. It was necesary to overthrow the whole authority of the gentry, to strike them to the ground and keep them there. There is revolutionary significance in all the actions which were labelled as "going too far" in this period. To put it bluntly, it is necessary to create terror for a while in every rural area, or otherwise it would be impossible to suppress the activities of the counter-revolutionaries in the countryside or overthrow the authority of the gentry. Proper limits have to be exceeded in order to right a wrong, or else the wrong cannot be righted. Those who talk about the peasants "going too far" seem at first sight to be different from those who say "It's terrible!" as mentioned earlier, but in essence they proceed from the same standpoint and likewise voice a landlord theory that upholds the interests of the privileged classes. Since this theory impedes the rise of the peasant movement and so disrupts the revolution, we must firmly oppose it.

The movement of the riffraff

The right-wing of the Kuomintang says, "The peasant movement is a movement of the riffraff, of the lazy peasants." This view is current in Changsha. When I was in the countryside, I heard the gentry say, "It is all right to set up peasant associations, but the people now running them are no good. They ought to be replaced!" This opinion comes to the same thing as what the right-wingers are saying; according to both it is all right to have a peasant movement (the movement is already in being and no one dare say otherwise), but they say that the people running it are no good and they particularly hate those in charge of the associations at lower levels, calling them "riffraff". In short, all those whom the gentry had despised, those whom they had trodden into the dirt, people with no place in society, people with no right to speak, have now audaciously lifted up their heads. They have not only lifted up their heads but taken power into their hands. They are now running the township peasant associations (at the lowest level), which they have turned into something fierce and formidable. They have raised their rough, work-soiled hands and laid them on the gentry. They tether the evil gentry with ropes, crown them with tall paper-hats and parade them through the villages . . . Not a day passes but they drum some harsh, pitiless words of denunciation into these gentry's ears. They are issuing orders and are running everything. Those who used to rank lowest now rank above everybody else; and so this is called "turning things upside down."

Vanguards of the revolution

We said above that the peasants have accomplished a revolutionary task which had been left unaccomplished for many years and have done an important job for the national revolution. But has this great revolutionary task, this important revolutionary work, been performed by all the peasants? No. There are three kinds of peasants, the rich, the middle and the poor peasants. The three live in different circumstances and so have different views about the revolution. . . . When the rich peasants join the associations, they generally enter the name of some sixty-or seventy-year-old member of the family, for they are in constant dread of "conscription". After joining, the rich peasants are not keen on doing any work for the associations. They remain in-active throughout.

How about the middle peasants? Theirs is a vacillating atti-tude. They think that the revolution will not bring them much good. They have rice cooking in their pots and no creditors knocking on their doors at midnight . . . It was not until the second period, when the peasant associations were already exercising great power, that the middle peasants came in. They show up better in the associations than the rich peasants but are not as yet very enthusiastic; they still want to wait and see. It is essential for the peasant associations to get the middle peasants to join and to do a good deal more explanatory work among them.

The poor peasants have always been the main force in the bitter fight in the countryside. They have fought militantly through the two periods of underground work and of open activity. They are the most responsive to Communist Party leadership. They are deadly enemies of the camp of the local tyrants and evil gentry and attack it without the slightest hesita-tion. . . . It is true the poor peasants are not afraid of losing anything. Many of them really have "neither a tile over their heads nor a speck of land under their feet". What, indeed, is there to keep them from joining the associations? According to the survey of Changsha County, the poor peasants comprise 70 per cent, the middle peasants 20 per cent, and the landlords and the rich peasants 10 per cent of the population in the rural areas. The 70 per cent, the poor peasants, may be sub-divided into two categories, the utterly destitute and the less destitute. The utterly destitute, comprising 20 per cent, are the completely dispossessed, that is, people who have neither land nor money, are without any means of livelihood, and are forced to leave home and become mercenaries or hired labourers or wandering beggars. The less destitute, the other 50 per cent, are the par-tially dispossessed, that is, people with just a little land or a little money who eat up more than they earn and live in toil and distress the year round, such as the handicraftsmen, the tenant-peasants (not including the rich tenant-peasants) and the semi-owner peasants.

This great mass of poor peasants, or altogether 70 per cent of the rural population, are the backbone of the peasant associations, the vanguard in the overthrow of the feudal forces and the heroes who have performed the great revolutionary task which for long years was left undone.

Without the poor peasant class (the "riffraff", as the gentry call them), it would have been impossible to bring about the present revoutionary situation in the countryside, or to overthrow the local tyrants and evil gentry and complete the democratic revolution. The poor peasants, being the most revolutionary group, have gained the leadership of the peasant associations. ... Leadership by the poor peasants is absolutely necessary. Without the poor peasants there would be no revolution. To deny their rôle is to deny the revolution. To attack them is to attack the revolution. They have never been wrong on the general direction of the revolution. They have discredited the local tryrants and evil gentry. They have beaten down the local tyrants and evil gentry, big and small, and kept them underfoot. Many of their deeds in the period of revolutionary action, which were labelled as "going too far", were in fact the very things the revolution required. Some county governments, county headquarters of the Kuomintang and county peasant associations in Hunan have already made a number of mistakes; some have even sent soldiers to arrest officials of the lower-level associations at the landlords' request. ... This mistake is very serious and feeds the arrogance of the reactionaries. To judge whether or not it is a mistake, you have only to see how joyful the lawless landlords become and how reactionary sentiments grow, wherever the chairmen or committee members of local peasant associations are arrested. We must combat the counter-revolutionary talk of a "movement of riffraff" and a "movement of lazy peasants" and must be especially careful not to commit the error of helping the local tyrants and evil gentry in their attacks on the poor peasant class.

Though a few of the poor peasant leaders undoubtedly did have shortcomings, most of them have changed by now. ... Only 15 per cent retain some bad habits. The most one can call these is "an unhealthy minority", and we must not echo the local tyrants and evil gentry in undiscriminatingly condemning them as "riffraff". This problem of the "unhealthy minority" can be tackled only under the peasant associations' own slogan of "strengthen discipline", by carrying on propaganda among the masses, by educating the "unhealthy minority", and by tightening the associations' discipline; in no circumstances should soldiers be arbitrarily sent to make such arrests as would damage the prestige of the poor peasants and feed the arrogance of the local tyrants and evil gentry. This point requires particular attention (1). . . .

Mao went on to examine the "fourteen great achievements" of the peasant movement which were as follows: hitting the landlords politically and economically; overthrowing the "feudal rule of the local tyrants", the authority of the heads of the district and their aides and the armed forces of the landlords, followed by the establishing of armed forces of peasants; overthrowing the supreme authority of the clan elders, religious authority and even masculine authority; eliminating banditry, abolishing exorbitant levies, generally cleaning-up social life by prohibiting gaming, gambling, opium-smoking, sumptuous feasts, and by controlling the sale of alcohol, development of the co-operative movement (supply, sale and credit), of the movement for education (by opening many schools), of community work (repair of roads and embankments) and of political propaganda. He concluded:

All the fourteen deeds enumerated above have been accomplished by the peasants under the leadership of the peasant associations. Would the reader please think it over and say whether any of them is bad in its fundamental spirit and revolutionary significance? Only the local tyrants and evil gentry, I think, will call them bad. Curiously enough, it is reported from Nanchang that Chiang Kai-shek, Chang Ching-chiang and other such gentlemen do not altogether approve of the activities of the Hunan peasants. This opinion is shared by Liu Yueh-chih and other right-wing leaders in Hunan, all of whom say, "They have simply gone Red." But where would the national revolution be without this bit of Red? To talk about "arousing the masses of the people" day in and day out and then to be scared to death when the masses do rise – what difference is there between this and Lord Sheh's love of dragons? (2)

While Mao was completing his report on the Hunan peasant movement, the political and military situation in Southern China was evolving rapidly.

The peasant revolt had shocked and angered a number of circles and the Communists' rôle in the affair aroused strong reactions within the Kuomintang, especially within its Right wing, now banded round Chiang Kai-shek, which had for some time been pressing for a breach with the Communist Party.

On the other side, among the Communists, two trends emerged:

Moscow (the Soviet government and the International) and therefore Borodin (in China) had only one desire: to colonize the Kuomintang from the inside, to place Communists at all the key-points in its organization and thus gradually to win control of the Kuomintang and China. After advocating the confiscation of lands in 1926, Borodin now came out against it for fear of alarming the Kuomintang and in order to be able to go on co-operating with it. The Chinese Communist Party leadership, with Ch'en Tu-hsiu, who was naturally hostile to the development of revolutionary action in the countryside, shared this point of view.

Another group, of which Mao Tse-tung was part, and which was backed by M. N. Roy, Indian representative of the International, held that the revolution in China could succeed only if the peasantry were won over, and that it was necessary to destroy the political and economic basis of feudalism – the landlords – and to involve the people in a struggle for independence and democracy by satisfying the peasants through the confiscation and redistribution of the landlords' lands.

This debate was far from academic because there was a threat of a rift between the two sides over the agrarian problem.

The Kuomintang Central Executive Committee in Hankow (Wuhan), in which the Communists still enjoyed an important rôle, was at odds with the foreigners, especially the English and

Americans, who were very powerful in the Yangtze valley. Greatly alarmed, the latter had applied for the despatch of gun-boats and they were more and more afraid that victory by the "Kuomintang revolutionaries" might take the form of a general elimination of Western positions in Central and Southern China. They knew that the Communists were now striving to gain control in the coastal area, especially in Shanghai, the Anglo-Franco-American headquarters, where there were large working-class masses.

While Chiang Kai-shek's army was moving towards the lower valley of the Yangtze, Chou En-lai was ordered by the Communist Party to organize an uprising in Shanghai. On 21 March 1927, a general strike paralysed the town and armed workers seized power. A few days later, when Chiang Kai-shek arrived at the gates of the city, he was able to enter without a struggle and receive the power of the workers' organizations set up by the Communists.

It was at this point that "China's fate" for the next twenty years was sealed. The growing influence which the Communist Party exercised over the Kuomintang, in Hankow as well as in Nanking and Shanghai, filled the Westerners with the gravest fears. In Shanghai, a city which was practically under their control and where the interests of the upper Chinese bourgeoisie or comprador class largely coincided with their own, a classic scene took place, in the best Chinese tradition. After all, to the Anglo-Franco-Americans, Chiang Kai-shek was merely a new "warlord", unquestionably more intelligent, more brilliant and more capable than the rest, but not necessarily different in "sensibility". Besides which, among the trumps which would enable him to settle this grave crisis was the fact of being Sun Yat-sen's "disciple", of having been the ally of the U.S.S.R., and of having summoned the Chinese people to the "anti-imperialist and anti-militarist revolution". Secret negotiations held in foreign concessions in Shanghai managed to convince Chiang Kai-shek and the Right wing of the Kuomintang that it was in their interests to turn on the Communists, before the latter managed to "colonize" the Nationalist Party. If Chiang

c

accepted the bargain, he would benefit from the support of the Chinese big bourgeoisie, which would not stint him financial backing to help him unite China under his aegis, as well as of certain secret societies and of the West who stated that they were prepared to make a few concessions to his "anti-imperialism".

There was a rapid denouement. On 12 April 1927, Chiang Kai-shek brought off his *coup d'état* in Shanghai, and flung his army and his police force against the Communists: there was a rash of arrests and executions. At least five thousand Communists were massacred in Shanghai alone. Chou En-lai, who was on the black list, narrowly escaped and a price was put on his head. But Ch'en Tu-hsiu's son was massacred along with the other Party leaders.

Chiang Kai-shek and the Right wing of the Kuomintang now no longer made any secret of their intention to break with the Communists all along the line, and also with the Soviet Union, whose indiscretions, evasions and a search made at the Soviet Embassy in Peking* revealed "imperialist" ambitions. Since Russia had betrayed China, Chiang Kai-shek declared, the latter could turn only to those powers resolved to treat her on an equal footing.

The Communists, ousted from the lower valley of the Yangtze, fell back on Hankow where they still hoped to restore the situation with the co-operation of the Left Kuomintang, which dominated the Central Executive Committee. But serious dissension broke out between them, especially over the agrarian problem. In order to maintain co-operation with the Left Kuomintang, co-operation desired by Stalin and Borodin, the Communist Party and its secretary-general Ch'en Tu-hsiu, advocated the cessation or shelving of all violent action in the countryside, and that among other things a brake should be put on the confiscation of the lands of the landlords and rich peasants, which Mao Tse-tung and the peasant associations wished to carry out in the hopes of winning the poor peasants over to the revolution.

---

*It was during this operation by Chang Tso-lin, the pro-Japanese warlord in Peking, and the repression which ensued that Li Ta-chao, one of the Party's founders, was captured and strangled. He was thirty-eight.

They also believed, against all reason, that they could rally the Left Kuomintang and part of the local military leaders and organize effective resistance against Chiang Kai-shek and the Right. This was the line that prevailed at the Fifth Congress of the Party held in Hankow in May 1927. Mao was excluded from the party for his activities in the countryside and received orders to leave Hunan. The Congress refused to adopt a resolution on the peasant problem which Mao had proposed and voted for a far more moderate motion. Nevertheless a Chinese Peasant Association was set up at this point and Mao became its first president.

But M. N. Roy of the International, who was in favour of "agrarian reform", brought things to a head. His intrigues, indiscretions and immoderate language turned the Hankow Kuomintang against the Communists. Yet it was the events in Hunan which precipitated the crisis.

Most of the officers in the local revolutionary army (Kuomintang) came from families of landlords and rich peasants in the province. The sometimes savage actions of peasant associations had filled them with anger and desire for revenge. On 21 May, a military uprising took place in Changsha, capital of Hunan. It was a success and led to repression. All union organizations, both peasant and labour, were banned and their offices sacked. The instigator of this move, Ho Chien, who was later made Kuomintang governor of the province, was, according to objective accounts, like a veritable wild beast. Tens of thousands of people, not only Communists but cadres of peasants', workers' and students' associations were massacred. In a few weeks, fifteen thousand of the twenty thousand members of the Communist Party in the province met their deaths*. In the countryside, the landlords' specialized mercenary militia wreaked terrible vengeance, executing peasants by tens of thousands. From that day on, many peasants with no political affiliations turned to the Communists, merely out of a spirit of revenge. In particular, an essentially peasant and already prestigious military leader,

*Note the striking analogy between these events in China in 1927, in Shanghai as well as in Hunan, and those in Indonesia in 1965.

Ho Long, who was in the Ko Lai Hui secret society and had until then remained loyal to the Hankow government, became genuinely angry, went over to the Communist Party, rallied it in August and became one of its great military leaders.

In July, Wang Ching-wei and the Left Kuomintang, warned by Roy that the Communists were contemplating a move towards the confiscation of the landlords' lands, broke off relations with the Communists and expelled them from the Kuomintang. The Marxists were now to be victims of repression in the Centre as well as in the East.

After the breach with Hankow, Ch'en Tu-hsiu, who had advocated "sticking to the Kuomintang", was totally discredited. He returned to Shanghai where he lived in hiding, until his arrest in 1929. Borodin left China for Moscow.

The policy of collaboration with the Kuomintang thus ended in a tragic fiasco and the Communists were now in a serious position both in the North and the South. Moreover, the Party forces, severely tested, were broken up into small fragments. Within the Party, because of the divergences between leaders, "Putschist", "leftist" trends emerged. As Peking historians to-day put it :

Regarding the Chinese revolution as a "permanent revolution" and the revolutionary situation in China as a "permanent up-surge", the Putschist comrades refused to organize an orderly retreat and, adopting the methods of commandism and relying only on a small number of Party members and a small section of the masses, erroneously attempted to stage a series of local uprisings throughout the country, which had no prospect of success (3).

Thus it was that the peasants in the eastern coastal area of Kwangtung rose up three times and established a "revolutionary power" in certain districts, which lasted until April 1928, and that peasant insurrections broke out in the south of Hunan and in Fukien. But other attempts were more serious and had far-reaching consequences.

On 1 August, in Nanchung, units of the revolutionary army

(Kuomintang), under the influence of the Communist Party, totalling about thirty thousand men, rose up and seized the city*. At their head were some men well-known today, Ho Long, Chu Teh, Chou En-lai, and Lin Piao, at nineteen already a colonel. . . . On 5 August these troops left Nanchang and moved towards the coast. They suffered a reverse at Swatow where the local military leaders, supported by foreign gunboats, drove them back. Chou En-lai then went to Canton where he organized the 11 December 1927 uprising. Workers and revolutionary soldiers now set up a "popular power" – the "Commune" – and were involved in fierce battles with the Kuomintang forces. The unequal struggle ended with the crushing of the Communists; Chou En-lai rejoined Chu Teh's troops who were falling back on Kiangsi and Hunan.

It was Mao Tse-tung who once again took the initiative in Hunan. He had been readmitted to the Party. On 7 August, an emergency conference of the Central Committe was held. Ch'en Tu-hsiu had been deposed as secretary-general of the Party. All hope of co-operation with the Kuomintang had been abandoned because, according to Mao, the Nationalist Party had "irretrievably become the tool of imperialism" and "could therefore no longer carry through the democratic revolution". A new line had been adopted.

But shortly afterwards, without the agreement of the Central Committee, Mao, having collected some armed detachments of workers, miners, peasants and soldiers, decided to launch "the Autumn Harvest Uprising" which was intended to establish Communist power in Hunan and to make it a province independent of the Kuomintang. The offensive, launched on 9 September 1927, between Changsha and the eastern part of the provinces, ended in bloody failure. Meeting in November, the Central Committee once again repudiated Mao and relieved him of his post as temporary member of the Central Committee.

Meanwhile Mao Tse-tung was involved in fierce fighting at the head of his armed detachments which he had christened the

*1 August 1927 is remembered as the day when the Chinese Red Army was founded.

"First Division of the First Corps of the Workers' and Peasants' Revolutionary Army". He retreated towards the East. In October, with about a thousand men, he managed to take refuge in the Tsingkiang Mountains, on the Hunan-Kiangsi border, a fairly vast area, thinly populated and inaccessible, where he formed the "revolutionary base in the Hunan-Kiangsi border area".

In April 1928, he was joined there by the troops of Chu Teh, Ch'en Yi, Chou En-lai and Lin Piao. Some months earlier, all had discarded the Kuomintang banner and were flying the Red flag.

4 Guerilla Warfare

The still disparate units collected by Mao Tse-tung, and those which had joined them, were able to seek momentary refuge in the Tsingkiang Mountains, but it was clear that the Kuomintang, determined to "eliminate" the Communists, especially those who persisted in wanting to wage an armed action and to take away a patch of land from the authority of the national government, would be unlikely to give them any respite.

The situation was very serious for the Communists. Mao described it in the simplest of terms :

Our work in the Hunan-Kiangsi border area began in October 1927. At the start, all our Party organizations in the counties were defunct. The local armed forces consisted only of the two units under Yuan Wen-tsai and Wang Tso in the vicinity of the Tsingkiang Mountains, each unit having sixty rifles in bad repair, while the peasant self-defence corps in the counties of Yunghsin, Lienhua, Chaling and Linghsien had been totally disarmed by the landlord class and the revolutionary ardour of the masses had been stifled (1). . . .

However, in November 1927, some progress was made. A first "Council of Delegates" (Soviet) was set up in Chaling and a first "government" (executive committee), known as the "Government of the Workers, Peasants and Soldiers", was elected. Intensive work was carried on during the winter, and Mao tells how "by February 1928, there were already Party committees". In all districts small local armed detachments had been set up, and in two districts "there were a good many guerilla uprisings against the landlords which aroused the masses, and all were fairly successful". Mao went on: "The organs of political power were called Governments of the Workers, Peasants and Soldiers. Soldiers' committees were set up in the army."

But although, after April–May 1928, the arrival of Chu Teh's forces in the Tsingkiang Mountains, would have enabled the creation of a "revolutionary base in the border region between Hunan and Kiangsi", not without violent fluctuations, the fundamental question was for a long while "Can Red political power exist in China*?"

An important section of the Party, and of the Central Committee, argued that in view of the sizeable military forces at Chiang Kai-shek's disposal and their overwhelming superiority in equipment, to resist with arms, to wage an armed action, was folly. It was necessary, according to this body of opinion, to go into hiding, wait for better days, rouse the masses by patient propaganda, exploiting the inevitable rivalries between "warlords" and "imperialist powers", and eventually rely on the support of the Soviet Union. One day the Party would emerge from the shadows and could perhaps, if not recover a legal existence, at least effectively manoeuvre the masses already won over to the cause of the revolution by propaganda.

Mao thought that this was mere illusion: to follow this path amounted, in his opinion, to putting oneself at the mercy of an enemy who, thanks to the army, police and secret services, could eliminate underground organizations, and he explained this, in

---

*The problems tackled in this chapter are the same as arose in Yugoslavia, 1941–5, in Vietnam since 1951, in Greece 1943–9, in Algeria 1954–61, in Cuba 1958–61 and which are now arising in Latin America, in the Portuguese African colonies and in Thailand.

a famous report, dated 5 October 1928, "Why is it that Red Political Power Exists in China?"

First, he showed that the nature of power in China had not radically altered with the victory of the Kuomintang* :

China is in urgent need of a bourgeois-democratic revolution, and this revolution can be completed only under the leadership of the proletariat. Because the proletariat failed to exercise firm leadership in the revolution of 1926–27 which started from Kwangtung and spread towards the Yangtze River, leadership was seized by the comprador and landlord classes and the revolution was replaced by counter-revolution. The bourgeois-democratic revolution thus met with a temporary defeat. This defeat was a heavy blow to the Chinese proletariat and peasantry and also a blow to the Chinese bourgeoisie (but not to the comprador and landlord classes).

According to the directives of the Communist International and the Central Committee of our Party, the content of China's democratic revolution consists in overthrowing the rule of imperialism and its warlord tools in China so as to complete the national revolution, and in carrying out the agrarian revolution so as to eliminate the feudal exploitation of the peasants by the landlord class. Such a revolutionary movement has been growing day by day since the Tsinan massacre in May 1928 (2).

Mao then emphasized that "the long-term survival in a country of one or more small areas under Red political power completely surrounded by a White regime is a phenomenon that has never occurred anywhere else in the world", but that he was concerned with another unusual phenomenon, namely, war within the White regime :

*In 1928, Chiang Kai-shek united China. After marrying Sung Mei-lin, an American-educated Chinese Protestant, he marched on the North, with the support of the British and Americans, to attack the pro-Japanese "warlords", especially Chang Tso-lin. To prevent Anglo-American influence from spreading to their area, the Japanese tried to block Chiang's advance at Tsinan in May 1928, but Chiang by-passed the obstacle, occupied Peking in June 1928 and Manchuria in December 1928. In July 1928, he moved the capital from Peking to Nanking.

It is a feature of semi-colonial China that, since the first year of the Republic (1912), the various cliques of old and new warlords have waged incessant wars against one another, supported by imperialism from abroad and by the comprador and landlord classes at home. Such a phenomenon is to be found in none of the imperialist countries not for that matter in any colony under direct imperialist rule, but only in a country like China which is under indirect imperialist rule. Two things account for its occurrence, namely a localized agricultural economy (not a unified capitalist economy) and the imperialist policy of marking off spheres of influence in order to divide and exploit. The prolonged splits and wars within the White regime provide a condition for the emergence and persistence of one or more small Red areas under the leadership of the Communist Party amidst the encirclement of the White regime. The independent regime carved out on the borders of Hunan and Kiangsi Provinces is one of many such small areas. In difficult or critical times some comrades often have doubts about the survival of Red political power and become pessimistic. The reason is that they have not found the correct explanation for its emergence and survival. If we realize that splits and wars will never cease within the White regime in China, we shall have no doubts about the emergence, survival and daily growth of Red political power.

The regions where China's Red political power has first emerged and is able to last for a long time have not been those unaffected by the democratic revolution, such as Szechuan, Kweichow, Yunnan and the northern provinces, but regions such as the provinces of Hunan, Kwangtung, Hupeh and Kiangsi, where the masses of workers, peasants and soldiers rose in great numbers in the course of the bourgeois-democratic revolution of 1926 and 1927. In many parts of these provinces trade unions and peasant associations were formed on a wide scale, and many economic and political struggles were waged by the working class and the peasantry against the landlord class and the bourgeoisie. This is why the people held political power for three days in the city of Canton and why independent regimes of peasants emerged in Haifeng and Lufeng, in eastern and southern Hunan, in the Hunan-Kiangsi border area and in Huangan, Hupeh Province. As for the present Red Army, it is a split-off from the National Revolutionary Army which underwent democratic political training and came under the influence of the masses of workers and peasants. . . .

Whether it is possible for the people's political power in small areas to last depends on whether the nation-wide revolutionary situation continues to develop. If it does, then the small Red areas will undoubtedly last for a long time, and will, moreover, inevitably become one of the many forces for winning nation-wide political power. If the nation-wide revolutionary situation does not continue to develop but stagnates for a fairly long time, then it will be impossible for the small Red areas to last long. . . .

The existence of a regular Red Army of adequate strength is a necessary condition for the existence of Red political power. If we have local Red Guards only but no regular Red Army, then we cannot cope with the regular White forces, but only with the landlords' levies. Therefore, even when the masses of workers and peasants are active, it is definitely impossible to create an independent regime, let alone an independent regime which is durable and grows daily, unless we have regular forces of adequate strength. It follows that the idea of "establishing independent regimes of the workers and the peasants by armed force" is an important one which must be fully grasped by the Communist Party and by the masses of workers and peasants in areas under the independent regime.

Another important condition in addition to the above is required for the prolonged existence and development of Red political power, namely that the Communist Party organization should be strong and its policy correct.

Splits and wars among the warlords weaken the power of the White regime. Thus opportunities are provided for the rise of Red political power in small areas. But fighting among the warlords does not go on every day. Whenever the White regime in one or more provinces enjoys temporary stability, the ruling classes there inevitably combine and do their utmost to destroy Red political power. In areas where all the necessary conditions for its establishment and persistence are not fulfilled, Red political power is in danger of being overthrown by the enemy (3). . . .

Mao Tse-tung, referring to the creation of a revolutionary base in the border area, then indicated the objectives of the "Special Committee of the Party" of which he had control:

Struggle resolutely against the enemy, set up political power in the middle section of the Lohsiao mountain range, and oppose flightism.

Deepen the agrarian revolution in areas under the independent regime.

Promote the development of the local Party organization with the help of the army Party organization and promote the development of the local armed forces with the help of the regular army.

Concentrate the Red Army units in order to fight the enemy confronting them when the time is opportune, and oppose the division of forces so as to avoid being destroyed one by one.

Adopt the policy of advancing in a series of waves to expand the area under the independent regime, and oppose the policy of expansion by adventurist advance.

Thanks to these proper tactics, to a terrain favourable to our struggle, and to the inadequate co-ordination between the troops invading from Hunan and those invading from Kiangsi, we were able to win a number of victories in the four months from April to July. . . .

Mao, in his optimism, thought it would be possible "to extend the influence of the agrarian revolution and of the people's political power in the border area to neighbouring areas" and that the revolutionary base would thus play a large rôle "through the insurrections of the workers and peasants" which would unfold in Hunan, Hupei and Kiangsi "for the seizure of political power in these three provinces. . . . (4)"

He concluded by underlining the need to consolidate the military bases in the mountainous region. "The way to consolidate these bases is, first, to construct adequate defences, second, to store sufficient grain, and third, to set up comparatively good Red Army hospitals. The Party in the border area must strive to perform these three tasks effectively*."

In another famous report, "The Struggle in the Tsingkiang

*Up until the Cultural Revolution at least, the Peking government used to take some of its African or Latin American guests to visit the Tsingkiang Mountains.

Mountains", dated 25 November 1928, Mao Tse-tung completed his earlier analysis: for the Red areas to subsist and develop, not only must the enemy be divided, we "also require the following conditions: (i) a sound mass base, (ii) a sound Party organization, (iii) a fairly strong Red army, (iv) terrain favourable to military operations, and (v) economic resources sufficient for sustenance" (5). What had above all to be avoided, he stressed, in a period of stabilization, was "to divide our forces for an adventurous advance, and the worst thing in local work (distributing land, establishing political power, expanding the Party and organizing local armed forces) is to scatter our personnel and neglect to lay a solid foundation in the central districts".

But Mao emphasized the considerable changes made since April 1928 with the forming of the "revolutionary base", and he went on:

Since April this year the Red areas have been gradually extended. . . . In the Red areas the greater part of the land has been distributed and the remainder was being distributed. Organs of political power were set up everywhere in the districts and townships. . . . Insurrectionary detachments of workers and peasants were organized in the villages, and Red Guards were formed at the district and county levels (6). . . .

But it was at this point that the storm was unleashed, in the shape of the Kuomintang offensive, and Mao's description of it sheds instructive light on the nature of the battle, the composition of the Red Army, and the problems which Mao and his group were up against during this "ordeal by fire":

In July the Kiangsi enemy forces launched attacks, and in August the Hunan and Kiangsi enemy forces jointly attacked the Tsingkiang Mountains. All the county towns and the plains in the border area were occupied by the enemy. The enemy's jackals – the peace preservation corps and the landlords' levies – ran amuck, and White terror raged throughout the towns and countryside. Most of the Party and government organizations collapsed. The rich peasants and the opportunists in the

Party went over to the enemy in great numbers . . . The enemy is attempting to destroy our base area by military attacks and economic blockade, and we are now preparing to defeat his attacks.

Since the struggle in the border area is exclusively military, both the Party and the masses have to be placed on a war footing. How to deal with the enemy, how to fight, has become the central problem in our daily life. An independent regime must be an armed one. Wherever such an area is located, it will be immediately occupied by the enemy if armed forces are lacking or inadequate, or if wrong tactics are used in dealing with the enemy. As the struggle is getting fiercer every day, our problems have become extremely complex and serious . . .

As to class origin, the Red Army consists partly of workers and peasants and partly of *lumpen*-proletarians. Of course, it is inadvisable to have too many of the latter. But they are able to fight, and as fighting is going on every day with mounting casualties, it is already no easy matter to get replacements even from among them. In these circumstances the only solution is to intensify political training.

The majority of the Red Army soldiers come from the mercenary armies, but their character changes once they are in the Red Army. First of all, the Red Army has abolished the mercenary system, making the men feel they are fighting for themselves and for the people and not for somebody else. So far the Red Army has no system of regular pay, but issues grain, money for cooking oil, salt, firewood and vegetables, and a little pocket money. Land has been allotted to all Red Army officers and men who are natives of the border area, but it is rather difficult to allot land to those from other parts of the country.

After receiving political education, the Red Army soldiers have become class-conscious, learned the essentials of distributing land, setting up political power, arming the workers and peasants, etc., and they know they are fighting for themselves, for the working class and the peasantry. Hence they can endure the hardships of the bitter struggle without complaint . . .

Ordinarily a soldier needs six months' or a year's training before he can fight, but our soldiers, recruited only yesterday, have to fight today with practically no training. Poor in military technique, they fight on courage alone. As long periods of rest and training are out of the question, the only thing to do is to try and avoid certain engagements if possible and thus gain time for training. We now have a corps of 150 people in training as lower-ranking officers, and we intend to make this course a permanent institution. . . . As the casualties among the lower cadres are heavy, captured enemy soldiers often become platoon leaders or company commanders in a very short time; some of those captured in February or March are already battalion commanders. . . .

The Hunan Provincial Committee has asked us to attend to the material conditions of the soldiers and make them at least a little better than those of the average worker or peasant. Actually they are worse. In addition to grain, each man receives only five cents a day for cooking oil, salt, firewood and vegetables, and even this is hard to keep up. The monthly cost of these items alone amounts to more than ten thousand silver dollars, which is obtained exclusively through expropriation of the local tyrants. We now have cotton padding for winter clothing for the whole army of five thousand men, but are still short of cloth. Cold as the weather is, many of our men are still wearing only two layers of thin clothing. Fortunately we are inured to hardships. . . .

After each engagement there are some wounded. Also many officers and men have fallen ill from malnutrition, exposure to cold or other causes. Our hospitals up in the mountains give both Chinese and Western treatment, but are short of doctors and medicines. At present they have over eight hundred patients. The Hunan Provincial Committee promised to obtain drugs for us, but so far we have received none. We still hope the Central Committee and the two Provincial Committees will send us a few doctors with Western training, and some iodine.

Apart from the rôle played by the Party, the reason why the Red Army has been able to carry on in such poor material conditions and such frequent engagements is its practice of democracy. The officers do not beat the men; officers and men receive equal treatment; soldiers are free to hold meetings and to speak out; trivial formalities have been done away with; and the accounts are open for all to inspect. The soldiers handle the mess arrangements and, out of the daily five cents for cooking oil, salt, firewood and vegetables, they can even save a little for pocket money, amounting to roughly six or seven coppers per person per day, which is called "mess savings". All this gives great satisfaction to the soldiers. The newly captured soldiers in particular feel that our army and the Kuomintang army are worlds apart. They feel spiritually liberated, even though material conditions in the Red Army are not equal to those in the White army. The very soldiers who had no courage in the White army yesterday are very brave in the Red Army today; such is the effect of democracy. The Red Army is like a furnace in which all captured soldiers are transmuted the moment they come over. In China the army needs democracy as much as the people do. Democracy in our army is an important weapon for undermining the feudal mercenary army.

The Party organization now has four levels, the company branch, the battalion committee, the regimental committee and the army committee. In a company there is the branch, with a group in each squad. The Party branch is organized on a company basis ... At present the company branches are short of good Party secretaries, and we ask the Central Committee to send us a number of activists from among those who can no longer function where they are now. Almost all the cadres from southern Hunan are doing Party work in the army. But since some of them were scattered during the retreat in southern Hunan in August, we now have no people to spare.

The local armed forces consist of Red Guards and insurrectionary detachments of workers and peasants. Armed with spears and shot-guns, these detachments are organized on a township basis, each township having one detachment whose strength varies with the population. Its job is to suppress counter-revolution, protect the township government and assist the Red Army and Red Guards in battle when the enemy appears. The insurrectionary detachments started in Yungshin as an underground force, but they have come into the open since we captured the entire county. The organization has now been extended to other counties in the border area and the name remains unchanged. The arms of the Red Guards are mainly five-round rifles but also include some nine-round and single-round rifles. There are 140 rifles in Ningkang, 220 in Yunghsin, 43 in Lienhau, 50 in Chaling, 90 in Linghsien, 130 in Suichuan and 10 in Wanan, making a total of 683. Most of the rifles have been supplied by the Red Army, but a small number were captured from the enemy by the Red Guards themselves. . . . At present the Red Guards in the counties still have far too few rifles, fewer than those of the landlords; the Red Army should continue to help them with arms. The Red Army should do everything, short of reducing its own fighting capacity, to help arm the people. We have laid it down that each battalion of the Red Army should consist of four companies, each with 75 rifles, and, counting the rifles of the special task company, machine-gun company, trench-mortar company, regimental headquarters, and the three battalion headquarters, each regiment will have 1,075 rifles. . . .

The principle for the Red Army is concentration, and that for the Red Guards is dispersion. At the present time when the reactionary regime is temporarily stable, the enemy can mass huge forces to attack the Red Army, and dispersion would not be to the Red Army's advantage. In our experience, the dispersion of forces has almost always led to defeat, while the concentration of forces to fight a numerically inferior, equal or slightly superior enemy force has often led to victory. . . .

The most effective method in propaganda directed at the enemy forces is to release captured soldiers and give the wounded medical treatment. Whenever soldiers, platoon leaders, or company or battalion commanders of the enemy forces are captured, we immediately conduct propaganda among them; they are divided into those wishing to stay and those wishing to leave, and the latter are given travelling expenses and set free. This immediately knocks the bottom out of the enemy's slander that "the Communist bandits kill everyone on sight". . . . Medical treatment for the enemy wounded also has a great effect. Clever people on the enemy side like Li Wen-pin have recently imitated us by stopping the killing of prisoners and by giving medical attention to the wounded. Nevertheless, our men rejoin us at the very next engagement, bringing their arms with them, and this has happened twice already. In addition, we do as much written propaganda as possible, for instance, painting slogans. Wherever we go, we cover the walls with them. But we are short of people who can draw. . . .

As for the military bases, the first base, the Tsingkiang

Mountains, is at the juncture of four counties, Ningkang, Lingh-sien, Suichuan and Yunghsin. . . . All these places used to be infested by bandits and deserters but have now been turned into our base area. Its population is under two thousand, and the yield of unhusked rice is less than ten thousand piculs (about 500 tons), and so the entire grain for the army has to be supplied from Ningkang, Yunghsin and Suichuan Counties. All the strategic passes in the mountains are fortified. Our hospitals, bedding, and clothing workshops, ordnance department and regimental rear offices are all here. At the present moment grain is being transported to the mountains from Ningkang. Provided we have adequate supplies, the enemy can never break in. The second base, the Chiulung Mountains, is at the juncture of the four counties of Ningkang, Yunghsin, Lienhua and Chaling. It is less important than the Tsingkiang Mountains, but serves as the rearmost base for the local armed forces of the four counties, and it too has been fortified. It is essential for an independent Red regime encircled by the White regime to make use of the strategic advantages offered by mountains. . . .

The land situation in the border areas. Roughly speaking, more than 60 per cent of the land belongs to the landlords and less than 40 per cent to the peasants . . . Given this land situation, it is possible to win the support of the majority for the confiscation and redistribution of all the land. . . . The land policy which has been adopted in the border areas is complete confiscation and thorough distribution (7). . . .

However, Mao pointed out that "people's political power" was not operating satisfactorily :

The executive committees of the township, district or even county governments were invariably elected at some kind of mass meeting. But mass meetings called on the spur of the moment can neither discuss questions nor help in training the masses politically, and, what is more, they are only too apt to be manipulated by intellectuals or careerists. . . .

At present, what the masses of the people generally under-stand by the "government of workers, peasants and soldiers" is the executive committee, because they are still unaware of the powers of the council, and think that the executive committee alone is the real power. An executive committee without a council behind it often acts without regard for the views of the masses, and there are instances everywhere of hesitation and compromise on the confiscation and redistribution of land, of squandering or embezzling funds, and of recoiling before the White forces or fighting only half-heartedly . . .

In the early days the small landlords and rich peasants scrambled to get on to government committees especially at the township level. Wearing red ribbons and feigning enthusiasm, they wormed their way into the government committees by trickery and seized control of everything, relegating the poor-peasant members to a minor role. They can be cleared out only when they are unmasked in the course of struggle and the poor peasants assert themselves. . . .

The role of the Communist Party was, according to Mao, not yet adequately defined. Of course, he said :

The Party enjoys immense prestige and authority among the masses, the government much less. The reason is that for the sake of convenience the Party handles many things directly and brushes aside the government bodies. There are many such instances. In some places there are no leading Party members' groups in the government organizations, while in others they exist but are not functioning properly. From now on the Party must carry out its task of giving leadership to the government; with the exception of propaganda, the Party's policies and the measures it recommends must be carried out through the government organizations (8). . . .

In another report, written a year later, in December 1929, "On Correcting Mistaken Ideas in the Party", Mao Tse-tung, recalling that "military affairs . . . are only one means of accomplishing political tasks", gave a striking definition of the role of the Red Army. He wrote :

They imagine that the task of the Red Army, like that of the White Army, is merely to fight. They do not understand that the Chinese Red Army is an armed body for carrying out the political tasks of the revolution. Especially at present, the Red Army should certainly not confine itself to fighting; besides fighting to destroy the enemy's military strength, it should shoulder such important tasks as doing propaganda among the masses, organizing the masses, arming them, helping them to establish revolutionary political power and setting up Party organizations. The Red Army fights not merely for the sake of fighting but in order to conduct propaganda among the masses, organize them, arm them, and help them to establish revolutionary political power. Without these objectives, fighting loses its meaning and the Red Army loses the reason for its existence (9)....

But the months went by and the situation hardly improved. Mao said in December 1928:

In the past year we have fought in many places and are keenly aware that the revolutionary tide is on the ebb in the country as a whole. While Red political power has been established in a few small areas, in the country as a whole the people lack the ordinary democratic rights, the workers, the peasants and even the bourgeois democrats do not have freedom of speech or assembly, and the worst crime is to join the Communist Party. Wherever the Red Army goes, the masses are cold and aloof, and only after our propaganda do they slowly move into action. . . . We have an acute sense of our isolation which we keep hoping will end (10) . . .

In 1929, fresh difficulties arose. The Tsingkiang Mountains were an excellent base for a small mobile army like Mao Tse-tung's or Chu Teh's. Enjoying good natural defences and resources adequate for a restricted armed force, it lent itself very well to guerilla activities, but with the Red Army's increase in numbers and especially with the violent offensive launched by the Whites against the base in late 1928, resources became inadequate and the situation difficult. It became necessary to force the blockade, to break through the encircling forces, and while P'eng Te-huai's units remained in the Tsingkiang Mountains, Mao and Chu Teh, with the lion's share of the troops, went and set up a larger base in Kiangsi and Fukien. But the general situation did not grow perceptibly better or the isolation less, and Mao could well have repeated at the beginning of 1930 what he wrote in November 1928. "Only by launching a political and economic struggle for democracy, which will involve the urban petty bourgeoisie, can we turn the revolution into a seething tide that will surge through the country," without however concealing the fact that "in China, a country with a predominantly agricultural economy . . . the use of military action (is necessary) to develop insurrection" (11).

It was at just such a critical moment, when discouragement began to enter the ranks of many cadres that Mao made his report, dated 5 January 1930, entitled: "A Single Spark can Start a Prairie Fire", of which long extracts are worth quoting:

Some comrades in our Party still do not know how to appraise the current situation correctly and how to settle the attendant question of what action to take. Though they believe that a revolutionary high tide is inevitable, they do not believe it to be imminent. Therefore, they disapprove of the plan to take Kiangsi and only approve of roving guerilla actions in the three areas on the borders of Fukien, Kwangtung and Kiangsi; at the same time, as they do not have a deep understanding of what it means to establish Red political power in the guerilla areas, they do not have a real understanding of the idea of accelerating the nation-wide revolutionary high tide through the consolidation and expansion of Red political power. They seem to think that, since the revolutionary high tide is still remote, it will be labour lost to attempt to establish political power by hard work. Instead, they want to extend our political influence through the easier method of roving guerilla actions, and, once the masses throughout the country have been won over, or more or less won over, they want to launch a nation-wide armed insurrection which, with the participation of the Red Army, would become a great nation-wide revolution. Their theory that we must first win over the masses on a country-wide scale and in all regions and then establish political power does not accord with the actual state of the Chinese revolution. . . . The establishment and expansion of the Red army, the guerilla forces and the Red areas is the highest form of peasant struggle under the leadership of the proletariat, the inevitable outcome of the growth of the semi-colonial peasant struggle, and undoubtedly the most important factor in accelerating the revolutionary high tide throughout the country. . . . The policy which merely calls for roving guerilla actions cannot accomplish the task of accelerating this nation-wide revolutionary high tide (12). . . .

Mao then indicated that political measures were indispensable:

These measures foreshadow in particular the establishing of base areas; of systematically setting up political power; of deepening the agrarian revolution; of expanding the people's armed forces by a comprehensive process of building up first the township Red Guards, then the district Red Guards, then the county Red Guards, then the local Red Army troops, all the way up to the regular Red Army troops; of spreading political power by advancing in a series of waves, etc., etc. Only thus is it possible to build the confidence of the revolutionary masses throughout the country, as the Soviet Union has built it throughout the world. Only thus is it possible to create tremendous difficulties for the reactionary ruling classes, shake their foundations and hasten their internal disintegration. Only thus is it really possible to create a Red Army which will become the chief weapon for the great revolution of the future. In short, only thus is it possible to hasten the revolutionary high tide.

Comrades who suffer from revolutionary impetuosity overestimate the subjective forces of the revolution and underestimate the forces of the counter-revolution. Such an appraisal stems mainly from subjectivism. In the end, it undoubtedly leads to putschism. On the other hand, underestimating the subjective forces of the revolution and overestimating the forces of the counter-revolution would also constitute an improper appraisal and be certain to produce bad results of another kind. Therefore, in judging the political situation in China it is necessary to understand the following:

i). Although the subjective forces of the revolution in China are now weak, so also are all organizations (organs of political power, armed forces, political parties, etc.) of the reactionary ruling classes, resting as they do on the backward and fragile social and economic structure of China. This helps to explain why revolution cannot break out at once in the countries of Western Europe where, although the subjective forces of revolution are now perhaps somewhat stronger than in China, the forces of the reactionary ruling classes are many times stronger. In China the revolution will undoubtedly move towards a high tide more rapidly, for although the subjective forces of the revolution at present are weak, the forces of the counter-revolution are relatively weak too.

ii). The subjective forces of the revolution have indeed been greatly weakened since the defeat of the revolution in 1927. The remaining forces are very small and those comrades who judge by appearances alone naturally feel pessimistic. But if we judge by essentials, it is quite another story. Here we can apply the old Chinese saying, "A single spark can start a prairie fire". In other words, our forces, although small at present, will grow very rapidly. In the conditions prevailing in China, their growth is not only possible but indeed inevitable, as the 30 May Movement and the Great Revolution which followed have fully proved. When we look at a thing, we must examine its essence and treat its appearance merely as an usher at the threshold, and once we cross the threshold, we must grasp the essence of the thing; this is the only reliable and scientific method of analysis.

iii). Similarly, in appraising the counter-revolutionary forces, we must never look merely at their appearance, but should examine their essence. In the initial period of our independent regime in the Hunan-Kiangsi border area, some comrades genuinely believed the incorrect appraisal made by the Hunan Provincial Committee and regarded the class enemy as not worth a rap; the two descriptive terms, "terribly shaky" and "extremely panicky", which are standing jokes to this day, were used by the Hunan Provincial Committee at the time (from May to June 1928) in appraising the Hunan ruler Lu Ti-ping. Such an appraisal necessarily led to putschism in the political sphere. But during the four months from November of that year to February 1929 . . . when the enemy's third "joint suppression expedition" was approaching the Tsingkiang Mountains, some comrades asked the question, "How long can we keep the Red Flag flying?"

As a matter of fact, the struggle in China between Britain, the United States and Japan had by then become quite open, and a state of tangled warfare between Chiang Kai-shek, the Kwangsi clique and Feng Yu-hsiang was taking shape; hence it was actually the time when the counter-revolutionary tide had begun to ebb and the revolutionary tide to rise again. Yet pessimistic ideas were to be found not only in the Red Army and local Party organizations; even the Central Committee was misled by appearances and adopted a pessimistic tone. Its February letter is evidence of the pessimistic analysis made in the Party at that time.

iv). The objective situation today is still such that comrades who see only the superficial appearance and not the essence of what is before them are liable to be misled. In particular, when our comrades working in the Red Army are defeated in battle or encircled or pursued by strong enemy forces, they often unwittingly generalize and exaggerate their momentary, specific and limited situation, as though the situation in China and the world as a whole gave no cause for optimism and the prospects of victory for the revolution were remote. The reason they seize on the appearance and brush aside the essence in their observation of things is that they have not made a scientific analysis of the essence of the overall situation. The question whether there will soon be a revolutionary high tide in China can be decided only by making a detailed examination to ascertain whether the contradictions leading to a revolutionary high tide are really developing (13). . . .

Mao was here compiling a list of the various contradictions of which China was the centre and showing that, as they developed and deepened, things were inescapably moving towards a revolutionary situation. And he went on :

Once we understand all these contradictions . . . we shall also see that the high tide of revolution against the imperialists, the warlords and the landlords is inevitable, and will come very soon. All China is littered with dry faggots which will soon be aflame. The saying, "A single spark can start a prairie fire", is an apt description of how the current situation will develop. . . . The Kuomintang's three "suppression" campaigns against the Tsingkiang Mountains was the high water mark reached by the counter-revolutionary tide. But there it stopped, and since then the counter-revolutionary tide has gradually receded while the revolutionary tide has gradually risen. Although our Party's fighting capacity and organizational strength have been weakened to the extent described by the Central Committee, they will be rapidly restored, and the passivity among comrades in the Party will quickly disappear as the counter-revolutionary tide gradually ebbs. The masses will certainly come over to us. The Kuomintang's policy of massacre only serves to "drive the fish into deep waters", as the saying goes, and reformism no longer has any mass appeal. It is certain that the masses will soon shed their illusions about the Kuomintang. In the emerging situation, no other party will be able to compete with the Communist Party in winning over the masses. . . . The tactics we have derived from the struggle of the past three years are indeed different from any other tactics, ancient or modern, Chinese or foreign. With our tactics, the masses can be aroused for struggle on an ever-broadening scale, and no enemy, however powerful, can cope with us. Ours are guerilla tactics. They consist mainly of the following points :

"Divide our forces to arouse the masses, concentrate our forces to deal with the enemy."

"The enemy advances, we retreat; the enemy camps, we harass; the enemy tires, we attack; the enemy retreats, we pursue."

"To extend stable base areas, employ the policy of advancing in waves; when pursued by a powerful enemy, employ the policy of circling around."

"Arouse the largest numbers of the masses in the shortest possible time and by the best possible methods."

These tactics are just like casting a net; at any moment we should be able to cast it or draw it in. We cast it wide to win over the masses and draw it in to deal with the enemy. Such are the tactics we have used for the past three years.

Here, "to cast the net wide" means to divide our forces within a short radius . . . As to dividing our forces over a wide radius, it is possible only on the two conditions that circumstances are comparatively favourable and the leading bodies fairly strong. For the purpose of dividing up our forces is to put us in a better position for winning over the masses, for deepening the agrarian revolution and establishing political power, and for expanding the Red Army and the local armed units. It is better not to divide our forces when this purpose cannot be attained or the division of our forces would lead to defeat and to the weakening of the Red Army. . . .

How then should we interpret the word "soon" in the statement, "there will soon be a high tide of revolution"? This is a common question among comrades. Marxists are not fortunetellers. They should, and indeed can, only indicate the general direction of future developments and changes; they should not and cannot fix the day and the hour in a mechanistic way. But when I say that there will soon be a high tide of revolution in China, I am emphatically not speaking of something which in the words of some people "is possibly coming", something illusory, unattainable and devoid of significance for action. It is like a ship far out at sea whose mast-head can already be seen from the shore; it is like the morning sun in the east whose shimmering rays are visible from a high mountain top; it is like a child about to be born moving restlessly in its mother's womb (14).

Confrontation with Li Li-san

After 1930, Mao Tse-tung suffered something of an eclipse, and for nearly seven years it was as if his thought were curbed, troubled and even deprived of means of expression, because he neither said nor wrote anything of note. The Chinese Communist Party was at this stage passing through a sort of crisis, a sort of "infantile disorder", and Mao Tse-tung, who did not share the views of the dominant faction, naturally toed the "line", because of the rules of democratic centralism, but hardly ever expressed himself.

From 1930–34, it was the "Li Li-san line" that prevailed directly or indirectly in the Party.

Li Li-san, like Mao a Hunanese, had been with Chou En-lai in a group of young men who had gone to study in France from 1920–22, where an important section of the Chinese Communist Party had been trained. His personality had dominated the Central Committee ever since the Sixth Party Congress, held in Moscow in September 1928. Li Li-san's position, which enjoyed its greatest glory between June and September 1930, was roughly as follows: he recognized the usefulness of establishing Soviets in rural bases and conducting guerilla activities from them, but this could only be, in his opinion, a temporary phase until such time as circumstances once again became favourable for a general uprising which would overthrow the Kuomintang government throughout China. The Chinese revolution had to be carried out according to the classical Marxist schema: it was up to the urban working-class proletariat to execute it and control it. The peasantry could only contribute; moreover, it was incapable of doing anything worthwhile without working-class leadership. Armed uprisings in the countryside might have some use over a limited period, if only to set up and train a "Red Army". The decisive action had to take place in the great urban centres, which the Red Army would seize with the aid of the proletariat on the appointed day.

After a spell of discouragement, at the beginning of 1929, the Komintern, faced with the crisis of world capitalism which began at the end of 1929, had come to support this line and to favour a "revolutionary leap" (see the 26 October 1929 letter from Moscow to the Chinese Communist Party), and Li Li-san, in the following spring, interpreting the Soviet directives somewhat hastily, persuaded the Chinese Politburo that "powerful assaults by the Red Army" could now make a decisive contribution to victory. This was embodied in the famous Politburo resolution of 11 June 1930 (15).

Orders were now given to all the armed forces in the Communist Party, including Mao's, to attack the large towns in Central China, as a prelude to the general uprising, perhaps even (intervention by the "imperialists" being regarded as inevitable) to the world conflict between socialism and capitalism. Thus it was that P'eng Te-huai attacked Changsha which he took on 28 July and held for ten days. Chu Teh advanced on Nanchang and Ho Long on Wuhan (Hankow). But the Kuomintang quickly recovered itself and the Communists were obliged to retreat and retire to the "revolutionary bases" and in particular the one where, in February 1930, before the resounding triumph of the "Li Li-san line", Mao had proclaimed the "Soviet provincial government of Kiangsi".

This was a crushing defeat for the supporters of Li Li-san. The latter had to retire, and then, summoned to Moscow, had to leave China, where he did not return until 1945*. But his political line, overall leadership by the working-class proletariat in Chinese Communism, was preserved by the new control which Moscow imposed on the Chinese Communist Party in January 1931. These new, very "bolshevik" leaders, were extremely concerned about the "peasant mentality" and "guerilla spirit" which, according to them, prevailed in the "base" controlled by Mao. This was why, in autumn 1931, the Central Committee felt it advisable to leave Shanghai, where it was leading a dangerous clandestine existence, to go and settle in Kiangsi, whose base had successively broken up three Kuomintang offensives, from which it could control Mao Tse-tung and his group more effectively.

In November 1931, following on Komintern "suggestions", mainly dated 26 August 1931, it was decided to set up a "Chinese Central Soviet Government" and a "Chinese Soviet Republic". The latter was proclaimed on 7 November 1931 in Juichin. A council of People's Commissars was set up and Mao Tse-tung was elected its president. But this was for the Central Committee a way of eliminating him. His military tactics (guerilla warfare) were the object of growing criticism, as was his lack of enthusiasm for principally and rapidly developing the Red Army. Finally Mao's military eviction became almost complete in May 1933 when Chou En-lai was appointed political commissar of the Red Army, whose supreme command still belonged to Chu Teh. Mao remained president of the Executive Committee of the Chinese Soviet Republic, but it seems that his responsibilities were now far more economic than

---

*He turned up, chiefly in Manchuria, where he made friends with Kao Kang, and then in Peking (trade union activities). He committed suicide during the recent Cultural Revolution (*Le Monde,* 8 August 1967.)

military. He devoted himself in particular to reviving class struggle in the countryside* and agricultural production.

This decline in Mao's political and military position was rapidly followed by a deterioration in the military position of the Communists. After the Li Li-san offensive in 1930, Chiang Kai-shek, realizing the danger, had decided to "have done with the Reds". When the Central Committee of the Chinese Communist Party arrived in Kiangsi in October 1931, Mao and Chu Teh, thanks to the strategy and tactics of guerilla warfare which they had now perfected, succeeded, with relatively limited numbers of troops (30–40,000 men), in breaking the three "encirclement and suppression campaigns", the official name given them by Nanking, which the Kuomintang had launched against the Kiangsi base, the first with 100,000 men, in December 1930–January 1931, the second with 200,000 men in spring 1931, and the third, led personally by Chiang Kai-shek, with 300,000 men. This last operation, it is true, had to be temporarily abandoned by Nanking because of the Japanese attack in Manchuria in September 1931.

The "Chinese Soviet Republic", with its three million inhabitants, felt strong enough in 1932 to "benefit from the contradictions of capitalism", as recommended by the Komintern, and once again attack the Nanking Central Government. The Party leadership argued that times had changed and that a new method could be applied. Mao later gave the following resumé of the "argumentation by comrades" in favour of the new strategy :

Was it not better to defeat the enemy without abandoning territory? And was it not better still to defeat the enemy in his own areas, or on the borders between his areas and ours? . . . Now our own state had been established and our Red army had become a regular army. Our fight against Chiang Kai-shek had become a war between two states, between two great armies. History should not repeat itself, and everything pertaining to "guerilla-ism" should be totally discarded. The new

*Mao's peasant Marxism was still suspect.

principles were "completely Marxist", while the old had been created by guerilla units in the mountains, and there was no Marxism in the mountains (16). . . .

A state like the Chinese Soviet Republic could not "allow the enemy to come and smash the pots and pans" on its own ground. It was necessary from now on to "attack on all fronts", "seize key cities" by a "decisive battle". This offensive line, adopted at the beginning of 1932, led in 1933–4 to a series of disasters. The republic of Kiangsi, after trying to attack in various directions, was incapable of breaking the fourth (April–October 1933) and particularly the fifth and last "encirclement and suppression campaign" launched by the Kuomintang between October 1933 and October 1934, with 400,000 men and the aid of German experts such as General von Falkenhausen (17), and it became clear by October 1934 that the Kiangsi base, which was probably near to collapse, would have to be abandoned.

The decision was now made to escape to the North-West, where the Party had other "revolutionary bases" less easy to encircle.

On 16 October 1934, the Red Army and some cadres of the Party, 100,000 men in all, with a good deal of equipment, set off for the West leaving some detachments of guerillas in Kiangsi. This was the beginning of "The Long March of 25,000 *li*" (8,000 miles) which, after 368 days of fighting and forced marches across the most difficult of terrain – snow-covered mountains, swamps and burning deserts – and epic adventures – Lu Shan Pass, Luting Brige over the River Tatu – brought the Communists to Northern Shensi, round Pao An, seat of the Shensi-Kansu base, which Kao Kang had developed into an "anti-Japanese base". They were joined there, a year later, by other forces, but the Central Committee had been set up in Pao An by October 1935*.

During the journey, in January 1935, in Tsunyi (Kweichow),

---

*In December 1936, the Communists occupied Yenan and Northern Shensi, to which the "capital" was then moved.

Mao Tse-tung, taking advantage of an extended meeting of the Politburo, had criticized the tragic blunders committed and had captured the Party leadership. Thanks to his reaffirmed military tactics, he was able to bring the terrible ordeal of the Long March, which only 20,000 men survived, to a successful conclusion.

Once in Pao An, Mao, undisputed master of the Party for many years to come, was now able to learn from the years of struggle.

5 Strategy in Revolutionary War

In a key work, "Problems of Strategy in China's Revolutionary War", dated December 1936, Mao Tse-tung condensed all the experience of ten years of guerilla warfare and gave a genuine précis of strategy to all movements of armed resistance which have since emerged in the Third World.

When the "war began in autumn 1927", he said, "we then had no experience at all". After the defeats of Nanchang, Canton and Hunan (Autumn Harvest Uprising), some units of the Red Army had managed to cross into the Tsingkiang Mountains. He continued:

By May 1928, however, basic principles of *guerilla warfare,* simple in nature and suited to the conditions of the time, had already been evolved, that is, the sixteen-character formula: "The enemy advances, we retreat; the enemy camps, we harass; the enemy tires, we attack; the enemy retreats, we pursue." This sixteen-character formulation of military principles was accepted by the Central Committee before the Li Li-san line. Later our operational principles were developed a step further. At the time of our first counter-campaign against "encirclement and suppression" in the Kiangsi base area, the principle of "luring the enemy in deep" was put forward and, moreover, successfully applied. By the time the enemy's third "encircle-ment and suppression" campaign was defeated, a complete set of operational principles for the Red Army had taken shape. This marked a new stage in the development of our military principles, which were greatly enriched in content and under-went many changes in form, mainly in the sense that although they basically remained the same as in the sixteen-character formula, they transcended their originally simple nature. The sixteen-character formula covered the basic principles for combating "encirclement and suppression"; it covered the two stages of the strategic defensive and the strategic offensive, and within the defensive, it covered the two stages of the strategic retreat and the strategic counter-offensive. What came later was only a development of this formula (1).

Mao Tse-tung insisted on the fact that, to succeed in the military field – as well as in the others – "one must acquire a method". To him this method

is to familiarize ourselves with all aspects of the enemy situation and our own, to discover the laws governing the actions of both sides and to make use of these laws in our own opera-tions (2). . . .

Reading is learning, but applying is also learning and the more important kind of learning at that. Our chief method is to learn warfare through warfare. . . . A revolutionary war is a mass undertaking; it is often not a matter of first learning and then doing, but of doing and then learning, for doing is itself learning. There is a gap between the ordinary civilian and the soldier, but it is no Great Wall, and it can be quickly closed, and the way to close it is to take part in revolution, in war (3). . . . To cross the threshold is not difficult, and mastery, too, is possible provided one sets one's mind to the task and is good at learning.

What is important or decisive should be determined not by general or abstract considerations, but according to the concrete circumstances (4). . . .

In the ten years since our guerilla war began, every indepen-dent Red guerilla unit, every Red Army unit or every revo-lutionary base area has been regularly subjected by the enemy to "encirclement and suppression". The enemy looks upon the

Red Army as a monster and seeks to capture it the moment it shows itself. He is for ever pursuing the Red Army and for ever trying to encircle it. For ten years this pattern of warfare has not changed, and unless the civil war gives place to a national war, the pattern will remain the same till the day the enemy becomes the weaker contestant and the Red Army the stronger.

The Red Army's operations take the form of counter-campaigns against "encirclement and suppression", that is, strategic victory and victories in campaigns. The fight against each "encirclement and suppression" campaign constitutes a counter-campaign, which usually comprises several or even scores of battles, big and small. Until an "encirclement and suppression" campaign has been basically smashed, one cannot speak of strategic victory or of victory in the counter-campaign as a whole, even though many battles may have been won. The history of the Red Army's decade of war is a history of counter-campaigns against "encirclement and suppression".

In the enemy's "encirclement and suppression" campaigns and the Red Army's counter-campaigns against them, the two forms of fighting, offensive and defensive, are both employed and here there is no difference from any other war, ancient or modern, in China or elsewhere. The special characteristic of China's civil war, however, is the repeated alternation of the two forms over a long period of time. In each "encirclement and suppression" campaign, the enemy employs the offensive against the Red Army's defensive, and the Red Army employs the defensive against his offensive; this is the first stage of a counter-campaign against "encirclement and suppression". Then the enemy employs the defensive against the Red Army's offensive, and the Red Army employs the offensive against his defensive; this is the second stage of the counter-campaign. Every "encirclement and suppression" campaign has these two stages, and they alternate over a long period*.

---

*Criticizing Li Li-san in the same work, Mao stated that "in 1930, Comrade Li Li-san failed to understand the protracted nature of China's civil war and for that reason did not perceive the law that in the course of this war there is repetition over a long period of 'encirclement and suppression' campaigns and of their defeat . . . Hence, in an attempt to achieve rapid victory for the revolution, he ordered the Red Army,

By repeated alternation over a long period we mean the repetition of this pattern of warfare and these forms of fighting. This is a fact obvious to everybody. An "encirclement and suppression" campaign and a counter-campaign against it – such is the repeated pattern of the war. . . .

As for the content of a campaign or of a battle, it does not consist of mere repetition but is different each time. This, too, is a fact and obvious to everybody. In this connection it has become a rule that with each campaign and each counter-campaign, the scale becomes larger, the situation more complicated and the fighting more intense.

But this does not mean that there are no ups and downs. . . .

What constitutes a defeat for the Red Army? Strategically speaking, there is a defeat only when a counter-campaign against "encirclement and suppression" fails completely, but even then the defeat is only partial and temporary. For only the total destruction of the Red Army would constitute complete defeat in the civil war; but this has never happened. The loss of extensive base areas and the shift of the Red Army constituted a temporary and partial defeat, not a final and complete one. . . .

The proposition that a revolution or a revolutionary war is an offensive is of course correct. A revolution or a revolutionary war in its emergence and growth from a small force to a big force, from the absence of political power to the seizure of political power, from the absence of a Red Army to the creation of a Red Army, and from the absence of revolutionary base areas to their establishment, must be on the offensive and cannot be conservative; and tendencies towards conservatism must be opposed.

The only entirely correct proposition is that a revolution or a revolutionary war is an offensive but also involves defence and retreat. To defend in order to attack, to retreat in order to

---

which was still in its infancy, to attack Wuhan, and also ordered a nation-wide uprising. Then he committed the error of 'Left' opportunism." Mao, who made the same criticisms of Li Li-san's successors, said that this "Left" opportunism "did immense damage to the Chinese revolution".

advance, to move against the flanks in order to move against the front, and to take a roundabout route in order to get on to the direct route – this is inevitable in the process of development of many phenomena, especially military movements. . . .

When will the pattern of repeated "encirclement and suppression" campaigns come to an end? In my opinion, if the civil war is prolonged, this repetition will cease when a fundamental change takes place in the balance of forces. It will cease when the Red Army has become stronger than the enemy. Then we shall be encircling and suppressing the enemy and he will be resorting to counter-campaigns, but political and military conditions will not allow him to attain the same position as that of the Red Army in its counter-campaigns. It can be definitely asserted that by then the pattern of repeated "encirclement and suppression" campaigns will have largely, if not completely, come to an end. . . .

The strategic defensive

Why do we begin by discussing defence? After the failure of China's first national united front of 1924–7, the revolution became a most intense and ruthless class war. While the enemy ruled the whole country, we had only small armed forces; consequently from the very beginning we have had to wage a bitter struggle against his "encirclement and suppression" campaigns. Our offensives have been closely linked with our efforts to break them, and our fate depends entirely on whether or not we are able to do so. The process of breaking an "encirclement and suppression" campaign is usually circuitous and not as direct as one would wish. The primary problem and a serious one too, is how to conserve our strength and await an opportunity to defeat the enemy. Therefore, the strategic defensive is the most complicated and most important problem facing the Red Army in its operations.

In our ten years of war two deviations often arose with regard to the strategic defensive; one was to belittle the enemy, the other was to be terrified of him (5). . . .

Mao Tse-tung underlined the importance of psychological preparation of the population during this defensive phase:

Political mobilization is a problem of prime importance in the struggle against "encirclement and suppression". That is to say, we should tell the Red Army and the people in the base area clearly, resolutely and fully that the enemy's offensive is inevitable and imminent and will do serious harm to the people, but at the same time, we should tell them about his weaknesses, the factors favourable to the Red Army, our indomitable will to victory and our general plan of work. We should call upon the Red Army and the entire population to fight against the enemy's "encirclement and suppression" campaigns and defend the base area. Except where military secrets are concerned, political mobilization must be carried out openly, and, what is more, every effort should be made to extend it to all who might possibly support the revolutionary cause. . . .

With regard to politically alien elements we should not be off our guard, but neither should we be unduly apprehensive of treachery on their part and adopt excessive precautionary measures. Distinction should be made between the landlords, the merchants and the rich peasants, and the main point is to explain things to them politically and win their neutrality, while at the same time organizing the masses of the people to keep an eye on them. Only against the very few elements who are most dangerous should stern measures like arrest be taken. . . . What we need is an enthusiastic but calm state of mind and intense but orderly work.

A strategic retreat is a planned strategic step taken by an inferior force for the purpose of conserving its strength and biding its time to defeat the enemy, when it finds itself confronted with a superior force whose offensive it is unable to smash quickly. But military adventurists stubbornly oppose such a step and advocate "engaging the enemy outside the gates".

We all know that when two boxers fight, the clever boxer usually gives a little ground at first, while the foolish one rushes in furiously and uses up all his resources at the very start, and in the end he is often beaten by the man who has given ground. . . .

The object of strategic retreat is to conserve military strength and prepare for the counter-offensive. Retreat is necessary because not to retreat a step before the onset of a strong enemy inevitably means to jeopardize the preservation of one's own forces. In the past, however, many people were stubbornly opposed to retreat, considering it to be an "opportunist line of pure defence". Our history has proved that their opposition was entirely wrong (6). . . .

Mao reiterated that, especially when a retreat is being made, the active support of the civil population must be obtained:

This means having a base area. Therefore, when the enemy launches a full-scale offensive, the Red Army generally withdraws from the White area into the base area, because that is where the population is most active in supporting the Red Army against the White army. Also, there is a difference between the borders and the central district of a base area; in the latter, the people are better at blocking the passage of information to the enemy, better at reconnaissance, transportation, joining in the fighting, and so on. . . .

One advantage of operating on interior lines is that it makes it possible for the retreating army to choose terrain favourable to itself and force the attacking army to fight on its terms. In order to defeat a strong army, a weak army must carefully choose favourable terrain as a battleground. But this condition alone is not enough and must be accompanied by others. The first of these is popular support. . . .

Another essential condition for a weak army fighting a strong one is to pick out the enemy's weaker units for attack. But at the beginning of the enemy's offensive we usually do not know which of his advancing columns is the strongest and which the second strongest, which is the weakest and which the second weakest, and so a process of reconnaissance is required. . . .

If the attacking enemy is far more numerous and much stronger than we are, we can accomplish a change in the balance of forces only when the enemy has penetrated deeply into our base area and tasted all the bitterness it holds for him. As the chief of staff of one of Chiang Kai-shek's brigades remarked during the third "encirclement and suppression" campaign, "Our stout men have worn themselves thin and our thin men have worn themselves to death." Or, in the words of Chen Ming-shu, Commander-in-Chief of the Western Route of the Kuomintang's "Encirclement and Suppression" Army, "Everywhere the National Army gropes in the dark, while the Red Army walks in broad daylight." By then the enemy army, although still strong, is much weakened, its soldiers are tired, its morale is sagging and many of its weak spots are revealed. But the Red Army, though weak, has conserved its strength and stored up its energy, and is waiting at its ease for the fatigued enemy. At such a time it is generally possible to attain a certain parity between the two sides, or to change the enemy's absolute superiority to relative superiority and our absolute inferiority to relative inferiority, and occasionally even to become superior to the enemy. When fighting against the third "encirclement and suppression" campaign in Kiangsi, the Red Army executed a retreat to the extreme limit (to concentrate in the rear section of the base area); if it had not done so, it could not have defeated the enemy because the enemy's "encirclement and suppression" forces were then over ten times the size of the Red Army. When Sun Wu Tzu said, "Avoid the enemy when he is full of vigour, strike when he is fatigued and withdraws," he was referring to tiring and demoralizing the enemy so as to reduce his superiority.

Finally, the object of retreat is to induce the enemy to make mistakes or to detect his mistakes. One must realize that an enemy commander, however wise, cannot avoid making some mistakes over a relatively long period of time, and hence it is always possible for us to exploit the openings he leaves us. The enemy is liable to make mistakes, just as we ourselves sometimes miscalculate and give him openings to exploit. In addition, we can induce the enemy to make mistakes by our own actions, for instance by "counterfeiting an appearance", as Sun Wu Tzu called it, that is, by making a feint to the east but attacking in the west. If we are able to do this, the terminal point for the retreat cannot be rigidly limited to a definite area. Sometimes when we have retreated to the predetermined area and not yet found openings to exploit, we have to retreat farther and wait for the enemy to give us an opening.

The favourable conditions which we seek by retreating are in general those stated above (7)....

It is extremely difficult to convince the cadres and the people of the necessity of strategic retreat ... [but, Mao argued:] It often happens that only by loss can loss be avoided; this is the principle of "Give in order to take". If what we lose is territory and what we gain is victory over the enemy, plus recovery and also expansion of our territory, then it is a paying proposition. In a business transaction, if a buyer does not "lose" some money, he cannot obtain goods; if a seller does not "lose" some goods, he cannot obtain money. The losses incurred in a revolutionary movement involve destruction, and what is gained is construction of a progressive character. Sleep and rest involve loss of time, but energy is gained for tomorrow's work. If any fool does not understand this and refuses to sleep, he will have no energy the next day, and that is a losing proposition. . . .

The same holds true on the question of bringing damage on the people. If you refuse to let the pots and pans of some households be smashed over a short period of time, you will cause the smashing of the pots and pans of all the people to go on over a long period of time. If you are afraid of unfavourable short-term political repercussions, you will have to pay the price in unfavourable long-term political repercussions. After the October Revolution, if the Russian Bolsheviks had acted on the opinions of the "Left Communists" and refused to sign the peace treaty with Germany, the new-born Soviets would have been in danger of early death.

Such seemingly revolutionary "Left" opinions originate from the revolutionary impetuosity of the petty-bourgeois intellectuals as well as from the narrow conservatism of the peasant small producers. People holding such opinions look at problems only one-sidedly and are unable to take a comprehensive view of the situation as a whole; they are unwilling to link the interests of today with those of tomorrow or the interests of the part with those of the whole, but cling like grim death to the partial and the temporary. Certainly, we should cling tenaciously to the partial and the temporary when, in the concrete circumstances of the time, they are favourable – and especially when they are decisive – for the whole current situation and the whole period, or otherwise we shall become advocates of letting things slide and doing nothing about them. That is why a retreat must have a terminal point. We must not go by the short-sightedness of the small producer. We should learn the wisdom of the Bolsheviks. The naked eye is not enough, we must have the aid of the telescope and the microscope. The Marxist method is our telescope and microscope in political and military matters. . . .

Strategic retreat is aimed solely at switching over to the counter-offensive and is merely the first stage of the strategic offensive. The decisive link in the entire strategy is whether victory can be won in the stage of the counter-offensive which follows (8).

Strategic counter-offensive

To defeat the offensive of an enemy who enjoys absolute superiority we rely on the situation created during the stage of our strategic retreat, a situation which is favourable to ourselves, unfavourable to the enemy and different from that at the beginning of his offensive.

To bring about victory or defeat a decisive battle between the two armies is necessary. Only a decisive battle can settle the question as to which army is the victor and which the vanquished. This is the sole task in the stage of strategic counter-offensive. The counter-offensive is a long process, the most fascinating, the most dynamic, and also the final stage of a defensive campaign (9). . . .

Our army's experience in these five counter-campaigns against "encirclement and suppression" prove that the first battle in the counter-offensive is of the greatest importance for the Red Army, which is on the defensive, if it is to smash a large and powerful enemy "suppression" force. Victory or defeat in the first battle has a tremendous effect upon the entire situation, all the way to the final engagement. Hence we arrive at the following conclusions.

First, the first battle must be won. We should strike only when positively certain that the enemy's situation, the terrain and popular support are all in our favour and not in his. Otherwise we should rather fall back and carefully bide our time. There will always be opportunities; we should not rashly accept battle (10). . . .

Second, the plan for the first battle must be the prelude to, and an organic part of, the plan for the whole campaign. Without a good plan for the whole campaign it is absolutely impossible to fight a really good first battle. That is to say, even though victory is won in the first battle, if the battle harms

rather than helps the campaign as a whole, such a victory can only be reckoned a defeat (as in the case of the battle of Hsunkou in the fifth campaign). Hence, before fighting the first battle one must have a general idea of how the second, third, fourth and even the final battle will be fought, and consider what changes will ensue in the enemy's situation as a whole if we win, or lose, each of the succeeding battles. Although the result may not – and, in fact, definitely will not – turn out exactly as we expect, we must think everything out carefully and realistically in the light of the general situation on both sides. Without a grasp of the situation as a whole, it is impossible to make any really good move on the chessboard.

Third, one must also consider what will happen in the next strategic stage of the war. Whoever directs strategy will not be doing his duty if he occupies himself only with the counter-offensive and neglects the measures to be taken after it succeeds, or in case it fails. In a particular strategic stage, he should take into consideration the succeeding stages, or, at the very least, the following one. . . . However, it is absolutely essential to have a long-term plan which has been thought out in its general outline and which covers an entire strategic stage or even several strategic stages. Failure to make such a plan will lead to the mistake of hesitating and allowing oneself to be tied down, which in fact serves the enemy's strategic objects and reduces one to a passive position. It must be borne in mind that the enemy's supreme command is not lacking in strategic insight. Only when we have trained ourselves to be a head taller than the enemy will strategic victories be possible. . . . In short, in the stage of retreat we must see ahead to the stage of the counter-offensive, in the stage of the counter-offensive we must see ahead to that of the offensive, and in the stage of the offensive we must again see ahead to a stage of retreat. Not to do so but to confine ourselves to considerations of the moment is to court defeat.

The first battle must be won. The plan for the whole campaign must be taken into account. And the strategic stage that comes next must be taken into account. These are the three principles we must never forget when we begin a counter-offensive, that is, when we fight the first battle. . . .

No matter how complicated, grave and harsh the circumstances, what a military leader needs most of all is the ability to function independently in organizing and employing the forces under his command. . . .

The initiative is not something imaginary but is concrete and material. Here the most important thing is to conserve and mass an armed force that is as large as possible and full of fighting spirit. . . .

Concentration of troops

Concentration of troops, mobile warfare, war of quick decision and war of annihilation are all necessary conditions for the full achievement of this aim. And of these, concentration of troops is the first and most essential.

This concentration is necessary for the purpose of reversing the situation as between the enemy and ourselves. . . . Previously it was the enemy who was advancing and we who were retreating; now we seek a situation in which we advance and he retreats. . . . We can turn a big "encirclement and suppression" campaign waged by the enemy against us into a number of small, separate campaigns of encirclement and suppression waged by us against the enemy . . . We can change the enemy's strategic superiority over us into our superiority over him in campaigns and battles . . . This is what we call . . . encirclement and suppression within "encirclement and suppression", blockade within blockade, the offensive within the defensive, superiority within inferiority, strength within weakness, advantage within disadvantage, and initiative within passivity. The winning of victory in the strategic defensive depends basically on this measure – concentration of troops. . . . The Chinese Red Army which entered the arena of the civil war as a small and weak force, has since repeatedly defeated its powerful antagonist and won victories that have astonished the world, and it has done so by relying largely on the employment of concentrated strength. Any one of its great victories can prove this point. When we say, "Pit one against ten, pit ten against a hundred", we are speaking of strategy, of the whole war and the over-all balance of forces, and in the strategic sense that is just what we have been doing. However, we are not speaking of campaigns and tactics, in which we must never do so. Whether in counter-offensives or offensives, we should always concentrate a big force to strike at one part of the enemy forces. . . . *Our strategy is "pit one against ten" and our tactics are "pit ten against one"* – this is one of our fundamental principles for gaining mastery over the enemy (11).

That is not to say we must have numerical superiority on every occasion. In certain circumstances, we may go into battle with a relatively or absolutely inferior force. Take the case of going into battle with a relatively inferior force when we have only a rather small Red Army force in a certain area (it is not that we have more troops and have not concentrated them). . . . In our *surprise* attack on this segment of the enemy flank, the principle of using a superior force against an inferior force, of using the many to defeat the few, still applies. The same principle also applies when we go into battle with an absolutely inferior force, for example, when a guerilla force makes a surprise attack on a large White army force, but is attacking only a small part of it. . . .

We use the few to defeat the many – this we say to the rulers of China as a whole. We use the many to defeat the few – this we say to each separate enemy force on the battle-field. That is no longer a secret, and in general the enemy is by now well acquainted with our way. However, he can neither prevent our victories nor avoid his own losses, because he does not know when and where we shall act. This we keep secret. The Red Army generally operates by surprise attacks. . . .

The kind of concentration of forces we advocate does not mean the abandonment of people's guerilla warfare. . . . Considering the revolutionary war as a whole, the operations of the people's guerillas and those of the main forces of the Red Army complement each other like a man's right arm and left arm, and if we had only the main forces of the Red Army without the people's guerillas, we would be like a warrior with only one arm. In concrete terms, and especially with regard to military operations, when we talk of the people in the base area as a factor, we mean that we have an armed people. That is the main reason why the enemy is afraid to approach our base area (12). . . .

Mobile warfare

Mobile warfare or positional warfare? Our answer is mobile warfare. So long as we lack a large army or reserves of ammunition, and so long as there is only a single Red Army force to do the fighting in each base area, positional warfare is generally useless to us. For us, positional warfare is generally inapplicable in attack as well as in defence.

One of the outstanding characteristics of the Red Army's operations, which follows from the fact that the enemy is powerful while the Red Army is deficient in technical equipment, is the absence of fixed battle lines.

The Red Army's battle lines are determined by the direction in which it is operating. As its operational direction often shifts, its battle lines are fluid. Though the main direction does not change in a given period of time, within its ambit the secondary directions may shift at any moment; when we find ourselves checked in one direction, we must turn to another. If after a time, we also find ourselves checked in the main direction, then we must change it too.

In a revolutionary civil war, there cannot be fixed battle lines . . . because the vicissitudes of victory and defeat, advance and retreat, preclude it. . . .

Fluidity of battle lines leads to fluidity in the size of our base areas. Our base areas are constantly expanding and contracting, and often as one base area falls another rises. This fluidity of territory is entirely a result of the fluidity of the war.

Fluidity in the war and in our territory produces fluidity in all fields of construction in our base areas. Construction plans covering several years are out of the question. Frequent changes of plan are all in the day's work.

It is to our advantage to recognize this characteristic. We must base our planning on it and must not have illusions about a war of advance without any retreats, take alarm at any temporary fluidity of our territory or of the rear areas of our army, or endeavour to draw up detailed long-term plans. We must adapt our thinking and our work to the circumstances, be ready to sit down as well as to march on, and always have our marching rations handy. It is only by exerting ourselves in today's fluid way of life that tomorrow we can secure relative stability, and eventual full stability. . . .

Our workers' and peasants' democratic republic is a state, but today it is not yet a full-fledged one. Today we are still in the period of strategic defensive in the civil war, the form of our political power is still far from that of a full-fledged stage, our army is still much inferior to the enemy both in numbers and technical equipment, our territory is still very small, and our enemy is constantly out to destroy us and will never rest content till he has done so. In defining our policy on the basis of these facts, we should not repudiate guerilla-ism in general terms, but should honestly admit the guerilla character of the Red Army. It is no use being ashamed of this. On the contrary, this guerilla character is precisely our distinguishing feature, our strong point, and our means of defeating the enemy. We should be prepared to discard it, but we cannot do so today. . . .

"Fight when you can win, move away when you can't win" – this is the popular way of describing our mobile warfare today. There is no military expert anywhere in the world who approves only of fighting and never of moving, though few people do as much moving as we do. We generally spend more time in moving than in fighting and would be doing well if we fought an average of one sizeable battle a month. All our "moving" is for the purpose of "fighting", and all our strategy and tactics are built on "fighting". Nevertheless, there are times when it is inadvisable for us to fight. In the first place, it is inadvisable to fight when the force confronting us is too large; second, it is sometimes inadvisable to fight when the force confronting us, though not so large, is very close to other enemy forces; third, it is generally inadvisable to fight an enemy force that is not isolated and is strongly entrenched; fourth, it is inadvisable to continue an engagement in which there is no prospect of victory. In any one of these situations we are prepared to move away. Such moving away is both permissible and necessary. For our recognition of the necessity of moving away is based on our recognition of the necessity of fighting. Herein lies the fundamental characteristic of the Red Army's mobile warfare (13). . . .

War of quick decision

A strategically protracted war and campaigns or battles of quick decision are two aspects of the same thing, two principles which should receive equal and simultaneous emphasis in civil wars and which are also applicable in anti-imperialist wars.

Because the reactionary forces are very strong, revolutionary forces grow only gradually, and this fact determines the protracted nature of our war. Here impatience is harmful and advocacy of "quick decision" incorrect. To wage a revolutionary war for ten years, as we have done, might be surprising in other countries, but for us it is like the opening sections in an "eight-legged essay" – the "presentation, amplification and preliminary exposition of the theme" – and many exciting parts are yet to follow. No doubt developments in the future will be greatly accelerated under the influence of domestic and international conditions. . . . But we should not expect successes overnight. . . . As China's reactionary forces are backed by many imperialist powers, our revolutionary war will continue to be a protracted one until China's revolutionary forces have built up enough strength to breach the main positions of our internal and external enemies, and until the international revolutionary forces have crushed or contained most of the international reactionary forces. To proceed from this point in formulating our strategy of long-term warfare is one of the important principles guiding our strategy.

The reverse is true of campaigns and battles – here the principle is not protractedness but quick decision. Quick decision is sought in campaigns and battles, and this is true at all times and in all countries. In a war as a whole, too, quick decision is sought at all times and in all countries, and a long drawn-out war is considered harmful.

For these reasons we have to fight battles of quick decision. It is unusual for us to conclude a battle in a few hours, or in a day or two. . . .

A quick decision cannot be achieved simply by wanting it, but requires many specific conditions. The main requirements are: adequate preparations, seizing the opportune moment, concentration of superior forces, encircling and outflanking tactics, favourable terrain, and striking at the enemy when he is on the move, or when he is stationary but has not yet consolidated his positions. Unless these requirements are satisfied, it is imposible to achieve quick decision in a campaign or battle (14).

War of annihilation

It is inappropriate to advocate a "contest of attrition" for the Chinese Red Army today. A "contest of treasures" not between Dragon Kings but between a Dragon King and a beggar would be rather ludicrous. For the Red Army which gets almost all its supplies from the enemy, war of annihilation is the basic policy. Only by annihilating the enemy's effective strength can we smash his "encirclement and suppression" campaigns and expand our revolutionary base areas. Inflicting casualties is a means of annihilating the enemy, or otherwise there would be no sense to it. We incur losses ourselves in inflicting casualties on the enemy, but we replenish ourselves by annihilating his units, thereby not only making good our losses but adding to the strength of our army. A battle in which the enemy is routed is not basically decisive in a contest with a foe of great strength. A battle of annihilation, on the other hand, produces a great and immediate impact on any enemy. Injuring all of a man's ten fingers is not as effective as chopping off one, and routing ten enemy divisions is not as effective as annihilating one of them. . . .

War of annihilation entails the concentration of superior forces and the adoption of encircling or outflanking tactics. We cannot have the former without the latter. Conditions such as popular support, favourable terrain, a vulnerable enemy force and the advantage of surprise are all indispensable for the purpose of annihilation. . . .

In establishing our own war industry we must not allow ourselves to become dependent on it. Our basic policy is to rely on the war industries of the imperialist countries and of our domestic enemy. We have a claim on the output of the arsenals of London as well as of Hanyang, and, what is more, it is delivered to us by the enemy's transport corps. This is the sober truth, it is not a jest (15).

"Economic work"

While thus formulating the strategic principles of "guerilla warfare", Mao Tse-tung did not lose sight of its economic aspects. In a series of speeches and articles in 1933 and 1934, he had defined the "economic bases" of guerilla warfare:

All our present efforts should be directed towards gaining victory in the revolutionary war . . . they should be directed towards securing the material conditions which will guarantee food and other supplies for the Red Army, towards bettering the life of the people and so stimulating their more active participation in the revolutionary war, towards organizing the masses on the economic front and educating them so as to provide fresh mass strength for the war, and towards consolidating the worker-peasant alliance and the democratic dictatorship of workers and peasant and strengthening proletarian leadership by building up the economy. Such economic construction is essential for the attainment of all these objectives. . . . Without building up the economy it is impossible to secure the material prerequisites for the revolutionary war, and the people will become exhausted in the course of a long war. Just consider! The enemy is enforcing an economic blockade, unscrupulous merchants and reactionaries are disrupting our finance and commerce, and the trade of our Red areas with the outside is seriously hampered. Will not the revolutionary war be seriously affected unless these difficulties are overcome? Salt is very dear, and sometimes even unobtainable. Rice is cheap in the autumn and winter, but it becomes terribly dear in spring and summer. All this directly affects the life of the workers and peasants and prevents any improvement. And does it not affect our basic line – the alliance of workers and peasants? If the workers and peasants become dissatisfied with their living conditions, will it not affect the expansion of our Red Army and the mobilization of the masses for the revolutionary war? . . . To dispense with economic construction would weaken the war effort. . . .

We should send our grain surplus out of the Red areas in a planned way (i.e., not in unlimited quantities) and bring in necessities from the White areas, thus avoiding exploitation by unscrupulous merchants. We must all do our best to develop agriculture and handicrafts and increase the output of farm implements and lime in order to ensure a bigger crop next year, and we must restore the output of such local products as wolfram, timber, camphor, paper, tobacco, linen, dried mushrooms and peppermint oil to former levels, and market them in the White areas in quantity. . . . What we are talking about and trying to do is to develop agriculture and the handicrafts, and send out grain and wolfram in exchange for salt and cloth. . . .

It is thus clear that, at the present stage, economic construction must revolve around our central task, the revolutionary war. Today the revolutionary war is our central task, which economic construction should serve, centre on and be subordinated to. . . . Not until the civil war is over will it be possible and necessary to regard economic construction as the centre of all our work. In the midst of a civil war, it is sheer delusion to try to carry out such peace-time economic construction as can and should be done in the future but not at present. The tasks for the present are those urgently demanded by the war. Every one of them should serve the war; none is a peace-time undertaking separate from the war. . . .

We must mobilize the masses by various organizational means. . . . We must not be bureaucratic in our methods of mobilizing the masses. Bureaucratic leadership cannot be tolerated in economic construction any more than in any other branch of our revolutionary work. The ugly evil of bureaucracy, which no comrade likes, must be thrown into the cesspit (16). . . .

It should be pointed out that in the present conditions agriculture occupies first place in our economic construction; it is by agriculture that we solve both the most important problem of food, and the problem of raw materials such as cotton, hemp, sugar-cane and bamboo, which are needed for the making of clothes, sugar, paper and other necessities. The care of forests and the increase of livestock are also an important part of agriculture. . . . We must actively lead the peasants in solving such difficult and essential problems in production as labour power, draught oxen, fertilizer, seed and irrigation. In this connection our fundamental task is to adjust the use of labour power in an organized way and to encourage women to do farm work. The necessary measures to solve the problem of labour power are organizing mutual-aid groups and ploughing teams and mobilizing and encouraging the whole rural population to help during the busy spring and summer ploughing seasons. Another big problem is that quite a large proportion (about 25 per cent) of the peasants are short of draught oxen. We must attend to organizing draught oxen co-operatives, encouraging the peasants without oxen to buy them for their common use through voluntary subscription to shares. Irrigation, which is the lifeblood of agriculture, also merits close attention. Of course, we cannot as yet bring up the question of state or collective farming, but it is urgently necessary to set up small experimental farms, agricultural research schools and exhibitions of farm produce. . . . We have an extensive market of our own because of the mass demand in our areas. We should systematically restore and develop handicrafts and also certain industries, firstly to supply our own needs and secondly for trade with the outside. . . . The most significant fields are tobacco, paper, wolfram, camphor, farm implements and fertilizers (such as lime). Moreover, in our present circumstances we should not neglect the manufacture of our own cotton cloth, medicines and sugar. . . . Some industries have been set up which were previously non-existent, such as paper-making, cloth-making and sugar-refining. . . . To relieve the shortage of salt, people have begun to extract it from nitre. . . .

Our economy is made up of three sectors, state enterprise, co-operative enterprise and private enterprise.

At present, state enterprise is limited to what is possible and essential. State-operated industry and commerce have begun to grow and they have boundless prospects.

As regards the private sector of the economy, we shall not hamper it, indeed, we shall promote and encourage it, so long as it does not transgress the legal limits set by our government. For the development of private enterprise is essential to the interests of the state and the people at the present stage. Needless to say, private enterprise is now preponderant and will inevitably continue to occupy a dominant position for a considerable time. Today, private undertakings in the Red areas are small in scale. . . .

Co-operative enterprise is growing rapidly. . . . Consumers' co-operatives and grain co-operatives head the list, with producers' co-operatives coming next. Credit co-operatives have just started functioning. When the co-operative and the state enterprises become co-ordinated and grow over a long period of time, they will gradually prevail and assume leadership over the private sector. Therefore, the greatest possible development of state enterprise and the extensive development of co-operative enterprise must go hand in hand with encouraging the development of private enterprise.

With the support of the masses, we have issued economic construction bonds to the value of three million yuan in order to develop state enterprise and assist the co-operatives. Such reliance on the strength of the masses is the only possible way to solve the problem of funds for economic construction at this time.

To increase our revenue by developing the economy is a basic principle of our financial policy; it has already brought tangible results. . . .

Thrift should be the guiding principle in our government expenditure. It should be made clear to all government workers that corruption and waste are very great crimes. Our campaigns against corruption and waste have already achieved some results, but further efforts are required. Our system of accounting must be guided by the principle of saving every copper for the war effort, for the revolutionary cause and for our economic construction (17). . . .

Four days later, on 27 January 1934, Mao Tse-tung returned to the basic problem of mobilizing the masses through economic progress:

The revolutionary war is a war of the masses; it can be waged only by mobilizing the masses and relying on them.

If we only mobilize the people to carry on the war and do nothing else, can we succeed in defeating the enemy? Of course not. If we want to win, we must do a great deal more. We must lead the peasants' struggle for land and distribute the land to them, heighten their labour enthusiasm and increase agricultural production, safeguard the interests of the workers, establish co-operatives, develop trade with outside areas, and solve the problems facing the masses – food, shelter and clothing, fuel, rice, cooking oil and salt, sickness and hygiene, and marriage. In short, all the practical problems in the masses' everyday life should claim our attention. If we attend to these problems, solve them and satisfy the needs of the masses, we shall really become organizers of the well-being of the masses, and they will truly rally round us and give us their warm support. Comrades, will we then be able to arouse them to take part in the revolutionary war? Yes, indeed we will. . . .

I earnestly suggest to this congress that we pay close attention to the well-being of the masses, from the problems of land and labour to those of fuel, rice, cooking oil and salt. The women want to learn ploughing and harrowing. Whom can we get to teach them? The children want to go to school. Have we set up primary schools? The wooden bridge over there is too narrow and people may fall off. Should we not repair it? Many people suffer from boils and other ailments. What are we going to do about it? All such problems concerning the well-being of the masses should be placed on our agenda. We should discuss them, adopt and carry out decisions and check up on the results. We should convince the masses that we represent their interests, that our lives are intimately bound up with theirs. We should help them to proceed from these things to an understanding of the higher tasks which we have put forward, the tasks of the revolutionary war, so that they will support the revolution and spread it throughout the country, respond to our political appeals and fight to the end for victory in the revolution. The masses in Changkang say, "The Communist Party is really good! It has thought of everything on our behalf." The comrades in Changkang Township are an example to all of us. . . . They have won the genuine affection of the broad masses, who support their call for war mobilization. Do we want to win the support of the masses? Do we want them to devote their strength to the front? If so, we must be with them, arouse their enthusiasm and initiative, be concerned with their well-being, work earnestly and sincerely in their interests and solve all their problems of production and everyday life – the problems of salt, rice, housing, clothing, childbirth, etc. If we do so the masses will surely support us and regard the revolution as their most glorious banner, as their very life. In the event of a

Kuomintang attack on the Red areas they will fight the Kuomintang to the death. There can be no doubt about this. . . .

Mao then taunted the Kuomintang which was trying to erect "bastions of iron" around the Red areas :

Comrades ! What is a true bastion of iron ? It is the masses, the millions upon millions of people who genuinely and sincerely support the revolution. That is the real iron bastion which no force can smash, no force whatsoever. The counter-revolution cannot smash us; on the contrary, we shall smash it. Rallying millions upon millions of people round the revolutionary government and expanding our revolutionary war, we shall wipe out all counter-revolution and take over the whole of China . . . overthrow the rule of imperialism and the Kuomintang throughout the country (18).

A little later on, Mao Tse-tung stated :

The Chinese Communist Party has led China's revolutionary war courageously and resolutely, and for fifteen long years has demonstrated to the whole nation that it is the people's friend, fighting at all times in the forefront of the revolutionary war in defence of the people's interests and for their freedom and liberation. . . . The enemy in this war is not imperialism alone but also the alliance of the big bourgeoisie and the big landlords. . . .This revolutionary war is led by the Communist Party alone, which has established absolute leadership over it. This absolute leadership is the most important condition enabling the revolutionary war to be carried through firmly to the end. Without it, it is inconceivable that the revolutionary war could have been carried on with such perseverance (19). . . .

With the establishment of the Red Army and the central bodies of the Communist Party in the North-West, an entirely new phase of the civil war began. But external threats from imperialism had by now eclipsed those of the Kuomintang. Japan had deliberately and thoroughly set about the conquest of China. To the Chinese people the war was now a "War of Resistance", a "War of National Liberation".

6 Philosophy of the Revolution

By the beginning of 1937, when the Chinese Communist Party began to organize its base in the North-West in depth, the Chinese Revolution had already gained a wealth of experience, its general leadership was clear and its main bearings drawn. It was a question of building a new, independent and democratic China, from which injustice, feudal and bureaucratic oppression, and cultural and economic stagnation would gradually be suppressed or eliminated. The moving spirits in the "game" were known and the obstacles listed. Most illusions had vanished. Everyone knew that the decisive battle of the future would be between the Kuomintang and the Communist Party. But there was still a long way to go before the battle started.

The Kuomintang was more than ever "the government of China". Abroad, the Chinese people's resistance to Japanese expansion won the Kuomintang new sympathy from the West. At home, Chiang Kai-shek was in control of an overwhelming force, far superior to the Communist Party's. Ten years of fighting and repression had however not brought him victory, and in December 1936, in Sian, he had even had to come to terms with the enemy.

Success for the Communist Party was not yet even in sight. Its concern was still with survival. The Party, in its North-West base, *was now primarily an army*, an army which had accomplished the "Long March"; an army which thanks to its rifles and its political commissar had unquestionably established a "Red regime", but in a rural and sparsely inhabited region. Engrossed with many urgent material tasks and guerilla activity, the Party had been unable to give its cadres the entire theoretical training necessary, and the years 1930–5 bore witness to how dogmatism can sometimes lead to disaster. Lenin had rightly said: "Without revolutionary theory, there can be no revolutionary movement." Now the Chinese Communist Party did not yet have any theory of its own. It was living on imported and often poorly assimilated ideas. It now had to take advantage of the momentary respite provided by circumstances to forge ideological weapons better adapted to the terrain and the environment.

To this end and in order to train a large number of "determined, anti-Japanese" revolutionary cadres, the Party Central Committee founded an "Anti-Japanese Red Army Institute" in Wayaopao in Northern Shensi in June 1936. In early 1937, this institute was transferred to Yenan and rechristened the "Military and Political Anti-Japanese Chinese People's Institute". Known familiarly as *Kangta*, this institute and its twelve branches, established in guerilla bases, trained, between 1937 and 1945, more than a hundred thousand revolutionary cadres which played a decisive rôle in the years to come (1).

It was in this institute that Mao Tse-tung gave the series of theoretical lectures which he collected and amplified, several months later, into two "philosophical essays", fundamental first for the understanding of his life and work, then for the future course of the Chinese Revolution: "On Practice", dated July 1937, and "On Contradiction", dated August 1937 (2).

Mao Tse-tung was not merely the generous and sympathetic "agrarian reformer" seen at the time by certain Americans. The philosophy which he taught was basically Marxist-Leninist. The two essays are sprinkled with references to Marx, Engels, Lenin and Stalin. But Mao was also able at times to quote from the Chinese classics, Chinese legends and to link his ideas with those of ancient Greek philosophers.

Once rid of the dross which often weighs them down, the text of these essays gives the reader, in a dense but most accessible form, a genuine world conception (*Weltanschauung*), a complete "philosophy" of the Revolution, of a revolution in fact permanent.

Perceptual knowledge and rational knowledge

Mao began with an analysis of knowledge :

Man's knowledge depends mainly on his activity in material production, through which he comes gradually to understand the phenomena, the properties and the laws of nature, and the relations between himself and nature; and through his activity in production he also gradually comes to understand, in varying degrees, certain relations that exist between man and man. None of this knowledge can be acquired apart from activity in production. . . .

Man's social practice is not confined to activity in production, but takes many other forms – class struggle, political life, scientific and artistic pursuits; in short, as a social being, man participates in all spheres of the practical life of society. Thus man, in varying degrees, comes to know the different relations between man and man, not only through his material life but also through his political and cultural life (both of which are intimately bound up with material life). Of these other types of social practice, class struggle in particular, in all its various forms, exerts a profound influence on the development of man's knowledge. In class society everyone lives as a member of a particular class, and every kind of thinking, without exception, is stamped with the brand of a class.

Marxists hold that in human society activity in production develops step by step from a lower to a higher level, that is, from the shallower to the deeper, from the one-sided to the many-sided. . . .

Marxists hold that man's social practice alone is the criterion of the truth of his knowledge of the external world. What actually happens is that man's knowledge is verified only when he achieves the anticipated results in the process of social practice (material production, class struggle or scientific experiment).

If a man wants to succeed in his work, that is, to achieve the anticipated results, he must bring his ideas into correspondence with the laws of the objective external world; if they do not correspond, he will fail in his practice. After he fails, he draws his lessons, corrects his ideas to make them correspond to the laws of the external world, and can thus turn failure into success; this is what is meant by "failure is the mother of success" and "a fall into the pit, a gain in your wit" . . . The Marxist philosophy of dialectical materialism has two outstanding characteristics. One is its class nature : it openly avows that dialectical materialism is in the service of the proletariat. The other is its practicality : it emphasizes the dependence of theory on practice, emphasizes that theory is based on practice and in turn serves practice. The truth of any knowledge or theory is determined not by subjective feelings, but by objective results in social practice. Only social practice can be the criterion of truth. The standpoint of practice is the primary and basic standpoint in the dialectical-materialist theory of knowledge.

But how then does human knowledge arise from practice and in turn serve practice? This will become clear if we look at the process of development of knowledge.

In the process of practice, man at first sees only the phenomenal side, the separate aspects, the external relations of things. . . . This is called the perceptual stage of cognition, namely, the stage of sense perceptions and impressions. . . . At this stage man cannot as yet form concepts, which are deeper, or draw logical conclusions.

As social practice continues, things that give rise to man's sense perceptions and impressions in the course of his practice are repeated many times; then a sudden change (leap) takes place in the brain in the process of cognition, and concepts are formed. Concepts are no longer the phenomena, the separate aspects and the external relations of things; they grasp the essence, the totality and the internal relations of things. Between concepts and sense perceptions there is not only a quantitative but also a qualitative difference. Proceeding further, by means of judgement and inference one is able to draw logical conclusions. . . . "Let me think it over", refers to man's use of concepts in the brain to form judgements and inferences. . . . This stage of conception, judgement and inference is the more important stage in the entire process of knowing a thing; it is the stage of rational knowledge. The real task of knowing is, through perception, to arrive at thought, to arrive step by step at the comprehension of the internal contradictions of objective things, of their laws and of the internal relations between one process and another, that is, to arrive at logical knowledge. . . . Therefore, logical knowledge is capable of grasping the development of the surrounding world in its totality, in the internal relations of all its aspects. . . .

The perceptual and the rational are qualitatively different, but are not divorced from each other; they are unified on the basis of practice (3).

Practice

Our practice proves that what is perceived cannot at once be comprehended and that only what is comprehended can be more deeply perceived. Perception only solves the problem of phenomena; theory alone can solve the problem of essence. The solving of both these problems is not separable in the slightest degree from practice. Whoever wants to know a thing has no way of doing so except by coming into contact with it, that is, by living (practising) in its environment. . . . Marxism could be the product only of capitalist society. Marx, in the era of laissez-faire capitalism, could not concretely know certain laws peculiar to the era of imperialism beforehand, because imperialism, the last stage of capitalism, had not yet emerged and the relevant practice was lacking; only Lenin and Stalin could undertake this task. . . . If you want to know a certain thing or a certain class of things directly, you must personally participate in the practical struggle to change reality, to change that thing or class of things, for only thus can you come into contact with them as phenomena; only through personal participation in the practical struggle to change reality can you uncover the essence of that thing or class of things and comprehend them. This is the path to knowledge which every man actually travels, though some people, deliberately distorting matters, argue to the contrary. . . . Knowledge is a matter of science, and no dishonesty or conceit whatsoever is permissible. What is required is definitely the reverse – honesty and modesty. If you want knowledge, you must take part in the practice of changing reality. If you want to know the taste of a pear, you must change the pear by eating it yourself. If you want to know the structure and properties of the atom, you must make physical and chemical experiments to change the state of the atom. If you want to know the theory and methods of revolution, you must take part in revolution. All genuine knowledge originates in direct experience. But one cannot have direct experience of everything; as a matter of fact, most of our knowledge comes from indirect experience, for example, all knowledge from past times and foreign lands. To our ancestors and to foreigners, such knowledge was – or is – a matter of direct experience, and this knowledge is reliable if in the course of their direct experience the requirement of "scientific abstraction", spoken of by Lenin, was – or is – fulfilled and objective reality scientifically reflected, otherwise it is not reliable. Hence a man's knowledge consists only of two parts, that which comes from direct experience and that which comes from indirect experience. Moreover, what is indirect experience for me is direct experience for other people. Consequently, considered as a whole, knowledge of any kind is inseparable from direct experience. All knowledge originates in perception of the objective external world through man's physical sense organs. Anyone who denies such perception, denies direct experience, or denies personal participation in the practice that changes reality, is not a materialist. That is why the "know-all" is ridiculous. There is an old Chinese saying, "How can you catch tiger cubs without entering the tiger's lair?" This saying holds true for man's practice and it also holds true for the theory of knowledge. There can be no knowledge apart from practice (4).

Mao Tse-tung here described the Chinese people's knowledge of imperialism. The first stage was one of superficial, perceptual knowledge, as shown in the indiscriminate anti-foreign struggles of the Movement of the Taiping Heavenly Kingdom, the Yi Ho Tuan Movement and so on. It was only in the second stage that the Chinese people reached the stage of rational knowledge, saw the internal and external contradictions of imperialism and saw the essential truth that imperialism had allied itself with China's comprador and feudal classes to oppress and exploit the great masses of the Chinese people. This knowledge began about the time of the 4 May Movement of 1919. . . .

Thus it can be seen that the first step in the process of cognition is contact with the objects of the external world; this belongs to the stage of perception. The second step is to synthesize the data of perception by arranging and reconstructing them; this belongs to the stage of conception, judgement and inference. It is only when the data of perception are very rich (not fragmentary) and correspond to reality (are not illusory) that they can be the basis for forming correct concepts and theories (5). . . .

After making his critique of "rationalism", idealistic as well as materialistic, Mao now took issue with empiricism.

This theory errs in failing to understand that, although the data of perception reflect certain realities in the objective world (I am not speaking here of idealist empiricism which confines experience to so-called introspection), they are merely one-sided and superficial, reflecting things incompletely and not reflecting their essence. Fully to reflect a thing in its totality, to reflect its essence, to reflect its inherent laws, it is necessary through the exercise of thought to reconstruct the rich data of sense perception, discarding the dross and selecting the essential, eliminating the false and retaining the true, proceeding from the one to the other and from the outside to the inside, in order to form a system of concepts and theories – it is necessary to make a leap from perceptual to rational knowledge. Such reconstructed knowledge is not more empty or more unreliable; on the contrary, whatever has been scientifically reconstructed in the process of cognition, on the basis of practice, reflects objective reality, as Lenin said, more deeply, more truly, more fully. As against this, vulgar "practical men" respect experience but despise theory, and therefore cannot have a comprehensive view of an entire objective process, lack clear direction and long-range perspective, and are complacent over occasional successes and glimpses of the truth. If such persons direct a revolution, they will lead it up a blind alley (6).

On contradiction

The law of contradiction in things, that is, the law of the unity of opposites*, is the basic law of materialist dialectics.

*Lenin defined it as: "the devision of a unity into mutually exclusive opposites and their reciprocal relation".

Lenin said, "Dialectics in the proper sense is the study of contradiction *in the very essence of objects....*" (7)

Mao Tse-tung stated that "Our present study of philosophy should therefore have the eradication of dogmatist thinking as its main objective" (8). However, he began by putting forward just such a dogma :

The world outlook of materialist dialectics hold that in order to understand the development of a thing we should study it internally and in its relations with other things. . . . The fundamental cause of the development of a thing is not external but internal; it lies in the contradictoriness within the thing. There is internal contradiction in every single thing, hence its motion and development. Contradictoriness within a thing is the fundamental cause of its development, while its interrelations and interactions with other things are secondary causes. . . . It is evident that purely external causes can only give rise to mechanical motion, that is, to changes in scale or quantity, but cannot explain why things differ qualitatively in thousands of ways and why one thing changes into another. As a matter of fact, even mechanical motion under external force occurs through the internal contradictoriness of things. Simple growth in plants and animals, their quantitative development, is likewise chiefly the result of their internal contradictions. . . . In a suitable temperature an egg changes into a chicken, but no temperature can change a stone into a chicken, because each has a different basis. . . . Similarly, social development is due chiefly not to external but to internal causes. . . . Changes in society are due chiefly to the development of the internal contradictions in society, that is, the contradiction between the productive forces and the relations of production, the contradiction between classes and the contradiction between the old and the new; it is the development of these contradictions that pushes society forward and gives the impetus for the supersession of the old society by the new. Does materialist dialectics exclude external causes? Not at all. It holds that external causes are the condition of change and internal causes are the basis of change, and that external causes become operative through internal causes. . . . The October Socialist Revolution ushered in a new epoch in world history as well as in Russian history. It exerted influence on internal changes in the other countries in the world, and, similarly and in a particularly profound way, on internal changes in China. These changes, however, were effected through the inner laws of development of these countries, China included. . . . In China in 1927, the defeat of the proletariat by the big bourgeoisie came about through the opportunism then to be found within the Chinese proletariat itself (inside the Chinese Communist Party). When we liquidated this opportunism, the Chinese revolution resumed its advance. Later, the Chinese revolution again suffered severe setbacks at the hands of the enemy, because adventurism had risen within our Party. When we liquidated this adventurism, our cause advanced once again. Thus it can be seen that to lead the revolution to victory, a political party must depend on the correctness of its own political line and the solidity of its own organization.

The dialectical world outlook emerged in ancient times both in China and in Europe. . . . Hegel . . . made most important contributions to dialectics, but his dialectic was idealist. It was not until Marx and Engels . . . had synthesized the positive achievements in the history of human knowledge and, in particular, critically absorbed the rational elements of Hegelian dialectics and created the great theory of dialectical and historical materialism that an unprecedented revolution occurred in the history of human knowledge. This theory was further developed by Lenin and Stalin. As soon as it spread to China, it wrought tremendous changes in the world of Chinese thought.

This dialectical world outlook teaches us primarily how to observe and analyse the movement of opposites in different things, and, on the basis of such analysis, to indicate the methods for resolving contradictions. It is therefore most important for us to understand the law of contradiction in things in a concrete way (9). . . .

The universality of contradiction

The universality or absoluteness of contradiction has a two-fold meaning. One is that contradiction exists in the process of development of all things, and the other is that in the process of development of each thing a movement of opposites exists from beginning to end. . . . Lenin defined the law of the unity of opposites as "the recognition (discovery) of the contradictory, *mutually exclusive,* opposite tendencies in *all* phenomena and processes of nature (*including* mind and society)". Are these ideas correct? Yes, they are. The interdependence of the contradictory aspects present in all things and the struggle between these aspects determine the life of all things and push their development forward. There is nothing that does not contain contradiction; without contradiction nothing could exist. . . .

In war, offence and defence, advance and retreat, victory and defeat are all mutually contradictory phenomena. One cannot exist without the other. The two aspects are at once in conflict and in interdependence, and this constitutes the totality of a war, pushes its development forward and solves its problems.

Every difference in men's concepts should be regarded as reflecting an objective contradiction. . . .

Opposition and struggle between ideas of different kinds constantly occur within the Party; this is a reflection within the Party of contradictions between classes and between the new and the old in society. If there were no contradictions in the Party and no ideological struggles to resolve them, the Party's life would come to an end.

Thus it is already clear that contradiction exists universally and in all processes, whether in the simple or in the complex forms of motion, whether in objective phenomena or ideological phenomena. . . . Contradiction is universal and absolute, it is present in the process of development of all things and permeates every process from beginning to end.

What is meant by the emergence of a new process? The old unity with its constituent opposites yields to a new unity with its constituent opposites, whereupon a new process emerges to replace the old. The old process ends and the new one begins. The new process contains new contradictions and begins its own history of the development of contradictions. . . .

Chinese Communists must learn this method; only then will they be able correctly to analyse the history and the present state of the Chinese revolution and infer its future.

The particularity of contradiction

Contradiction is present in the process of development of all things; it permeates the process of development of each thing from beginning to end. This is the universality and absoluteness of contradiction which we have discussed above. Now let us discuss the particularity and relativity of contradiction.

This problem should be studied on several levels.

First, the contradiction in each form of motion of matter has its particularity. . . . There is nothing in this world except matter in motion and this motion must assume certain forms. In considering each form of motion of matter, we must observe the points which it has in common with other forms of motion. But what is especially important and necessary, constituting as it does the foundation of our knowledge of a thing, is to observe what is particular to this form of motion of matter, namely, to observe the qualitative difference between this form of motion and other forms. Only when we have done so can we distinguish between things. Every form of motion contains within itself its own particular contradiction. . . . It is the internal cause or, as it may be called, the basis for the immense variety of things in the world. There are many forms of motion in nature, mechanical motion, sound, light, heat, electricity, dissociation, combination, and so on. All these forms are interdependent, but in its essence each is different from the others. The particular essence of each form of motion is determined by its own particular contradiction. This holds true not only for nature but also for social and ideological phenomena. Every form of society, every form of ideology, has its own particular contradiction and particular essence. . . .

As regards the sequence in the movement of man's knowledge, there is always a gradual growth from the knowledge of individual and particular things to the knowledge of things in general. Only after man knows the particular essence of many different things can he proceed to generalization and know the common essence of things. When man attains the knowledge of this common essence, he uses it as a guide and proceeds to study various concrete things which have not yet been studied, or studied thoroughly, and to discover the particular essence of each; only thus is he able to supplement, enrich and develop his knowledge of their common essence and prevent such knowledge from withering or petrifying. These are the two processes of cognition : one, from the particular to the general, and the other, from the general to the particular. Thus cognition always

E

moves in cycles and (so long as scientific method is strictly adhered to) each cycle advances human knowledge a step higher and so makes it more and more profound. . . .

Qualitatively different contradictions can only be resolved by qualitatively different methods. For instance, the contradiction between the proletariat and the bourgeoisie is resolved by the method of socialist revolution; the contradiction between the great masses of the people and the feudal system is resolved by the method of democratic revolution; the contradiction between the colonies and imperialism is resolved by the method of national revolutionary war; the contradiction between the working class and the peasant class in socialist society is resolved by the method of collectivization and mechanization in agriculture; contradiction within the Communist Party is resolved by the method of criticism and self-criticism; the contradiction between society and nature is resolved by the method of developing the productive forces. Processes change, old processes and old contradictions disappear, new processes and new contradictions emerge, and the methods of resolving contradictions differ accordingly. In Russia, there was a fundamental difference between the contradiction resolved by the February Revolution and the contradiction resolved by the October Revolution, as well as between the methods used to resolve them. The principle of using different methods to resolve different contradictions is one which Marxist-Leninists must strictly observe. The dogmatists do not observe this principle; they do not understand that conditions differ in different kinds of revolution and so do not understand that different methods should be used to resolve different contradictions; on the contrary, they invariably adopt what they imagine to be an unalterable formula and arbitrarily apply it everywhere, which only causes setbacks to the revolution or makes a sorry mess of what was originally well done.

In order to reveal the particularity of the contradictions in any process in the development of a thing, in their totality or interconnections, that is, in order to reveal the essence of the process, it is necessary to reveal the particularity of the two aspects of each of the contradictions in that process; otherwise it will be impossible to discover the essence of the process. . . .

There are many contradictions in the course of development

of any major thing. For instance, in the course of China's bourgeois-democratic revolution, where the conditions are exceedingly complex, there exists the contradiction between all the oppressed classes in Chinese society and imperialism, the contradiction between the great masses of the people and feudalism, the contradiction between the proletariat and the bourgeoisie, the contradiction between the peasantry and the urban petty bourgeoisie on the one hand and the bourgeoisie on the other, the contradiction between the various reactionary ruling groups, and so on. These contradictions cannot be treated in the same way, since each has its own particularity; moreover, the *two* aspects of *each* contradiction cannot be treated in the same way since each aspect has its own characteristics. We who are engaged in the Chinese revolution should not only understand the particularity of these contradictions in their totality, that is, in their interconnections, but should also study the two aspects of each contradiction as the only means of understanding the totality. When we speak of understanding each aspect of a contradiction, we mean understanding what specific position each aspect occupies, what concrete forms it assumes in its interdependence and in its contradiction with its opposite, and what concrete methods are employed in the struggle with its opposite, when the two are both interdependent and in contradiction, and also after the interdependence breaks down.

It is of great importance to study these problems. Lenin meant just this when he said that *the most essential thing in Marxism, the living soul of Marxism, is the concrete analysis of concrete conditions* (10). Our dogmatists have violated Lenin's teachings; they never use their brains to analyse anything correctly, and in their writings and speeches they always use stereotypes devoid of content, thereby creating a very bad style of work in our Party.

In studying a problem, we must shun subjectivity, one-sidedness and superficiality. To be subjective means not to look at problems objectively, that is, not to use the materialist viewpoint in looking at problems. . . . To be one-sided means not to look at problems all-sidedly, for example, to understand only China but not Japan, only the Communist Party but not the Kuomintang, only the proletariat but not the bourgeoisie, only the peasants but not the landlords, only the favourable conditions but not the difficult ones, only the past but not the future, only individual parts but not the whole, only the defects but not the achievements, only the plaintiff's case but not the defendant's, only underground revolutionary work but not open revolutionary work, and so on. In a word, it means not to understand the characteristics of both aspects of a contradiction. This is what we mean by looking at a problem one-sidedly. Or it may be called seeing the part but not the whole, seeing the trees but not the forest. That way it is impossible to find the method for resolving a contradiction, it is impossible to accomplish the tasks of the revolution, to carry out assignments well or to develop inner-Party ideological struggle correctly. When Sun Wu Tzu said in discussing military science, "Know the enemy and know yourself, and you can fight a hundred battles with no danger of defeat"*, he was referring to the two sides in a battle. Wei Cheng of the Tang Dynasty also understood the error of one-sidedness when he said "Listen to both sides and you will be enlightened, heed only one side and you will be benighted." But our comrades often look at problems one-sidedly and so they often run into snags. In the novel *Shui Hu Chuan*, Sung Chiang thrice attacked Chu Village. Twice he was defeated because he was ignorant of the local conditions and used the wrong method. Later he changed his method; first he investigated the situation, and he familiarized himself with the maze of roads, then he broke up the alliance between the Li, Hu and Chu Villages and sent his men in disguise into the enemy camp to lie in wait, using a stratagem similar to that of the Trojan Horse in the foreign story. And on the third occasion he won. There are many examples of materialist dialectics in *Shui Hu Chuan*, of which the episode of the three attacks on Chu Village is one of the best†. Lenin said: ". . . in order really to know an object we must embrace, study, all its sides, all connections and 'mediations'. We shall never achieve this completely, but the demand for all-sidedness is a safeguard against mistakes and rigidity."

*Sun Wu Tzu was a famous Chinese military scientist in the 5th century BC, who wrote a treatise on war containing thirteen chapters (see chap. 3).
†*Shui Hu Chuan* (*Heroes of the Marshes*), a famous 14th century Chinese novel, describes a peasant war in the vicinity of Liangshanpo, where

We should remember his words. To be superficial means to consider neither the characteristics of a contradiction in its totality nor the characteristics of each of its aspects; it means to deny the necessity for probing deeply into a thing and minutely studying the characteristics of its contradiction, but instead, merely to look from afar and, after glimpsing the rough outline, immediately to try to resolve the contradiction (to answer a question, settle a dispute, handle work, or direct a military operation). This way of doing things is bound to lead to trouble. . . .

The fundamental contradiction in the process of development of a thing and the essence of the process determined by this fundamental contradiction will not disappear until the process is completed; but in a lengthy process the conditions usually differ at each stage. The reason is that, although the nature of the fundamental contradiction in the process of development of a thing and the essence of the process remain unchanged, the fundamental contradiction becomes more and more intensified as it passes from one stage to another in the lengthy process. In addition, among the numerous major and minor contradictions which are determined or influenced by the fundamental contradiction, some become intensified, some are temporarily or partially resolved or mitigated, and some new ones emerge; hence the process is marked by stages. If people do not pay attention to the stages in the process of development of a thing, they cannot deal with its contradictions properly. . . .

Take the process of China's bourgeois-democratic revolution, which began with the Revolution of 1911; it, too, has several distinct stages. In particular, the revolution in its period of bourgeois leadership and the revolution in its period of proletarian leadership represent two vastly different historical stages. In other words, proletarian leadership has fundamentally changed the whole face of the revolution, has brought about a new alignment of classes, given rise to a tremendous upsurge in the peasant revolution, imparted thoroughness to the revolution against imperialism and feudalism, created the possibility of the

---

Sung Chiang, leader of the peasant uprising and hero of the novel, established his base. Chu Chao-feng, the head of this village, was a despotic landlord. (*Heroes of the Marshes* is one of Mao Tse-tung's favourite novels, cf. chap. i.)

transition from the democratic revolution to the socialist revolution, and so on. None of these was possible in the period when the revolution was under bourgeois leadership. Although no change has taken place in the nature of the fundamental contradiction in the process as a whole, i.e., in the anti-imperialist, anti-feudal, democratic-revolutionary nature of the process (the opposite of which is its semi-colonial and semi-feudal nature), nonetheless this process has passed through several stages of development in the course of more than twenty years; during this time many great events have taken place – the failure of the Revolution of 1911 and the establishment of the regime of the Northern warlords, the formation of the first national united front and the revolution of 1924–7, the break-up of the united front and the desertion of the bourgeoisie to the side of the counter-revolution, the wars among the new warlords, the Agrarian Revolutionary War, the establishment of the second national united front and the War of Resistance Against Japan. These stages are marked by particular features such as the intensification of certain contradictions (e.g., the Agrarian Revolutionary War and the Japanese invasion of the four north-eastern provinces), the partial or temporary resolution of other contradictions (e.g., the destruction of the Northern warlords and our confiscation of the land of the landlords), and the emergence of yet other contradictions (e.g., the conflicts among the new warlords, and the landlords' recapture of the land after the loss of our revolutionary base areas in the south).

In studying the particularities of the contradictions at each stage in the process of development of a thing, we must not only observe them in their interconnections or their totality, we must also examine the two aspects of each contradiction. For instance, consider the Kuomintang and the Communist party (11). . . .

Here Mao Tse-tung showed how the Kuomintang, revolutionary and vigorous at the outset, when it represented "the alliance of various classes for the democratic revolution", changed after 1927 "into its opposite and became a reactionary bloc of the landlords and the big bourgeoisie". The Communist Party also underwent changes and transformations:

Without studying both these sets of features we cannot understand the particular relations between the two parties during the various stages of their development, namely, the establishment of a united front, the break-up of the united front, and the establishment of another united front. What is even more fundamental for the study of the particular features of the two parties is the examination of the class basis of the two parties and the resultant contradictions which have arisen between each party and the other forces at different periods. . . . If we do not study the particular features of both aspects of the contradiction, we shall fail to understand not only the relations of each party with the other forces, but also the relations between the two parties. . . .

The relationship between the universality and the particularity of contradiction is the relationship between the general character and the individual character of contradiction. By the former we mean that contradiction exists in and runs through all processes from beginning to end; motion, things, processes, thinking – all are contradictions. To deny contradiction is to deny everything. This is a universal truth for all times and all countries, which admits of no exception. Hence the general character, the absoluteness of contradiction. But this general character is contained in every individual character; without individual character there can be no general character. If all individual character were removed, what general character would remain? It is because each contradiction is particular that individual character arises. All individual character exists conditionally and temporarily, and hence is relative.

This truth concerning general and individual character, concerning absoluteness and relativity, is the quintessence of the problem of contradiction in things; failure to understand it is tantamount to abandoning dialectics.

The principal contradiction and the principal aspect of a contradiction

There are many contradictions in the process of development of a complex thing, and one of them is necessarily the principal contradiction whose existence and development determine or influence the existence and development of the other contradictions.

For instance, in capitalist society the two forces in contradiction, the proletariat and the bourgeoisie, form the principal contradiction. The other contradictions, such as those between the remnant feudal class and the bourgeoisie, between the peasant petty bourgeoisie and the bourgeoisie, between the proletariat and the peasant petty bourgeoisie, between the non-monopoly capitalists and the monopoly capitalists, between bourgeois democracy and bourgeois fascism, among the capitalist countries and between imperialism and the colonies, are all determined or influenced by this principal contradiction.

In a semi-colonial country such as China, the relationship between the principal contradiction and the non-principal contradictions presents a complicated picture.

When imperialism launches a war of aggression against such a country, all its various classes, except for some traitors, can temporarily unite in a national war against imperialism. At such a time, the contradiction between imperialism and the country concerned becomes the principal contradiction, while all the contradictions among the various classes within the country (including what was the principal contradiction, between the feudal system and the great masses of the people) are temporarily relegated to a secondary and subordinate position. So it was in China in the Opium War of 1840, the Sino-Japanese War of 1894 and the Yi Ho Tuan War of 1900, and so it is now in the present Sino-Japanese War.

But in another situation, the contradictions change position. When imperialism carries on its oppression not by war, but by milder means – political, economic and cultural – the ruling classes in semi-colonial countries capitulate to imperialism, and the two form an alliance for the joint oppression of the masses of the people. At such a time, the masses often resort to civil war against the alliance of imperialism and the feudal classes, while imperialism often employs indirect methods rather than direct action in helping the reactionaries in the semi-colonial countries to oppress the people, and thus the internal contradictions become particularly sharp. This is what happened in China in the Revolutionary War of 1911, the Revolutionary War of 1924–7, and the ten years of Agrarian Revolutionary War after 1927. Wars among the various reactionary ruling groups in the semi-colonial countries, e.g., the wars among the warlords in China, fall into the same category.

When a revolutionary civil war develops to the point of threatening the very existence of imperialism and its running dogs, the domestic reactionaries, imperialism often adopts other methods in order to maintain its rule; it either tries to split the revolutionary front from within or sends armed forces to help the domestic reactionaries directly. At such a time, foreign imperialism and domestic reaction stand quite openly at one pole while the masses of the people stand at the other pole, thus forming the principal contradiction which determines or influences the development of the other contradictions. The assistance given by various capitalist countries to the Russian reactionaries after the October Revolution is an example of armed intervention. Chiang Kai-shek's betrayal in 1927 is an example of splitting the revolutionary front.

But whatever happens, there is no doubt at all that at every stage in the development of a process, there is only one principal contradiction which plays the leading rôle.

Hence, if in any process there are a number of contradictions, one of them must be the principal contradiction playing the leading and decisive rôle, while the rest occupy a secondary and subordinate position. Therefore, in studying any complex process in which there are two or more contradictions, we must devote every effort to finding its principal contradiction. Once this principal contradiction is grasped, all problems can be readily solved. This is the method Marx taught us in his study of capitalist society. Likewise Lenin and Stalin taught us this method when they studied imperialism and the general crisis of capitalism and when they studied the Soviet economy. There are thousands of scholars and men of action who do not understand it, and the result is that, lost in a fog, they are unable to get to the heart of a problem and naturally cannot find a way to resolve its contradictions.

As we have said, one must not treat all the contradictions in a process as being equal but must distinguish between the principal and the secondary contradictions, and pay special attention to grasping the principal one. But, in any given contradiction, whether principal or secondary, should the two contradictory aspects be treated as equal? Again, no. In any contradiction the development of the contradictory aspects is uneven. Sometimes they seem to be in equilibrium, which is however only temporary and relative, while unevenness is basic. Of the two contradictory aspects, one must be principal and the other secondary. The principal aspect is the one playing the leading rôle in the contradiction. The nature of a thing is determined mainly by the principal aspect of a contradiction, the aspect which has gained the dominant position.

But this situation is not static; the principal and the non-principal aspects of a contradiction transform themselves into each other and the nature of the thing changes accordingly. In a given process or at a given stage in the development of a contradiction, A is the principal aspect and B is the non-principal aspect; at another stage or in another process the rôles are reversed – a change determined by the extent of the increase or decrease in the force of each aspect in its struggle against the other in the course of the development of a thing.

We often speak of "the new superseding the old". The supersession of the old by the new is a general, eternal and inviolable law of the universe. . . . In each thing there is contradiction between its new and its old aspects, and this gives rise to a series of struggles with many twists and turns. As a result of these struggles, the new aspect changes from being minor to being major and rises to predominance, while the old aspect changes from being major to being minor and gradually dies out. And the moment the new aspect gains dominance over the old, the old thing changes qualitatively into a new thing. It can thus be seen that the nature of a thing is mainly determined by the principal aspect of the contradiction, the aspect which has gained predominance. When the principal aspect which has gained predominance changes, the nature of a thing changes accordingly.

In capitalist society, capitalism has changed its position from being a subordinate force in the old feudal era to being the dominant force, and the nature of society has accordingly changed from feudal to capitalist. In the new, capitalist era, the feudal forces changed from their former dominant position to a subordinate one, gradually dying out. Such was the case, for example, in Britain and France. With the development of the productive forces, the bourgeoisie changes from being a new class playing a progressive rôle to being an old class playing a reactionary rôle, until it is finally overthrown by the proletariat and becomes a class deprived of privately owned means of production and stripped of power, when it, too, gradually dies out. The proletariat, which is much more numerous than the bourgeoisie and grows simultaneously with it but under its rule, is a new force which, initially subordinate to the bourgeoisie, gradually gains strength, becomes an independent class playing the leading rôle in history, and finally seizes political power and becomes the ruling class. Thereupon the nature of society changes and the old capitalist society becomes the new socialist society. This is the path already taken by the Soviet Union, a path that all other countries will inevitably take.

Look at China, for instance. Imperialism occupies the principal position in the contradiction in which China has been reduced to a semi-colony, it oppresses the Chinese people, and China has been changed from an independent country into a semi-colonial one. But this state of affairs will inevitably change; in the struggle between the two sides, the power of the Chinese people which is growing under the leadership of the proletariat will inevitably change China from a semi-colony into an independent country, whereas imperialism will be overthrown and old China will inevitably change into New China.

The change of old China into New China also involves a change in the relation between the old feudal forces and the new popular forces within the country. The old feudal landlord class will be overthrown, and from being the ruler it will change into being the ruled; and this class, too, will gradually die out. From being the ruled, the people, led by the proletariat, will become the rulers. Thereupon, the nature of Chinese society will change into a new democratic society. . . . In 1927, the people's forces, led by the Communist Party, were greatly reduced numerically under the attacks of Kuomintang reaction, but with the elimination of opportunism within their ranks they gradually grew again. In the revolutionary base areas under Communist leadership, the peasants have been transformed from being the ruled to being the rulers, while the landlords have undergone a reverse transformation. It is always so in the world, the new displacing the old, the old being superseded by the new, the old being eliminated to make way for the new, and the new emerging out of the old.

At certain times in the revolutionary struggle, the difficulties outweigh the favourable conditions and so constitute the principal aspect of the contradiction and the favourable conditions constitute the secondary aspect. But through their efforts the revolutionaries can overcome the difficulties step by step and open up a favourable new situation; thus a difficult situation yields place to a favourable one. . . .

When we engage in study, the same holds good for the contradiction in the passage from ignorance to knowledge. At the very beginning of our study of Marxism, our ignorance of or scanty acquaintance with Marxism stands in contradiction to knowledge of Marxism. But by assiduous study, ignorance can be transformed into knowledge, scanty knowledge into substantial knowledge and blindness in the application of Marxism into mastery of its application. . . .

For instance, in the contradiction between the productive forces and the relations of production, the productive forces are the principal aspect. . . . Whoever denies this is not a materialist. But it must also be admitted that in certain conditions, such aspects as the relations of production, theory and the superstructure in turn manifest themselves in the principal and decisive rôle. When it is impossible for the productive forces to develop without a change in the relations of production, then the change in the relations of production plays the principal and decisive rôle. The creation and advocacy of revolutionary theory plays the principal and decisive rôle in those times of which Lenin said, "Without revolutionary theory there can be no revolutionary movement." When a task, no matter which, has to be performed, but there is as yet no guiding line, method, plan or policy, the principal and decisive thing is to decide on a guiding line, method, plan or policy. When the superstructure (politics, culture, etc.) obstructs the development of the economic base, political and cultural changes become principal and decisive. Are we going against materialism when we say this? No. The reason is that while we recognize that in the general development of history the material determines the mental and social being determines social consciousness, we also – and indeed must – recognize the reaction of mental on material things, of social consciousness on social being and of the superstructure on the economic base. This does not go against materialism; on the contrary, it avoids mechanical materialism and firmly upholds dialectical materialism. . . .

Nothing in this world develops absolutely evenly; we must oppose the theory of even development or the theory of equilibrium. Moreover, it is these concrete features of a contradiction and the changes in the principal and non-principal aspects of a contradiction in the course of its development that manifest the force of the new superseding the old. The study of the various states of unevenness in contradictions, of the principal and non-principal contradictions and of the principal and non-principal aspects of a contradiction constitutes an essential method by which a revolutionary political party correctly determines its strategic and tactical policies both in political and in military affairs (12).

The identity and struggle of the aspects of a contradiction

Identity, unity, coincidence, interpenetration, interdependence (or mutual dependence for existence), interconnection or mutual co-operation – all these different terms mean the same thing and refer to the following two points: first, the existence of each of the two aspects of a contradiction in the process of the development of a thing presupposes the existence of the other aspect, and both aspects coexist in a single entity; second, in given conditions, each of the two contradictory aspects transforms itself into its opposite. This is the meaning of identity.

Lenin said: "*Dialectics* is the teaching which shows how *opposites* can be and how they happen to be (how they become) *identical* – under what conditions they are identical, transforming themselves into one another – why the human mind should take these opposites not as dead, rigid, but as living, conditional, mobile, transforming themselves into one another (13)."

What does this passage mean?

The contradictory aspects in every process exclude each other, struggle with each other and are in opposition to each other. . . .

The fact is that no contradictory aspect can exist in isolation. Without its opposite aspect, each loses the condition for its existence. Just think, can any one contradictory aspect of a thing or of a concept in the human mind exist independently? Without life, there would be no death; without death, there would be no life. Without "above", there would be no "below"; without "below", there would be no "above". Without misfortune, there would be no good fortune; without good fortune, there would be no misfortune. Without facility, there would be no difficulty; without difficulty, there would be no facility. Without landlords, there would be no tenant-peasants; without tenant-peasants, there would be no landlords. Without the bourgeoisie, there would be no proletariat; without the proletariat, there would be no bourgeoisie. Without imperialist oppression of nations, there would be no colonies or semi-colonies; without colonies or semi-colonies there would be no imperialist oppression of nations. It is so with all opposites; in given conditions on the one hand they are opposed to each other, and on the other they are interconnected, interpenetrating, interpermeating and interdependent, and this character is described as identity. . . .

But is it enough to say merely that each of the contradictory aspects is the condition for the other's existence, that there is identity between them and that consequently they can co-exist in a single entity? No, it is not. The matter does not end with their dependence on each other for their existence; what is more important is their transformation into each other. That is to say, in given conditions, each of the contradictory aspects within a thing transforms itself into its opposite, changes its position to that of its opposite. This is the second meaning of the identity of opposites. . . .

Our agrarian revolution has been a process in which the landlord class owning the land is transformed into a class that has lost its land, while the peasants who once lost their land are tranformed into small holders who have acquired land, and it will be such a process once again. In given conditions having and not having, acquiring and losing, are interconnected; there is identity of the two sides. Under socialism, private peasant ownership is transformed into the public ownership of socialist agriculture; this has already taken place in the Soviet Union, as it will take place everywhere else. There is a bridge leading from private property to public property, which in philosophy is called identity, or transformation into each other, or interpenetration. . . .

War and peace, as everybody knows, transform themselves

into each other. War is transformed into peace . . . Peace is transformed into war. . . . Why is this so? Because in class society such contradictory things as war and peace have an identity in given conditions.

All contradictory things are interconnected; not only do they co-exist in a single entity in given conditions, but in other given conditions, they also transform themselves into each other. This is the full meaning of the identity of opposites. . . .

The fact is that the unity or identity of opposites in objective things is not dead or rigid, but is living, conditional, mobile, temporary and relative; in given conditions, every contradictory aspect transforms itself into its opposite. Reflected in man's thinking, this becomes the Marxist world outlook of materialist dialectics. It is only the reactionary ruling classes of the past and present and the metaphysicians in their service who regard opposites not as living, conditional, mobile and transforming themselves into one another, but as dead and rigid, and they propagate this fallacy everywhere to delude the masses of the people, thus seeking to perpetuate their rule. . . .

Such is the problem of identity. What then is struggle? And what is the relation between identity and struggle?

All processes have a beginning and an end, all processes transform themselves into their opposites. The constancy of all processes is relative, but the mutability manifested in the transformation of one process into another is absolute.

There are two states of motion in all things, that of relative rest and that of conspicuous change. Both are caused by the struggle between the two contradictory elements contained in a thing. When the thing is in the first state of motion, it is undergoing only quantitative and not qualitative change and consequently presents the outward appearance of being at rest. When the thing is in the second state of motion, the quantitative change of the first state has already reached a culminating point and gives rise to the dissolution of the thing as an entity and thereupon a qualitative change ensues, hence the appearance of a conspicuous change. Such unity, solidarity, combination, harmony, balance, stalemate, deadlock, rest, constancy, equilibrium, solidity, attraction, etc., as we see in daily life, are all the appearances of things in the state of quantitative change, the transformation of one process into another. Things are constantly transforming themselves from the first into the second state of motion; the struggle of opposites goes on in both states but the contradiction is resolved through the second state. That is why we say that the unity of opposites is conditional, temporary and relative, while the struggle of mutually exclusive opposites is absolute. . . . To quote Lenin, ". . . there *is* an absolute *in* the relative" (14).

The place of antagonism in contradiction

The question of the struggle of opposites includes the question of what is antagonism. Our answer is that antagonism is one form, but not the only form, of the struggle of opposites.

In human history, antagonism between classes exists as a particular manifestation of the struggle of opposites. Consider the contradiction between the exploiting and the exploited classes. Such contradictory classes coexist for a long time in the same society, be it slave society, feudal society or capitalist society, and they struggle with each other; but it is not until the contradiction between the two classes develops to a certain stage that it assumes the form of open antagonism and develops into revolution. The same holds for the transformation of peace into war in class society.

Before it explodes, a bomb is a single entity in which opposites coexist in given conditions. The explosion takes place only when a new condition, ignition, is present. An analogous situation arises in all those natural phenomena which finally assume the form of open conflict to resolve old contradictions and produce new things.

It is highly important to grasp this fact. It enables us to understand that revolutions and revolutionary wars are inevitable in class society and that without them, it is impossible to accomplish any leap in social development and to overthrow the reactionary ruling classes and therefore impossible for the people to win political power. Communists must expose the deceitful propaganda of the reactionaries, such as the assertion that social revolution is unnecessary and impossible. They must firmly uphold the Marxist-Leninist theory of social revolution and enable the people to understand that social revolution is not only entirely necessary but also entirely practicable, and that the whole history of mankind and the triumph of the Soviet Union have confirmed this scientific truth.

However, we must make a concrete study of the circumstances of each specific struggle of opposites and should not arbitrarily apply the formula discussed above to everything. Contradiction and struggle are universal and absolute, but the methods of resolving contradictions, that is, the forms of struggle, differ according to the differences in the nature of the contradictions. Some contradictions are characterized by open antagonism, others are not. In accordance with the concrete development of things, some contradictions which were originally non-antagonistic develop into antagonistic ones, while others which were originally antagonistic develop into non-antagonistic ones.

As already mentioned, so long as classes exist, contradictions between correct and incorrect ideas in the Communist Party are reflections within the Party of class contradictions. At first, with regard to certain issues, such contradictions may not manifest themselves as antagonistic. But with the development of class struggle, they may grow and become antagonistic. The history of the Communist Party of the Soviet Union shows us that the contradictions between the correct thinking of Lenin and Stalin and the fallacious thinking of Trotsky, Bukharin and others did not at first manifest themselves in an antagonistic form, but that later they did develop into antagonism. There are similar cases in the history of the Chinese Communist Party. At first the contradictions between the correct thinking of many of our Party comrades and the fallacious thinking of Ch'en Tu-hsiu, Chang Kuo-tao and others also did not manifest themselves in an antagonistic form, but later they did develop into antagonism. At present the contradiction between correct and incorrect thinking in our Party does not manifest itself in an antagonistic form, and if comrades who have committed mistakes can correct them, it will not develop into antagonism. Therefore, the Party must on the one hand wage a serious struggle against erroneous thinking, and on the other give the comrades who have committed errors ample opportunity to wake up. This being the case, excessive struggle is obviously inappropriate. But if the people who have committed errors persist in them and aggravate them, there is the possibility that this contradiction will develop into antagonism.

Economically, the contradiction between town and country is an extremely antagonistic one both in capitalist society, where under the rule of the bourgeoisie the towns ruthlessly plunder the countryside, and in the Kuomintang areas in China, where under the rule of foreign imperialism and the Chinese big comprador bourgeoisie the towns most rapaciously plunder the countryside. But in a socialist country and in our revolutionary base areas this antagonistic contradiction has changed into one that is non-antagonistic; and when communist society is reached it will be abolished (15).

After recapitulating the basic points in this exposé, Mao Tse-tung added:

If, through study, we achieve a real understanding of the essentials explained above, we shall be able to demolish dogmatist ideas which are contrary to the basic principles of Marxism-Leninism and detrimental to our revolutionary cause, and our comrades with practical experience will be able to organize their experience into principles and avoid repeating empiricist errors (16). . . .

Return to practice

If the dialectical-materialist movement of knowledge were to stop at rational knowledge, only half the problem would be dealt with. And as far as Marxist philosophy is concerned, only the less important half at that. Marxist philosophy holds that the most important problem does not lie in understanding the laws of the objective world and thus being able to explain it, but in applying the knowledge of these laws actively to change the world. From the Marxist viewpoint, theory is important, and its importance is fully expressed in Lenin's statement, "Without revolutionary theory there can be no revolutionary movement (17)." But Marxism emphasizes the importance of theory precisely and only because it can guide action. If we have a correct theory but merely prate about it, pigeonhole it and do not put it into practice, then that theory, however good, is of no significance. Knowledge begins with practice, and theoretical knowledge is acquired through practice and must then return to practice. The active function of knowledge manifests itself not only in the active leap from perceptual to rational knowledge, but – and this is more important – it must manifest itself in the leap from rational knowledge to revolutionary practice. The knowledge which grasps the laws of the world, must be redirected to the practice of changing the world, must be applied anew to the practice of production, in the practice of revolutionary class struggle and revolutionary national struggle and in the practice of scientific experiment. This is the process of testing and developing theory, the continuation of the whole process of cognition.

The problem of whether theory corresponds to objective reality is not, and cannot be, completely solved in the movement of knowledge from the perceptual to the rational, mentioned above. The only way to solve this problem completely is to redirect rational knowledge to social practice, apply theory to practice and see whether it can achieve the objectives one has in mind. Many theories of natural science are held to be true not only because they were so considered when natural scientists originated them, but because they have been verified in subsequent scientific practice. Similarly, Marxism-Leninism is held to be true not only because it was so considered when it was scientifically formulated by Marx, Engels, Lenin and Stalin but because it has been verified in the subsequent practice of revolutionary class struggle and revolutionary national struggle. Dialectical materialism is universally true because it is impossible for anyone to escape from its domain in his practice. The history of human knowledge tells us that the truth of many theories is incomplete and that this incompleteness is remedied through the test of practice. Many theories are erroneous and it is through the test of practice that their errors are corrected. That is why practice is the criterion of truth and why "the standpoint of life, of practice, should be first and fundamental in the theory of knowledge (18)." Stalin has well said, "Theory becomes purposeless if it is not connected with revolutionary practice, just as practice gropes in the dark if its path is not illumined by revolutionary theory (19)."

When we get to this point, is the movement of knowledge completed? Our answer is: it is and yet it is not. When men in society throw themselves into the practice of changing a certain objective process (whether natural or social) at a certain stage of its development, they can, as a result of the reflection of the objective process in their brains and the exercise of their subjective activity, advance their knowledge from the perceptual to the rational, and create ideas, theories, plans or programmes which correspond in general to the laws of that objective process. They then apply these ideas, theories, plans or programmes in practice in the same objective process. And if they can realize the aims they have in mind, that is, if in that same process of practice they can translate, or on the whole, translate, those previously formulated ideas, theories, plans or programmes into fact, then the movement of knowledge may be considered completed with regard to this particular process. . . . But generally speaking, whether in the practice of changing nature or of changing society, men's original ideas, theories, plans or programmes are seldom realized without any alteration. . . . In many instances, failures have to be repeated many times before errors in knowledge can be corrected and correspondence with the laws of the objective process achieved, and consequently before the subjective can be transformed into the objective, or in other words, before the anticipated results can be achieved in practice. But when that point is reached, no matter how, the movement of human knowledge regarding a certain objective process at a certain stage of its development may be considered completed.

However, so far as the progression of the process is concerned, the movement of human knowledge is not completed. Every process, whether in the realm of nature or of society, progresses and develops by reason of its internal contradiction and struggle, and the movement of human knowledge should also progress and develop along with it. As far as social movements are concerned, true revolutionary leaders must not only be good at correcting their ideas, theories, plans or programmes when errors are discovered, as has been indicated above, but when a certain objective process has already progressed and changed from one stage of development to another, they must also be good at making themselves, and all their fellow-revolutionaries progress and change in their subjective knowledge along with it, that is to say, they must ensure that the proposed new revolutionary tasks and new working programmes correspond to the new changes in the situation. In a revolutionary period the situation changes very rapidly; if the knowledge of revolutionaries does not change rapidly in accordance with the changed situation, they will be unable to lead the revolution to victory.

It often happens, however, that thinking lags behind reality; this is because man's cognition is limited by numerous social conditions. We are opposed to die-hards in the revolutionary ranks whose thinking fails to advance with changing objective circumstances and has manifested itself historically as Right opportunism. These people fail to see that the struggle of opposites has already pushed the objective process forward while their knowledge has stopped at the old stage. This is characteristic of the thinking of all die-hards. Their thinking is divorced from social practice, and they cannot march ahead to guide the chariot of society; they simply trail behind, grumbling that it goes too fast and trying to drag it back or turn it in the opposite direction.

We are also opposed to "Left" phrase-mongering. The thinking of "Leftists" outstrips a given stage of development of the objective process; some regard their fantasies as truth, while others strain to realize in the present an ideal which can only be realized in the future. They alienate themselves from the current practice of the majority of the people and from the realities of the day, and show themselves adventurist in their actions.

Idealism and mechanical materialism, opportunism and adventurism, are all characterized by the breach between the subjective and the objective, by the separation of knowledge from practice. The Marxist-Leninist theory of knowledge, characterized as it is by scientific social practice, cannot but resolutely oppose these wrong ideologies. Marxists recognize that in the absolute and general process of development of the universe, the development of each particular process is relative, and that hence, in the endless flow of absolute truth man's knowledge of a particular process at any given stage of development is only relative truth. The sum total of innumerable relative truths constitutes absolute truth.

The development of an objective process is full of contradictions and struggles, and so is the development of the movement of human knowledge. All the dialectical movements of the objective world can sooner or later be reflected in human knowledge. In social practice, the process of coming into being, developing and passing away is infinite and so is the process of coming into being, developing and passing away in human knowledge. As man's practice which changes objective reality in accordance with given ideas, theories, plans or programmes, advances further and further, his knowledge of objective reality likewise becomes deeper and deeper. The movement of change in the world of objective reality is never-ending and so is man's cognition of truth through practice. Marxism-Leninism has in no way exhausted truth but ceaselessly opens up roads to the knowledge of truth in the course of practice. Our conclusion is the concrete, historical unity of the subjective and the objective, of theory and practice, of knowing and doing, and we are opposed to all erroneous ideologies, whether "Left" or Right, which depart from concrete history (20).

Correct ideas

Where do correct ideas come from? Do they drop from the skies? No. Are they innate in the mind? No. They come from social practice, and from it alone; they come from three kinds of social practice, the struggle for production, the class struggle and scientific experiment. It is man's social being that determines his thinking. Once the correct ideas characteristic of the advanced class are grasped by the masses, these ideas turn into a material force which changes society and changes the world. . . .

It was not enough to move from perceptual knowledge to conceptual knowledge. It was not yet sure that theories, policies, plans or measures "correctly reflect the laws of the objective world; it is not yet possible to know if they are right or not . . ." It was now a question of moving from consciousness back to matter, from ideas back to existence, in which the knowledge gained in the first stage is applied in social practice to ascertain whether the theories, policies, plans or measures meet with the anticipated success. Generally speaking, those that succeed are correct and those that fail are incorrect, and this is especially true of man's struggle with nature. In social struggle, the forces representing the advanced class sometimes suffer defeat not because their ideas are incorrect but because, in the balance of forces engaged in struggle they are not as powerful for the time being as the forces of reaction; they are therefore temporarily defeated, but they are bound to triumph sooner or later. Man's knowledge makes another leap through the test of practice. This leap is more important than the previous one*. For it is this leap alone that can prove the correctness or incorrectness of the first leap, i.e., of the ideas, theories, policies, plans or measures formulated in the course of reflecting the objective external world. There is no other way of testing truth. Furthermore, the one and only purpose of the proletariat in knowing the world is to change it. Often, a correct idea can be arrived at only after many repetitions of the process leading from matter to consciousness and then back to matter, that is, leading from practice to knowledge and then back to practice (21). . . .

Discover the truth through practice, and again through practice verify and develop the truth. Start from perceptual knowledge and actively develop it into rational knowledge; then start from rational knowledge and actively guide revolutionary practice to change both the subjective and the objective world. Practice, knowledge, again practice, and again knowledge. This form repeats itself in endless cycles, and with each cycle the content of practice and knowledge rises to a higher level. . . .

In the present epoch of the development of society the responsibility of correctly knowing and changing the world has been placed by history upon the shoulders of the proletariat and its party. This process, the practice of changing the world, which is determined in accordance with scientific knowledge, has already reached a historic moment in the world and in China, a great moment unprecedented in human history, that is, the moment for completely banishing darkness from the world and from China and for changing the world into a world of light such as never previously existed. The struggle of the proletariat and the revolutionary people to change the world comprises the fulfilment of the following tasks: to change the objective world and, at the same time, their own subjective

*From perceptual knowledge to rational knowledge.

world – to change their cognitive ability and change the relations between the subjective and the objective world. Such a change has already come about in one part of the globe, in the Soviet Union. There the people are pushing forward this process of change. The people of China and the rest of the world either are going through, or will go through, such a process. And the objective world which is to be changed also includes all the opponents of change, who, in order to be changed, must go through a stage of compulsion before they can enter the stage of voluntary, conscious change. The epoch of world communism will be reached when all mankind voluntarily and consciously changes itself and the world (22).

What direction was Mao Tse-tung's thought to take once the leader was entrenched in Yenan? How was it to be put into practice? What objectives was the man who had now become the leader of Chinese Communism to set?

7 Mao Tse-tung defines "New Democracy"

When the Chinese Communist Party Central Committee settled in Yenan in December 1936, China had already reached a new, very important stage in her history. The Kuomintang regime in Nanking seemed to have consolidated; it had practically eliminated most of the areas of armed rebellion south of the Yangtze, and was plagued only by the survival of the revolutionary base in the North-West interior, where the Communist Party, reduced to forty thousand members after the Long March, was trying to bind its wounds and to regather its strength.

The principal threat was now from abroad. Japan, since 1931 master of Manchuria, now Manchukuo, a Nippon protectorate, embarked on the conquest of Northern China. In 1935, she succeeded in removing it from the effective authority of the central government by creating an "autonomous government" there, which was in fact manipulated by Tokyo. Resistance against Japan had become China's major problem, because, as Mao said, if China becomes a Japanese colony, Chinese of all or almost all classes will be reduced to slavery. Class struggle therefore had to be subordinated to the struggle for national independence. Moreover, in endeavouring to assume the leadership of the anti-Japanese struggle, Mao knew that he had a chance of winning over the forces of Chinese nationalism to the advantage of the Communist Party. Circumstances provoked a *crise de conscience* in the population. On 9 December 1935, students demonstrated in Peking and called on the nation to resist foreign conquest. But the Kuomintang equivocated, changed course and even appeared to seek some compromise with Japan. It was in fact more concerned with its "domestic" enemies, and the nation began to judge its attitude with severity.

In August 1935, to combat world Fascism, the Seventh Komintern Congress had advocated the setting up of popular fronts and "governments of national defence". In May 1936, in accordance with this line, which it approved, the Chinese Communist Party proposed co-operation against Japan to Chiang Kai-shek. It got a cold reception. But in December 1936, Chiang Kai-shek, arriving in the North-West to end the collaboration which was going on between his troops and the Communists, was captured in Sian. He was freed, after long negotiations, in exchange for a promise to resist Japan, resistance for which the Communists were prepared to support him provided he stopped fighting them. Chiang agreed to the bargain; and when in February 1937 the Communist Party drew up proposals for a new Kuomintang-Communist Party alliance against Japan, Chiang called a halt to operations against the Communists in the spring of the same year.

The Japanese reacted to the prospect of a China united against them. On 7 July 1937, the Lukiukiao incident, six miles south-west of Peking, was the cue for a major war by Japan against China, which was, according to Tokyo, an undertaking to persuade China to collaborate harmoniously with Japan.

Once again the Kuomintang seemed to be in search of a compromise. But the Communists reacted bluntly*: compromises were no longer acceptable; the time had come to fight. The

---

*It was at this juncture, July–August 1937, that Mao Tse-tung found time to write his two philosophical essays: "On Practice" and "On Contradiction" (see previous chapter).

resolution adopted by the Party on 25 August 1937 stated that it was necessary to mobilize the nation to win the war. On 22 September, an agreement was signed between Chiang and Mao on the bases proposed by the Communist Party in February. The supreme Communist authority gave up its title of "Workers' and Peasants' Revolutionary Government" and became the "autonomous government of the Border Region", the "Red Army" changed its name and became the "National Revolutionary Army". The Communist Party agreed to end its agrarian policy of confiscating the landlords' lands and to revert to a policy of reducing rents and interest rates. It finally abandoned its policy of insurrection against the central government. In return, the latter halted its operations against the Communists, and recognized the existence of the "Border Region" and the Eighth Route Army. The latter was to be under the strategic directives of the Defence Council, in which the Communist Party would be represented. It was a rough draft of a united front against the foreign invader.

Though certain circles in Nanking and elsewhere had deluded themselves as to the relations in forces between China and Japan, the early months of the war put an end to their dreams. The Japanese seized Northern China, to the south of Peking, occupied Shanghai and Nanking (captured and sacked in December 1937), and advanced into the valleys of the Yangtze; then in October 1938 they took Hankow, forcing the Central Chinese Government to settle still further in the interior, in Chungking. Shortly afterwards, the Japanese, who had occupied several ports in Eastern China, landed at Canton and tried to unite all their forces operating in China. Only Communist guerilla units continued the struggle behind their lines. China had been forced to yield up most of her towns and ports, her rich and fertile areas and was practically isolated from the world outside.

Confronted with this situation, which had taken such a swift and dramatic turn, Mao Tse-tung tried to view the problems in both a complete and realistic way. In his opinion, it was as necessary to guard against excessive pessimism, which generated defeatism, as against absurd optimism; he stated: "The theory of China's inevitable subjugation is groundless. China will not be defeated but she can conquer only at the cost of a "protracted war" (1).

"On Protracted War" is the title of a work combining the speeches which Mao made in Yenan from 26 May to 3 June 1938 to the Association for the Study of the War of Resistance against Japan. It contains certain passages essential to the undertanding of Mao Tse-tung's work.

Not that we would not like a quick victory; everybody would be in favour of driving the "devils" out overnight. But we point out that, in the absence of certain definite conditions, quick victory is something that exists only in one's mind and not in objective reality, and that it is a mere illusion, a false theory. Accordingly, having made an objective and comprehensive appraisal of all the circumstances concerning both the enemy and ourselves, we point out that the only way to final victory is the strategy of protracted war, and we reject the groundless theory of quick victory. We maintain that we must strive to secure all the conditions indispensable to final victory, and the more fully and the earlier these conditions are secured, the surer we shall be of victory and the earlier we shall win it. We believe that only in this way can the course of the war be shortened, and we reject the theory of quick victory, which is just idle talk (2). . . .

There are three factors contributing to China's perseverance in the War of Resistance. In the first place, the Communist Party, which is the reliable force leading the people to resist Japan. Next, the Kuomintang, which depends on Britain and the United States and hence will not capitulate to Japan unless they tell it to. Finally, the other political parties and groups, most of which oppose compromise and support the War of Resistance. With unity among these three, whoever compromises will be standing with the traitors, and anybody will have the right to punish him. All those unwilling to be traitors have no choice but to unite and carry on the War of Resistance to the end; therefore compromise can hardly succeed. . . . Except for Japan's allies and certain elements in the upper strata of other capitalist countries, the whole world is in favour of resistance, and not of compromise by China (3). . . .

That the war will be protracted is certain, but nobody can predict exactly how many months or years it will last, as this depends entirely upon the degree of the change in the balance of forces. All those who wish to shorten the war have no alternative but to work hard to increase our own strength and reduce that of the enemy. . . . There is no magic short-cut (4). . . .

Since the Sino-Japanese war is a protracted one and final victory will belong to China, it can reasonably be expected that this protracted war will pass through three stages. The first stage covers the period of the enemy's strategic offensive and our strategic defensive. The second stage will be the period of the enemy's strategic consolidation and our preparation for the counter-offensive. The third stage will be the period of our strategic counter-offensive and the enemy's strategic retreat (5). . . .

In this stage the form of fighting we should adopt is primarily mobile warfare, supplemented by guerilla and positional warfare (6). . . .

In the second stage, the enemy will attempt to safeguard the occupied areas and to make them his own by the fraudulent method of setting up puppet governments, while plundering the Chinese people to the limit; but again he will be confronted with stubborn guerilla warfare. Taking advantage of the fact that the enemy's rear is unguarded, our guerilla warfare will develop extensively in the first stage, and many base areas will be established, seriously threatening the enemy's consolidation of the occupied areas, and so in the second stage there will still be widespread fighting. In this stage, our form of fighting will be primarily guerilla warfare, supplemented by mobile warfare (7). . . .

Generally speaking, we should be prepared to see this stage last a comparatively long time and to weather its hardships. It will be a very painful period for China; the two big problems will be economic difficulties and the disruptive activities of the traitors. The enemy will go all out to wreck China's united front, and the traitor organizations in all the occupied areas will merge into a so-called "unified government". Owing to the loss of big cities and the hardships of war, vacillating elements within our ranks will clamour for compromise and pessimism will grow to a serious extent. Our tasks will then be to mobilize the whole people to unite as one man and carry on the war with unflinching perseverance, to broaden and consolidate the united front, sweep away all pessimism and ideas of compromise, promote the will to hard struggle and apply new wartime policies and so to weather the hardships. In the second stage we will have to call upon the whole country resolutely to maintain a united government, we will have to oppose splits and systematically improve fighting techniques, reform the armed forces, mobilize the entire people and prepare for the counter-offensive (8). . . .

The third stage will be the stage of the counter-offensive to recover our lost territories. Their recovery will depend mainly upon the strength which China has built up in the preceding stage and which will continue to grow in the third stage. But China's strength alone will not be sufficient, and we shall have to rely on the support of international forces and on the changes that will take place inside Japan, or otherwise we shall not be able to win; this adds to China's tasks in international propaganda and diplomacy. In the third stage, our war will no longer be one of strategic defensive, but will turn into a strategic counter-offensive manifesting itself in strategic offensives; and it will no longer be fought on strategically interior lines, but will shift gradually to strategically exterior lines. Not until we fight our way to the Yalu River can this war be considered over. The third stage will be the last in the protracted war. . . . Our primary form of fighting will still be mobile warfare, but positional warfare will rise to importance. . . . In the third stage guerilla warfare will again provide strategic support by supplementing mobile and positional warfare but it will not be the primary form as in the second stage. . . .

The war will be protracted and consequently ruthless in nature. The enemy will not be able to gobble up the whole of China but will be able to occupy many places for a considerable time. China will not be able to oust the Japanese quickly, but the greater part of her territory will remain in her hands. Ultimately the enemy will lose and we will win, but we shall have a hard stretch of road to travel (9). . . .

Among the forms of warfare in the anti-Japanese war, mobile warfare comes first and guerilla warfare second. When we say that in the entire war mobile warfare is primary and guerilla warfare supplementary we mean that the outcome of the war depends mainly on regular warfare, especially in its mobile form, and that guerilla warfare cannot shoulder the main responsibility in deciding the outcome. It does not follow, however, that the role of guerilla warfare is unimportant in the strategy of the war. Its rôle in the strategy of the war as a whole is second only to that of mobile warfare, for without its support we cannot defeat the enemy. In saying this we also have in mind the strategic task of developing guerilla warfare into mobile warfare. Thus the strategic role of guerilla warfare is twofold, to support regular warfare and to transform itself into regular warfare (10). . . .

From the viewpoint of all three stages in China's War of Resistance Against Japan, guerilla warfare is definitely indispensable. Our guerilla war will present a great drama unparalleled in the annals of war. For this reason, out of the millions of China's regular troops, it is absolutely necessary to assign at least several hundred thousand to disperse through all enemy-occupied areas, arouse the masses to arm themselves, and wage guerilla warfare in co-ordination with the masses (11). . . .

The anti-Japanese war is at once a war of attrition and a war of annihilation. . . . It is chiefly by using the method of attrition through annihilation that China can wage protracted war (12). . . .

The Chinese people will become tempered in the course of this long and ruthless war. The political parties taking part in the war will also be steeled and tested. The united front must be persevered in; only by persevering in the united front can we persevere in the war; and only by persevering in the united front and in the war can we win final victory. Only thus can all difficulties be overcome. After travelling the hard stretch of road we shall reach the highway to victory (13). . . .

In 1938–9, some currents of opinion in Chungking, London and Washington favoured alliance with the Chinese Communists against Japan, but with the signing of the German-Soviet pact on 23 August 1939 and the beginning of the war in Europe on 1 September, there was nothing to stop the Kuomintang from reverting to its previous distrust and even hostility.

However, the fate of China, invaded, sacked and dismembered by the Japanese, outweighed all personal or ideological considerations among the people. Public opinion pressed increasingly for united resistance against the invader.

In December 1939 and January 1940, in a series of lectures given in Yenan, "The Chinese Revolution and the Chinese Communist Party" and "On New Democracy", Mao Tse-tung, already to some extent adopting a post-war stance, once again defined, in a more precise way, the objectives of the Chinese Revolution :

The historical characteristic of the Chinese revolution lies in its division into the two stages, democracy and socialism. . . .

Clearly it follows from the colonial, semi-colonial and semi-feudal character of present-day Chinese society that the Chinese revolution must be divided into two stages. The first step is to change the colonial, semi-colonial and semi-feudal forms of society into an independent, democratic society. The second is to carry the revolution forward and build a socialist society. At present the Chinese revolution is taking the first step. . . . The first is no longer democracy in general, but democracy of the Chinese type, a new and special type, namely, New Democracy (14). . . .

First Mao pointed out "the chief targets or enemies at this stage of the Chinese revolution" :

They are imperialism and feudalism, the bourgeoisie of the imperialist countries and the landlord class of our country. For it is these two that are the chief oppressors, the chief obstacles to the progress of Chinese society at the present stage. The two are in collusion with each other in oppressing the Chinese people, and imperialism is the foremost and most ferocious enemy of the Chinese people, because national oppression by imperialism is the more onerous.

Since Japan's armed invasion of China, the principal enemy

of the revolution has been Japanese imperialism together with all the Chinese traitors and reactionaries in league with it, whether they have capitulated openly or are preparing to do so. . . .

It is evident, then, that the enemies of the Chinese revolution are very powerful. They include not only powerful imperialists and powerful feudal forces, but also, at times, the bourgeois reactionaries who collaborate with the imperialist and feudal forces to oppose the people. Therefore, it is wrong to underestimate the strength of the enemies of the revolutionary Chinese people.

In the face of such enemies, the Chinese revolution cannot be other than protracted and ruthless. With such powerful enemies, the revolutionary forces cannot be built up and tempered into a power capable of crushing them except over a long period of time. With enemies who so ruthlessly suppress the Chinese revolution, the revolutionary forces cannot hold their own positions, let alone capture those of the enemy, unless they steel themselves and display their tenacity to the full. It is therefore wrong to think that the forces of the Chinese revolutionary struggle can triumph overnight.

In the face of such enemies, the principal means of form of the Chinese revolution must be armed struggle, not peaceful struggle. For our enemies have made peaceful activity impossible for the Chinese people and have deprived them of all political freedom and democratic rights. Stalin says, "In China the armed revolution is fighting the armed counter-revolution. That is one of the specific features and one of the advantages of the Chinese revolution." This formulation is perfectly correct. Therefore, it is wrong to belittle armed struggle, revolutionary war, guerilla war and army work.

In the face of such enemies, there arises the question of revolutionary base areas. Since China's key cities have long been occupied by the powerful imperialists and their reactionary Chinese allies, it is imperative for the revolutionary ranks to turn the backward villages into advanced, consolidated base areas, into great military, political, economic and cultural bastions of the revolution from which to fight their vicious enemies who are using the cities for attacks on the rural districts, and in this way gradually to achieve the complete victory of the revolution

F

through protracted fighting; it is imperative for them to do so if they do not wish to compromise with imperialism and its lackeys but are determined to fight on, and if they intend to build up and temper their forces, and avoid decisive battles with a powerful enemy while their own strength is inadequate. Such being the case, victory in the Chinese revolution can be won first in the rural areas, and this is possible because China's economic development is uneven (her economy not being a unified capitalist economy), because her territory is extensive (which gives the revolutionary forces room to manoeuvre), because the counter-revolutionary camp is disunited and full of contradictions, and because the struggle of the peasants who are the main force in the revolution is led by the Communist Party, the party of the proletariat; but on the other hand, these very circumstances make the revolution uneven and render the task of winning complete victory protracted and arduous. Clearly then the protracted revolutionary struggle in the revolutionary base areas consists mainly in peasant guerilla warfare led by the Chinese Communist Party. Therefore, it is wrong to ignore the necessity of using rural districts as revolutionary base areas, to neglect painstaking work among the peasants, and to neglect guerilla warfare.

However, stressing armed struggle does not mean abandoning other forms of struggle; on the contrary, armed struggle cannot succeed unless co-ordinated with other forms of struggle. And stressing the work in the rural base areas does not mean abandoning our work in the cities and in the other vast rural areas which are still under the enemy's rule; on the contrary, without the work in the cities and in these other rural areas, our own rural base areas would be isolated and the revolution would suffer defeat. Moreover, the final objective of the revolution is the capture of the cities, the enemy's main bases, and this objective cannot be achieved without adequate work in the cities.

It is thus clear that the revolution cannot triumph either in the rural areas or in the cities without the destruction of the enemy's army, his chief weapon against the people. Therefore, besides annihilating the enemy's troops in battle, there is the important task of disintegrating them.

It is also clear that the Communist Party must not be

impetuous and adventurist in its propaganda and organizational work in the urban and rural areas which have been occupied by the enemy and dominated by the forces of reaction and darkness for a long time, but that it must have well-selected cadres working underground, must accumulate strength and bide its time there. In leading the people in struggle against the enemy, the Party must adopt the tactics of advancing step by step slowly and surely, keeping to the principle of waging struggles on just grounds, to our advantage, and with restraint, and making use of such open forms of activity as are permitted by law, decree and social custom; empty clamour and reckless action can never lead to success (15). . . .

In this lecture, Mao Tse-tung was once again analysing the forces in China capable of fighting or helping the revolution: landlords, bourgeoise, petty bourgeoise and peasants. This is how he referred to the poor peasants and the proletariat:

The poor peasants in China, together with the farm labourers, form about 70 per cent of the rural population. They are the broad peasant masses with no land or insufficient land, the semi-proletariat of the countryside, the biggest motive force of the Chinese revolution, the natural and most reliable ally of the proletariat and the main contingent of China's revolutionary forces. Only under the leadership of the proletariat can the poor and middle peasants achieve their liberation, and only by forming a firm alliance with the poor and middle peasants can the proletariat lead the revolution to victory. Otherwise neither is possible. The term "peasantry" refers mainly to the poor and middle peasants.

Among the Chinese proletariat, the modern industrial workers number from two and a half to three millions, the workers in small-scale industry and in handicrafts and the shop assistants in the cities total about twelve million, and in addition there are great numbers of rural proletarians (the farm labourers) and other propertyless people in the cities and the country-side (16). . . .

The Chinese proletariat is more resolute and thoroughgoing in revolutionary struggle than any other class because it is subjected to a threefold oppression (imperialist, bourgeois and feudal) which is marked by a severity and cruelty seldom found in other countries. Since there is no economic basis for social reformism in colonial and semi-colonial China as there is in Europe, the whole proletariat, with the exception of a few scabs, is most revolutionary. . . .

Because the Chinese proletariat by origin is largely made up of bankrupted peasants, it has natural ties with the peasant masses, which facilitates its forming a close alliance with them.

Therefore, in spite of certain unavoidable weaknesses, for instance, its smallness (as compared with the peasantry), its youth (as compared with the proletariat in the capitalist countries) and its low educational level (as compared with the bourgeoisie), the Chinese proletariat is nonetheless the basic motive force of the Chinese revolution. Unless it is led by the proletariat, the Chinese revolution cannot possibly succeed (17). . . .

The Chinese proletariat should understand that although it is the class with the highest political consciousness and sense of organization, it cannot win victory by its own strength alone. In order to win it, it must unite, according to varying circumstances, with all classes and strata that can take part in the revolution, and must organize a revolutionary united front. Among all the classes in Chinese society, the peasantry is a firm ally of the working class, the urban petty bourgeoisie is a reliable ally, while the national bourgeoisie is an ally in certain periods and to a certain extent (18). . . .

The Chinese revolution at the present stage must strive to create a democratic republic in which the workers, the peasants and the other sections of the petty bourgeoisie all occupy a definite position and play a definite role. In other words, it must be a democratic republic based on a revolutionary alliance of the workers, peasants, urban petty bourgeoisie and all others who are against imperialism and feudalism. Only under the leadership of the proletariat can such a republic be completely realized (19). . . .

In present-day China the bourgeois-democratic revolution is no longer of the old general type, which is now obsolete, but one of a new special type. We call this type the new-democratic revolution and it is developing in all other colonial and semi-colonial countries as well as in China. The new-democratic revolution is part of the world proletarian-socialist revolution, for it resolutely opposes imperialism, i.e., international capitalism. Politically it strives for the joint dictatorship of the revolutionary classes over the imperialists, traitors and reactionaries, and opposes the transformation of Chinese society into a society under bourgeois dictatorship. Economically, it aims at the nationalization of all the big enterprises and capital of the imperialists, traitors and reactionaries, and the distribution among the peasants of the land held by the landlords, while preserving private capitalist enterprise in general and not eliminating the rich-peasant economy. Thus, the new type of democratic revolution clears the way for capitalism on the one hand and creates the prerequisites for socialism on the other. The present stage of the Chinese revolution is a stage of transition between the abolition of the colonial, semi-colonial and semi-feudal society and the establishment of a socialist society, i.e., it is a process of new-democratic revolution. This process, begun only after the First World War and the Russian October Revolution, started in China with the 4 May Movement of 1919. A new-democratic revolution is an anti-imperialist and anti-feudal revolution of the broad masses of the people under the leadership of the proletariat. Chinese society can advance to socialism only through such a revolution; there is no other way.

The new-democratic revolution is vastly different from the democratic revolutions of Europe and America in that it results not in a dictatorship of the bourgeoisie but in a dictatorship of the united front of all the revolutionary classes under the leadership of the proletariat (20). . . .

The new-democratic revolution also differs from a socialist revolution in that it overthrows the rule of the imperialists, traitors and reactionaries in China but does not destroy any section of capitalism which is capable of contributing to the anti-imperialist, anti-feudal struggle (21). . . .

Every Communist ought to know that, taken as a whole, the Chinese revolutionary movement led by the Communist Party embraces the two stages, i.e., the democratic and the socialist revolutions which are two essentially different revolutionary processes, and that the second process can be carried through only after the first has been completed. The democratic revolution is the necessary preparation for the socialist revolution, and the socialist revolution is the inevitable sequel to the democratic revolution. The ultimate aim for which all communists strive is to bring about a socialist and communist society. A clear understanding of both the differences and the interconnections between the democratic and the socialist revolutions is indispensable to correct leadership in the Chinese revolution.

Except for the Communist Party, no political party (bourgeois or petty-bourgeois) is equal to the task of leading China's two great revolutions, the democratic and the socialist revolutions, to complete fulfilment (22). . . .

This amounts to saying that "no revolution can triumph without the leadership of the Chinese Communist Party".

In "On New Democracy", given in January 1940, Mao Tse-tung developed the same themes, adding some interesting details :

The proletariat, the peasantry, the intelligentsia and the other sections of the petty bourgeoisie undoubtedly constitute the basic forces determining China's fate. These classes, some already awakened and others in the process of awakening, will necessarily become the basic components of the state and governmental structure in the democratic republic of China, with the proletariat as the leading force. The Chinese democratic republic which we desire to establish now must be a democratic republic under the joint dictatorship of all antiimperialist and anti-feudal people led by the proletariat, that is, a new-democratic republic of the genuinely revolutionary new Three People's Principles with their Three Great Policies. . . . This form suits a certain historical period and is therefore transitional; nevertheless, it is a form which is necessary and cannot be dispensed with (23). . . .

We hope that China's anti-Japanese united front will be maintained and that, with the co-operation of all instead of the monopoly of a single clique, the anti-Japanese cause will be brought to victory. . . .

We Communists will never push aside anyone who is revolutionary; we shall persevere in the united front and practise long-term co-operation with all those classes, strata, political parties and groups and individuals that are willing to fight Japan to the end. But it will not do if certain people want to push aside the Communist Party; it will not do if they want to split the united front (24). . . .

Either you co-operate with the Communist Party or you oppose it. Opposition to communism is the policy of the Japanese imperialists and Wang Ching-wei, and if that is what you want, very well, they will invite you to join their Anti-Communist Company. But wouldn't that look suspiciously like turning traitor? You may say, "I am not following Japan, but some other country." That is just ridiculous. No matter whom you follow, the moment you oppose the Communist Party you become a traitor, because you can no longer resist Japan. If you say, "I am going to oppose the Communist Party independently," that is arrant nonsense. How can the "heroes" in a colony or semi-colony tackle a counter-revolutionary job of this magnitude without depending on the strength of imperialism? . . . If you oppose the Communist Party at a juncture when our national enemy is penetrating deep into our territory, the people will be after your hide; they will certainly show you no mercy. This much is certain, whoever wants to oppose the Communist Party must be prepared to be ground to dust. If you are not keen on being ground to dust, you had certainly better drop this opposition. This is our sincere advice to all the anti-Communist "heroes" (25). . . .

In the international situation of today, the "heroes" in the colonies and semi-colonies either line up on the imperialist front and become part of the forces of world counter-revolution, or they line up on the anti-imperialist front and become part of the forces of world revolution. They must be one or the other, for there is no third choice. . . .

We Communists will always persevere in long-term co-operation with all the true followers of the Three People's Principles and, while rejecting the traitors and the sworn enemies of communism, will never forsake any of our friends (26). . . .

At this point Mao Tse-tung harked back to the peasant question :

Stalin has said that *"in essence,* the national question is a peasant question". This means that the Chinese revolution is essentially a peasant revolution and that the resistance to Japan now going on is essentially peasant resistance. Essentially, the politics of New Democracy means giving the peasants their rights. . . . Essentially, mass culture means raising the cultural level of the peasants. The anti-Japanese war is essentially a peasant war. . . . Essentially it is the peasants who provide everything that sustains the resistance to Japan and keeps us going. By "essentially" we mean basically, not ignoring the other sections of the people, as Stalin himself has explained. As every schoolboy knows, 80 per cent of China's population are peasants. So the peasant problem becomes the basic problem of the Chinese revolution and the strength of the Chinese revolution. In the Chinese population the workers rank second to the peasants in number. There are several million industrial workers in China and several tens of millions of handicraft workers and agricultural labourers. China cannot live without her workers in the various industries, because they are the producers in the industrial sector of the economy. And the revolution cannot succeed without the modern industrial working class, because it is the leader of the Chinese revolution and is the most revolutionary class (27). . . .

Mao Tse-tung now went on to discuss the problem of "the new democratic culture" and he said :

A given culture is the ideological reflections of the politics and economics of a given society. There is in China an imperialist culture which is a reflection of imperialist rule, or partial rule, in the political and economic fields. This culture is fostered not only by the cultural organizations run directly by the imperialists in China but by a number of Chinese who have lost all sense of shame. Into this category falls all culture embodying a slave ideology. China also has a semi-feudal culture which reflects her semi-feudal politics and economy, and whose exponents include all those who advocate the worship of Confucius, the study of the Confucian canon, the old ethical code and the old ideas in opposition to the new culture and new ideas. Imperialist culture and semi-feudal culture are devoted brothers and have formed a reactionary cultural alliance against China's new culture. This kind of reactionary culture serves the imperialists and the feudal class and must be swept away. Unless it is swept away, no new culture of any kind can be built up. There is no construction without destruction, no flowing without damming and no motion without rest; the two are locked in a life-and-death struggle.

As for the new culture, it is the ideological reflection of the new politics and the new economy which it sets out to serve (28). . . .

New-democratic culture is national. It opposes imperialist oppression and upholds the dignity and independence of the Chinese nation. It belongs to our nation and bears our own national characteristics. It links up with the socialist and new-democratic cultures of all other nations and they are related in such a way that they can absorb something from each other and help each other to develop, together forming a new world culture; but as a revolutionary national culture it can never link up with any reactionary imperialist culture of whatever nation. To nourish her own culture China needs to assimilate a good deal of foreign progressive culture, not enough of which was done in the past. We should assimilate whatever is useful to us today not only from the present-day socialist and new-democratic cultures but also from the earlier cultures of other nations, for example, from the culture of the various capitalist countries in the Age of Enlightenment. However, we should not gulp any of this foreign material down uncritically, but must treat it as we do our food—first chewing it, then submitting it to the working of the stomach and intestines with their juices and secretions, and separating it into nutriment to be absorbed and waste matter to be discarded – before it can nourish us. To advocate "wholesale westernization" is wrong. China has suffered a great deal from the mechanical absorption of foreign material. Similarly, in applying Marxism to China, Chinese Communists must fully and properly integrate the universal truth of Marxism with the concrete practice of the Chinese revolution, or in other words, the universal truth of Marxism must be combined with specific national characteristics and acquire a definite national form if it is to be useful, and in no circumstances can it be applied subjectively as a mere formula. Marxists who make a fetish of formulas are simply playing the fool with Marxism and the Chinese revolution, and there is no room for them in the ranks of the Chinese revolution. Chinese culture should have its own form, its own national form. National in form and new-democratic in content – such is our new culture today.

New-democratic culture is scientific. Opposed as it is to all feudal and superstitious ideas, it stands for seeking truth from facts, for objective truth and for the unity of theory and practice. On this point, the possibility exists of a united front against imperialism, feudalism and superstition between the scientific thought of the Chinese proletariat and those Chinese bourgeois materialists and natural scientists who are progressive, but in no case is there a possibility of a united front with any reactionary idealism. In the field of political action Communists may form an anti-imperialist and anti-feudal united front with some idealists and even religious people, but we can never approve of their idealism or religious doctrines. A splendid old culture was created during the long period of Chinese feudal society. To study the development of this old culture, to reject its feudal dross and assimilate its democratic essence is a necessary condition for developing our new national culture and increasing our national self-confidence, but we should never swallow anything and everything uncritically. It is imperative to separate the fine old culture of the people which had a more or less democratic and revolutionary character from all the decadence of the old feudal ruling class. China's present new politics and new economy have developed out of her old politics and old economy, and her present new culture, too, has developed out of her old culture; therefore, we must respect our own history and must not lop it off. However, respect for history means giving it its proper place as a science, respecting its dialectical development, and not eulogizing the past at the expense of the present or praising every drop of feudal poison. As far as the masses and the young students are concerned, the essential thing is to guide them to look forward and not backward.

New-democratic culture belongs to the broad masses and is therefore democratic. It should serve the toiling masses of workers and peasants who make up more than 90 per cent of the nation's population and should gradually become their very own. There is a difference of degree, as well as a close link, between the knowledge imparted to the revolutionary cadres and the knowledge imparted to the revolutionary masses, between the raising of cultural standards and popularization. Revolutionary culture is a powerful revolutionary weapon for the broad masses of the people. It prepares the ground ideologically before the revolution comes and is an important, indeed essential, fighting front in the general revolutionary front during the revolution. People engaged in revolutionary cultural work are the commanders at various levels on this cultural front. . . . A revolutionary cultural worker who is not close to the people is a commander without an army, whose fire-power cannot bring the enemy down. To attain this objective, written Chinese must be reformed, given the requisite conditions, and our spoken language brought closer to that of the people, for the people, it must be stressed, are the inexhaustible source of our revolutionary culture. . . .

Combine the politics, the economy and the culture of New Democracy, and you have the new democratic republic, the Republic of China both in name and in reality, the New China we want to create (29).

However, the horizon was nothing like so clear, and the war dragged on extremely painfully for China, the Japanese not as yet having suffered any serious reverses. They had, as Mao had predicted, succeeded in winning over a far from negligible group of the Kuomintang, and a Chinese "puppet" government, led by Wang Ching-wei, was set up in Nanking in March 1940. England, faced with a German attack, had to reduce its aid to China. Alarmed, the U.S.S.R. signed a neutrality pact with Japan in April 1941, and by June 1941 the German invasion placed her in a very difficult position. More than ever, Moscow advised political discretion.

One of the results of the Anglo-Soviet alliance, concluded in July 1941, was that London and Moscow now both wanted the Chinese Communists to merge into the anti-Japanese front, which was led, according to the English and Russians, by the Kuomintang.

While the Chinese Communists were giving priority to the struggle against Japan and advocating union just as much as before, they remained as clear-sighted as ever. They knew that the Kuomintang was still dominated by military cliques, the landlords and the big bourgeoisie, backed by England and America, and that it would strive to crush the Communist Party at every opportunity. The latter could not therefore contemplate "merging" with a front, putting itself in a situation where it would be, as in 1927, at the mercy of the Kuomintang.

8 From Yenan to Peking: the struggle continues

The Communist Party now impressed itself on the people as the most determined force resisting the invader, and the new strategy applied by the latter, based on the slogan "Burn all, kill all, plunder all," increased their determination to hold on and exacerbated the hate of the Chinese masses. Anxious gradually to take over the leadership in the struggle, highly suspicious of Chungking, the Communist Party was able to retain its autonomy and its political and military freedom of action, come wind, come rain. A "rectification" campaign, begun in Yenan in February 1942, helped to preserve the "proletarian" character of the Border Area, as much in the field of political alignment as in that of culture.

Since Japan's declaration of war on the United States and England, China was no longer by herself. Her struggle now became an integral part of the Second World War. But with the arrival of fairly large numbers of American forces on the Chinese theatre of war, a new factor emerged : the Americans were in fact astonished to see the Kuomintang keeping so many forces in reserve against the Communists, so they put pressure on Chiang Kai-shek's government to make it throw its forces into the war against Japan. After Vice-President Wallace's visit to Chungking and his invitation to Chiang to co-operate with the Communists, an American military mission was attached to the Communist H.Q. in Yenan, along with an American diplomat, John S. Service, in August 1944. But Chiang reacted very vigorously to the American "suggestions" of placing the whole of the Chinese forces, whether nationalist or Communist, under a single *American* command. Washington gave way, recalled General Stillwell and Ambassador Gauss, and appointed a conservative ambassador, Patrick Hurley.

In spite of their defeats in the Pacific at the hands of the Americans, the Japanese continued to strike hard at China where the "allied" victory still seemed a very long way off. The Chinese Communist Party and its two armies did however achieve some notable successes, building up its principal and secondary revolutionary bases in the Nippon rear, consolidating its powers, and increasing its numbers of regular troops and guerillas. By the beginning of 1945, the Communists were said to control 91 million inhabitants in China and to have military forces of over 2 million combatants. Thus they faced the Chungking government with an increasingly serious problem. But the latter remained deaf to all suggestions, both Allied and Chinese, of forming a "coalition government" with the Communists.

However, at the Seventh Chinese Communist Party Congress in April 1945, Mao Tse-tung compiled a massive report on the theme: "On Coalition Government". The Chinese Communist Party was, according to him, ready to take part in one – on certain conditions.

The Yalta Conference, the Allied victory in Europe, the bombing-raids on Japan and MacArthur's progress made it clear that the final phase of the war against Japan was drawing near: the latter was about to be struck in the very heart of her Empire, at home.

On 6 August 1945, the Americans dropped the first atomic bomb on Hiroshima. On the 8th, the U.S.S.R. declared war on Japan. Within a few days the Soviet army routed Kwang Tung's

Japanese army in Manchuria, entered Korea and Northern China – Jehol, Chahar. On 10 August, the Japanese government announced its intention to surrender.

As the Communists prepared to accept the surrender of Japanese and "puppet"* forces wherever possible, Chiang Kai-shek ordered them to remain where they were and to await instructions. He forbade them at all costs to disarm the enemy. At the same time the Kuomintang invited the "puppet" troops and civil servants to join their ranks. On 13 August 1945, Mao reacted, denouncing the Kuomintang's attitude and insisting that it could lead only to civil war :

It is necessary to be soberly aware that the danger of civil war is extremely serious because Chiang Kai-shek's policy is already set. Chiang Kai-shek's policy is civil war. . . . The opponents of civil war consist only of the Chinese Communist Party and the Chinese people (1). . . .

Our policy is to give tit for tat. . . . Today we say, "If Chiang goes for us, we'll go for him. If Chiang stops, we'll stop too." We will act after his fashion. As Chiang Kai-shek is now sharpening his swords, we must sharpen ours too.

The right the people have won must never be lightly given up but must be defended by fighting. We don't want civil war. However, if Chiang Kai-shek insists on forcing civil war on the Chinese people, the only thing we can do is to take up arms and fight him in self-defence to protect the lives and property the rights and well-being of the people of the Liberated Areas. This will be a civil war he forces on us (2). . . .

The stage of the War of Resistance Against Japan is over and the new situation and task is domestic struggle. . . . From now on the struggle will be, build what sort of country? To build a new democratic country of the broad masses of the people under the leadership of the proletariat? Or to build a semi-colonial and semi-feudal country under the dictatorship of the big landlords and the big bourgeoisie? . . .

Chiang Kai-shek will face many difficulties if he tries to let loose a civil war. First in the Liberated Areas there are a hundred million people, a million troops and over two million

*These were the Nanking "government" forces led by Wang Ching-wei.

people's militia. Second, the politically conscious people in the Kuomintang areas are against civil war, and this is some kind of check on Chiang Kai-shek. Third, inside the Kuomintang also there is a section which is not in favour of civil war. The situation today is vastly different from that in 1927. In particular, the condition of our Party today is vastly different from what it was in 1927 (3). . . .

Today the level of political consciousness of the Chinese people is likewise very much higher. The prestige of our Party among the people has never been so great. Nevertheless, among the people, and chiefly among those living in the Japanese-occupied and Kuomintang areas, there are still a good many who believe in Chiang Kai-shek and have illusions about the Kuomintang and the United States of America, illusions which Chiang Kai-shek is working hard to spread. The fact that a section of the Chinese people is not yet politically conscious shows that much remains to be done in our propaganda and organizational work. The political awakening of the people is not easy. It requires much earnest effort on our part to rid their minds of wrong ideas. We should sweep backward ideas from the minds of the Chinese people, just as we sweep our rooms. Dust never vanishes of itself without sweeping. . . .

It is up to us to organize the people. As for the reactionaries in China, it is up to us to organize the people to overthrow them. Everything reactionary is the same; if you don't hit it, it won't fall. This is also like sweeping the floor; as a rule, where the broom does not reach, the dust will not vanish of itself. . . .

Some of our comrades put their faith only in political influence, fancying that problems can be solved merely by influence. That is blind faith. Bells don't ring until you strike them. Tables don't move until you shift them. . . . The enemy and puppet troops never handed over their arms until our troops fought them. Only where the broom reaches can political influence produce its full effect. Our broom is the Communist Party, the Eighth Route Army and the New Fourth Army. Broom in hand, you must learn to sweep; don't lie in bed, fancying that a gust of wind will somehow rise and blow all the dust away. . . . There is an old saying in China, "Rise at dawn and sweep the courtyard." Dawn is the breaking of a new day. Our forefathers told us to rise and start sweeping at the very break of day. They were setting us a task. Only by thinking and acting in this way will we benefit and find work to do. China has a vast territory, and it is up to us to sweep it clean inch by inch (4). . . .

In an attempt to prevent civil war, negotiations between the Kuomintang and the Communist Party took place in Chungking in October 1945. They led to an agreement on 10 October. But this agreement remained a dead letter one. In spite of efforts by the American "mediator", George Marshall, civil war flared up again in China in January 1946. The Kuomintang, which had more than five million men and plenty of American equipment, thought that it would be easily able to deal with the Communist Party which had only two to three million men – largely militiamen – and far less modern and powerful arms. It enjoyed considerable successes at first, capturing Yenan in March 1947, but the Communist Party was able to recover the offensive in spring 1948 from the new base areas which it had rapidly organized in the North and North-East (Manchuria). Shattered, the Kuomintang armies soon had to abandon the North-West, then Manchuria, but they were already faced by powerful Communist forces in the so-called "central" plains. On 20 January 1949, Peking surrendered and Chiang Kai-shek intimated that he was ready to discuss peace. The Communist armies, breaking towards the South, reached the Yangtze.

The negotiations now held between the Communist Party and the Kuomintang broke down because of the intransigence of both sides. It is significant that at this point Mao was faced with a strong resurgence within the Party of certain "leftist deviationist" trends, which had already had a harmful influence in matters of agrarian reform. In spring 1949, the Party Left, of which Liu Shao-ch'i seemed to be leader, went so far as to demand actual capitulation by the Kuomintang. Instead of winning the support of the majority of the Kuomintang and the transfer of "legal power" to the Communist Party, which would have avoided any serious dissent with Formosa or Canton, the Party headquarters kept up its demands, provoking a breach.

The Communist armies crossed the Yangtze and occupied Nanking and Shanghai. Late in 1949, having driven the Kuomintang from the mainland, they won control of every part of the Chinese mainland, except Tibet. But Chiang Kai-shek had sought refuge in Formosa, taking with him a semblance of Chinese legality, and claiming for years to be the only government in China. The "Leftists" in the Communist Party had made a political mistake of the first order.

Few people in China were aware of it at the time. The end of the fighting and the collapse of the Kuomintang regime were enough to delight the masses.

On 1 October 1949, the People's Republic of China was proclaimed in Peking and a government set up under the leadership of Mao Tse-tung. The latter, in a speech on 30 June 1949, had already defined "the people's democratic dictatorship":

All the experience the Chinese people have accumulated through several decades teaches us to enforce the people's democratic dictatorship, that is, to deprive the reactionaries of the right to speak and let the people alone have that right.

Who are the people? At the present stage in China, they are the working class, the peasantry, the urban petty bourgeoisie and the national bourgeoisie. These classes, led by the working class and the Communist Party, unite to form their own state and elect their own government; they enforce their dictatorship over the running dogs of imperialism – the landlord class and bureaucrat-bourgeoisie, as well as the representatives of those classes, the Kuomintang reactionaries and their accomplices – suppress them, allow them only to behave themselves and not to be unruly in word or deed. If they speak or act in an unruly way, they will be promptly stopped and punished. Democracy is practised within the ranks of the people, who enjoy the rights of freedom of speech, assembly, association and so on. The right to vote belongs only to the people, not to the reactionaries. The combination of these two aspects, democracy for the people and dictatorship over the reactionaries, is the people's democratic dictatorship.

Why must things be done this way? The reason is quite clear to everybody. If things were not done this way, the revolution would fail, the people would suffer, the country would be conquered (5). . . .

Imperialism still exists, because domestic reaction still exists, because classes still exist in our country. Our present task is to strengthen the people's state apparatus – mainly the people's army, the people's police and the people's courts – in order to consolidate national defence and protect the people's interests. Given this condition, China can develop steadily, under the leadership of the working class and the Communist Party, from an agricultural into an industrial country and from a new-democratic into a socialist and communist society, can abolish classes and realize the Great Harmony. The state apparatus, including the army, the police and the courts, is the instrument by which one class oppresses another. It is an instrument for the oppression of antagonistic classes, it is violence and not "benevolence". "You are not benevolent!" Quite so. We definitely do not apply a policy of benevolence to the reactionaries and towards the reactionary activities of the reactionary classes. Our policy of benevolence is applied only within the ranks of the people, not beyond them to the reactionaries or to the reactionary activities of reactionary classes.

The people's state protects the people. Only when the people have such a state can they educate and remould themselves on a country-wide scale by democratic methods and, with everyone taking part, shake off the influence of domestic and foreign reactionaries (which is still very strong, will survive for a long time and cannot be quickly destroyed), rid themselves of the bad habits and ideas acquired in the old society, not allow themselves to be led astray by the reactionaries, and continue to advance – to advance towards a socialist and communist society.

Here, the method we employ is democratic, the method of persuasion, not of compulsion (6). . . .

As for the members of the reactionary classes and individual reactionaries, so long as they do not rebel, sabotage or create trouble after their political power has been overthrown, land and work will be given to them as well in order to allow them to live and remould themselves through labour into new people. If they are not willing to work, the people's state will compel them to work. Propaganda and educational work will be done among them too and will be done, moreover, with as much care and thoroughness as among the captured army officers in the past. This, too, may be called a "policy of benevolence" if you like, but it is imposed by us on the members of the enemy classes and cannot be mentioned in the same breath with the work of self-education which we carry on within the ranks of the revolutionary people.

Such remoulding of members of the reactionary classes can be accomplished only by a state of the people's democratic dictatorship under the leadership of the Communist Party. When it is well done, China's major exploiting classes, the landlord class and the bureaucratic-bourgeoisie (the monopoly capitalist class), will be eliminated for good. There remains the national bourgeoisie; at the present stage, we can already do a good deal of suitable educational work with many of them. When the time comes to realize socialism, that is, to nationalize private enterprise, we shall carry the work of educating and remoulding them a step further. The people have a powerful state apparatus in their hands – there is no need to fear rebellion by the national bourgeoisie.

The serious problem is the education of the peasantry. The peasant economy is scattered, and the socialization of agriculture, judging by the Soviet Union's experience, will require a long time and painstaking work. Without socialization of agriculture, there can be no complete, consolidated socialism. The steps to socialize agriculture must be co-ordinated with the development of a powerful industry having state enterprise as its backbone. The state of the people's democratic dictatorship must systematically solve the problems of industrialization(7). . . .

Revolutionary dictatorship and counter-revolutionary dictatorship are by nature opposites, but the former was learned from the latter. Such learning is very important. If the revolutionary people do not master this method of ruling over the counter-revolutionary classes, they will not be able to maintain their state power, domestic and foreign reaction will overthrow that power and restore its own rule over China, and disaster will befall the revolutionary people.

The people's democratic dictatorship is based on the alliance of the working class, the peasantry and the urban petty bourgeoisie, and mainly on the alliance of the workers and the peasants, because these two classes comprise 80 to 90 per cent of China's population. . . .

The people's democratic dictatorship needs the leadership of the working class. For it is only the working class that is most far-sighted, most selfless and most thoroughly revolutionary. The entire history of revolution proves that without the leadership of the working class revolution fails and with the leadership of the working class revolution triumphs. In the epoch of imperialism, in no country can any other class lead any genuine revolution to victory. This is clearly proved by the fact that the many revolutions led by China's petty bourgeoisie and national bourgeoisie all failed.

The national bourgeoisie at the present stage is of great importance. Imperialism, a most ferocious enemy, is still standing alongside us. China's modern industry still forms a very small proportion of the national economy. No reliable statistics are available, but it is estimated, on the basis of certain data, that before the War of Resistance against Japan the value of output of modern industry constituted only about 10 per cent of the total value of output of the national economy. To counter imperialist oppression and to raise her backward economy to a higher level, China must utilize all the factors of urban and rural capitalism that are beneficial and not harmful to the national economy and the people's livelihood; and we must unite with the national bourgeoisie in common struggle. Our present policy is to regulate capitalism, not to destroy it. But the national bourgeoisie cannot be the leader of the revolution, nor should it have the chief rôle in state power. The reason it cannot be the leader of the revolution and should not have the chief rôle in state power is that the social and economic position of the national bourgeoisie determines its weakness; it lacks foresight and sufficient courage and many of its members are afraid of the masses. . . . In the epoch of imperialim the petty bourgeoisie and the national bourgeoisie cannot lead any genuine revolution to victory.

Our twenty-eight years have been quite different. We have had much valuable experience. A well-disciplined Party armed with the theory of Marxism-Leninism, using the method of self-criticism and linked with the masses of the people; an army under the leadership of such a Party; a united front of all revolutionary classes and all revolutionary groups under the leadership of such a Party – these are the three main weapons with which we have defeated the enemy. They distinguish us from our predecessors. . . . We have travelled a tortuous road. We have struggled against opportunist deviations in our Party, both Right and Left. Whenever we made serious mistakes on these three matters, the revolution suffered setbacks. Taught by mistakes and setbacks, we have become wiser and handle our affairs better. It is hard for any political party or person to avoid mistakes, but we should make as few as possible. Once a mistake is made, we should correct it, and the more quickly and thoroughly the better (8). . . .

Twenty-eight years of our Party are a long period in which we have accomplished only one thing – we have won basic victory in the revolutionary war. This calls for celebration, because it is the people's victory, because it is a victory in a country as large as China. But we still have much work to do; to use the analogy of a journey, our past work is only the first step in a long march of ten thousand *li*. Remnants of the enemy have yet to be wiped out. The serious task of economic construction lies before us. We shall soon put aside some of the things we know well and be compelled to do things we don't know well. This means difficulties. The imperialists reckon that we will not be able to manage our economy; they are standing by and looking on, awaiting our failure.

We must overcome difficulties, we must learn what we do not know. We must learn to do economic work from all who know how, no matter who they are. We must esteem them as teachers, learning from them respectfully and conscientiously. We must not pretend to know when we do not know. We must not put on bureaucratic airs. If we dig into a subject for several months, for a year or two, for three or five years, we shall eventually master it. At first some of the Soviet Communists also were not very good at handling economic matters and the imperialists awaited their failure too. But the Communist Party of the Soviet Union emerged victorious and, under the leadership of Lenin and Stalin, it learned not only how to make the revolution but also how to carry on construction. It has built a great and splendid socialist state. The Communist Party of the Soviet Union is our best teacher and we must learn from it. The situation both at home and abroad is in our favour, we can rely fully on the weapon of the people's democratic dictatorship, unite the people throughout the country, the reactionaries excepted, and advance steadily to our goal (9).

This composite article is strange in certain respects. It is tougher, especially in its first part, than Mao's earlier texts, and particularly those given in this chapter. It has, it must be admitted, a rather "Stalinist" character. This once again prompts us to ask the question: what happened within the Chinese Communist Party in spring 1949? To what extent did the elements, which could be called "Stalinist" or "neo-Stalinist", and were supposed to have included Liu Shao-ch'i, get the better of the genuine "Maoists"? The new tone of Mao's 30 June 1949 article suggests that he must in any case have been aware of a new, strong "leftist" trend.

The regime now grew and consolidated. Its first major decisions naturally concerned the peasants. An agrarian reform law, promulgated on 30 April 1950, began the complete and general withdrawal of power from the landlords, whose lands were confiscated and redistributed (though not those of the rich peasants).

The Korean war, which broke out at this precise moment, at the end of June 1950, and in which China intervened at the end of October, was a long and harsh ordeal which enabled the "Stalinists" in the party to obtain increasing influence in the apparatus at home and enabled them to secure the country in the "steel corset" of "Party dictatorship" and not that of the people. The purification of counter-revolutionaries was savagely carried out. On the other hand, Liu Shao-ch'i and his friends gradually managed to gain control of the Party apparatus, of which Mao remained apparent leader*. In autumn 1953, the Party broke the "conspiracy" by Kao Kang, who had become the genuine dictator of Manchuria, which he had, it was said, more or less established as his private fief and in which he was suspected of playing a Soviet rather than a Chinese game (10).

*In 1967, Mao admitted that "ever since 1952 the Party had become cut off from the masses". (Instructions by President Mao, 29 April 1967, c.f. *Le Monde*, 23 May 1967.)

By 1954, the regime was establishing stable institutions. The Constitution was promulgated in this year and came into full force. Mao Tse-tung was elected president of the Republic. Chou En-lai took over the presidency of the Council of State. Liu Shao-ch'i assumed the Party presidency and presided over the Central Committee.

In 1955, the regime, regarding itself as sufficiently consolidated, gradually moved from a "people's democratic dictatorship" to a "proletarian dictatorship". It decided to embark – certainly more quickly than Mao had originally envisaged – on the second stage of the revolution, that of socialist transformation. However, it was Mao who gave the signal to establish the co-operative system instead of individual economy throughout the Chinese countryside*.

In 1956, with the Eighth Congress, the Party took a firm grip on the power of its apparatus and its bureaucracy. But on 26 May of the same year the slogan "Let a hundred flowers blossom, let a hundred schools of thought contend!" was proclaimed. Strange as it may seem, the world did not seem to suspect the existence of "contradictions" within the Chinese Communist Party. However, before the end of the year a major crisis shook the whole of the Communist world: "destalinization" began, with noisy repercussions by the new leader of the U.S.S.R., Nikita S. Khrushchev; and the popular uprising in socialist Hungary in October 1956.

In the great palaces of Peking where the men from the Tsingkiang Mountains and Yenan now reigned, it was hard not to ask questions. In China, too, a party led by intellectuals but devoted to the proletariat was exercising "dictatorship" in the people's name. But who were the new masters? And what were they now to do, *faced* by the people?

Faced by the vast sea of 600 million souls of which this people now consisted, what did the Party represent? Fifteen million

---

*"In October 1954, the Communist Party Central Committee decided to multiply the number of co-operatives by six and to raise them from 100,000 to 600,000" (Mao Tse-tung, *On the Problem of Agricultural Co-operation*, 31 July 1955 report, Peking, 1966, p. 5).

persons, one for every forty Chinese. The golden rule, for Mao Tse-tung, had not changed; to practise and keep practising the "mass line". The Hungarian experience had proved how a "proletarian dictatorship", a "revolutionary party" could become divorced from the people, and through its excesses, even fling the people on the side of counter-revolution.

The conclusions which Mao Tse-tung drew from the Hungarian affair are in what is without doubt the most important speech that he made after attaining power, "On the Correct Handling of Contradictions Among the People", in February 1957. Here are the most significant passages from it :

Never before has our country been as united as it is today. . . . The old days of national disunity and chaos which the people detested have gone, never to return. Led by the working class and the Communist Party, our six hundred million people, united as one, are engaged in the great task of building socialism. The unification of our country, the unity of our people and the unity of our various nationalities – these are the basic guarantees of the sure triumph of our cause. However, this does not mean that contradictions no longer exist in our society. To imagine that none exist is a naive idea which is at variance with objective reality. We are confronted by two types of social contradictions – those between ourselves and the enemy and those among the people themselves. The two are totally different in their nature.

To understand these two different types of contradictions correctly, we must first be clear on what is meant by "the people" and what is meant by "the enemy". The concept of "the people" varies in content in different countries and in different periods of history in the same country. Take our own country for example. During the War of Resistance against Japan, all those classes, strata and social groups opposing Japanese aggression came within the category of the people, while the Japanese imperialists, the Chinese traitors and the pro-Japanese elements were all enemies of the people. During the War of Liberation, the U.S. imperialists and their running dogs – the bureaucrat-capitalists, the landlords and the Kuomintang reactionaries who represented these two classes – were the enemies of the people, while the other classes, strata and social groups, which opposed these enemies, all came within the category of the people. At the present stage, the period of building socialism, the classes, strata and social groups which favour, support and work for the cause of socialist construction all come within the category of the people, while the social forces and groups which resist the socialist revolution and are hostile to or sabotage socialist construction are all enemies of the people.

The contradictions between ourselves and the enemy are antagonistic contradictions. Within the ranks of the people, the contradictions among the working people are non-antagonistic, while those between the exploited and the exploiting classes have a non-antagonistic aspect in addition to an antagonistic aspect. There have always been contradictions among the people, but their content differs in each period of the revolution and in the period of socialist construction. In the conditions prevailing in China today, the contradictions among the people comprise the contradictions within the working class, the contradictions within the peasantry, the contradictions within the intelligentsia, the contradictions between the working class and the peasantry, the contradictions between the workers and peasants on the one hand and the intellectuals on the other, the contradictions between the working class and other sections of the working people on the one hand and the national bourgeoisie on the other, the contradictions within the national bourgeoisie, and so on. Our People's Government is one that genuinely represents the people's interests, it is a government that serves the people. Nevertheless, there are still certain contradictions between the government and the people. These include contradictions among the interests of the state, the interests of the collective and the interests of the individual; between democracy and centralism; between the leadership and the led; and the contradiction arising from the bureaucratic style of work of certain government workers in their relations with the masses. All these are also contradictions among the people. Generally speaking, the people's basic identity of interests underlies the contradictions among the people (11). . . .

Our state is a people's democratic dictatorship. . . . The aim of this dictatorship is to protect all our people so that they can devote themselves to peaceful labour and build China into a socialist country with a modern industry, agriculture, science and culture. Who is to exercise this dictatorship? Naturally, the working class and the entire people under its leadership. Dictatorship does not apply within the ranks of the people. The people cannot exercise dictatorship over themselves, nor must one section of the people oppress another. Law-breaking elements among the people will be punished according to law, but this is different in principle from the exercise of dictatorship to suppress enemies of the people. . . . Our Constitution lays it down that citizens of the People's Republic of China enjoy freedom of speech, of the press, assembly, association, procession, demonstration, religious belief and so on. Our Constitution also provides that the organs of state must practise democratic centralism, that they must rely on the masses and that their personnel must serve the people.

Our socialist democracy is democracy in the broadest sense such as is not to be found in any capitalist country. Our dictatorship is the people's democratic dictatorship led by the working class and based on the worker-peasant alliance. That is to say, democracy operates within the ranks of the people, while the working class, uniting with all others, enjoying civil rights, and in the first place with the peasantry, enforces dictatorship over the reactionary classes and elements and all those who resist socialist transformation and oppose socialist construction. By civil rights, we mean, politically, the rights of freedom and democracy.

But this freedom is freedom with leadership and this democracy is democracy under centralized guidance, not anarchy. Anarchy does not accord with the interests or wishes of the people (12). . . .

Within the ranks of the people, we cannot do without freedom, nor can we do without discipline; . . . the people enjoy extensive democracy and freedom, but at the same time they have to keep within the bounds of socialist discipline. All this is well understood by the broad masses of the people.

In advocating freedom with leadership and democracy under centralized guidance, we in no way mean that coercive measures should be taken to settle ideological questions or questions involving the distinction between right and wrong among the people. All attempts to use administrative orders or coercive measures to settle ideological questions or questions of right and wrong are not only ineffective but harmful. We cannot abolish religion by administrative decree or force people not to believe in it. We cannot compel people to give up idealism any more than we can force them to believe in Marxism. The only way to settle questions of an ideological nature or controversial issues among the people is by the democratic method, the method of discussing, of criticism, of persuasion and education, and not by the method of coercion or repression (13). . . .

This democratic method of resolving contradictions among the people was epitomized in 1942 in the formula "unity, criticism, unity". To elaborate, it means starting from the desire for unity, resolving contradictions through criticism or struggle and arriving at a new unity on a new basis. In our experience this is the correct method of resolving contradictions among the people. . . .

The essential thing is to start from the desire for unity. For without this desire for unity the struggle is certain to get out of hand. Wouldn't this be the same as "ruthless struggle and merciless blows"? And what Party unity would there be left? . . . In other words, "learn from past mistakes to avoid future ones and cure the sickness to save the patient" (14).

In order to settle problems within the ranks of the people, "the method we employ is democratic, the method of persuasion, not of compulsion" . . .

Many dare not openly admit that contradictions still exist among the people of our country, although it is these very contradictions that are pushing our society forward. Many do not admit that contradictions continue to exist in a socialist society, with the result that they are handicapped and passive when confronted with social contradictions; they do not understand the socialist society will grow more united and consolidated through the ceaseless process of the correct handling and resolving of contradictions. For this reason we need to explain things to our people, and to our cadres in the first place, in order to help them understand the contradictions in a socialist society and learn to use correct methods for handling these contradictions (15). . . .

Our socialist system has only just been set up; it is not yet fully established or fully consolidated. . . . The superstructure consisting of the state system and laws of the people's democratic dictatorship and the socialist ideology guided by Marxism-Leninism plays a positive rôle in facilitating the victory of socialist transformation and the establishment of the socialist organization of labour; it is suited to the socialist economic base, that is, to socialist relations of production. But survivals of bourgeis ideology, certain bureaucratic ways of doing things in our state organs and defects in certain links in our state institutions are in contradiction with the socialist economic base. We must continue to resolve all such contradictions in the light of our specific conditions. Of course, new problems will emerge as these contradictions are resolved. And further efforts will be required to resolve the new contradictions. . . . Time is needed for our socialist system to become established and consolidated, for the masses to become accustomed to the new system, and for the government workers to learn and acquire experience (16). . . .

"Let a hundred flowers blossom, let a hundred schools of thought contend" and "long-term co-existence and mutual supervision" – how did these slogans come to be put forward? They were put forward in the light of China's specific conditions, on the basis of the recognition that various kinds of contradictions still exist in socialist society, and in response to the country's urgent need to speed up its economic and cultural development. Letting a hundred flowers blossom and a hundred schools of thought contend is the policy for promoting the progress of the arts and the sciences and a flourishing socialist culture in our land. Different forms and styles in art should develop freely and different schools in science should contend freely. We think it is harmful to the growth of art and science if administrative measures are used to impose one particular style of art or school of thought and to ban another. Questions of right and wrong in the arts and sciences should be settled through free discussion in artistic and scientific circles and through practical work in these fields. They should not be settled in summary fashion. A period of trial is often needed to determine whether something is right or wrong. Throughout history, new and correct things have often failed at the outset to win recognition from the majority of people and have had to develop by twists and turns in struggle. Often correct and good things have first been regarded not as fragrant flowers but as poisonous weeds. Copernicus' theory of the solar system and Darwin's theory of evolution were once dismissed as erroneous and had to win through over bitter opposition. Chinese history offers many similar examples. In a socialist society, conditions for the growth of the new are radically different from and far superior to those in the old society. Nevertheless, it still often happens that new, rising forces are held back and rational proposals constricted. Moreover, the growth of new things may be hindered in the absence of deliberate suppression simply through lack of discernment. It is therefore necessary to be careful about questions of right and wrong in the arts and sciences, to encourage free discussion and avoid hasty conclusions. We believe that such an attitude can help to ensure a relatively smooth development of the arts and sciences.

Marxism, too, has developed through struggle. At the beginning, Marxism was subjected to all kinds of attack and regarded as a poisonous weed. It is still being attacked and is still regarded as a poisonous weed in many parts of the world. In the socialist countries, it enjoys a different position. But non-Marxist and, moreover, anti-Marxist ideologies exist even in these countries. In China, although in the main socialist transformation has been completed with respect to the system of ownership, and although the large-scale and turbulent class struggles of the masses characteristic of the previous revolutionary periods have in the main come to an end, there are still remnants of the overthrown landlord and comprador classes, there is still a bourgeoisie, and the remoulding of the petty bourgeoisie has only just started. The class struggle is by no means over. The class struggle between the proletariat and the bourgeoisie, the class struggle between the different political forces, and the class struggle in the ideological field between the proletariat and the bourgeoisie will continue to be long and tortuous and at times will even become very acute. The proletariat seeks to transform the world according to its own world outlook, and so does the bourgeoisie. In this respect, the question of which will win, socialism or capitalism, is still not really settled. Marxists are still a minority among the entire population, as well as among the intellectuals. Therefore, Marxism must still develop through struggle. Marxism can develop only through struggle, and not only is this true of the past and the present, it is necessarily true of the future as well. What is correct invariably develops in the course of struggle with what is wrong. The true, the good and the beautiful always exist by contrast with the false, the evil and the ugly, and grow in strugggle with the latter. As soon as a wrong kind is rejected and a particular truth accepted by mankind, new truths begin their struggle with new errors. Such struggles will never end. This is the law of development of truth and, naturally, of Marxism as well.

It will take a fairly long period of time to decide the issue in the ideological struggle between socialism and capitalism in our country. The reason is that the influence of the bourgeoisie and of the intellectuals who come from the old society will remain in our country for a long time to come, and so will their class ideology. If this is not sufficiently understood, or is not understood at all, the gravest mistakes will be made and the necessity of waging the struggle in the ideological field will be ignored. Ideological struggle is not like other forms of struggle. The only method to be used in this struggle is that of painstaking reasoning and not crude coercion (17). . . .

People may ask, since Marxism is accepted as the guiding ideology by the majority of the people in our country, can it be criticized? Certainly it can. Marxism is scientific truth and fears no criticism. If it did, and if it could be overthrown by cricitism, it would be worthless. In fact, aren't idealists criticizing Marxism every day and in every way? . . . Marxists should not be afraid of criticism from any quarter. Quite the contrary, they need to temper and develop themselves and win new positions in the teeth of criticism and in the storm and stream of struggle. Fighting against wrong ideas is like being vaccinated – a man develops greater immunity from disease as a result of vaccination. Plants raised in hot-houses are unlikely to be sturdy. Carrying out the policy of letting a hundred flowers blossom and a hundred schools of thought contend will not weaken but strengthen the leading position of Marxism in the ideological field.

What should our policy be towards non-Marxist ideas? . . . Will it do to ban such ideas and deny them any opportunity for expression? Certainly not. It is not only futile but very harmful to use summary methods in dealing with ideological questions among the people, with questions concerned with man's mental world. You may ban the expression of wrong ideas, but the ideas will still be there. On the other hand, if correct ideas are pampered in hot-houses without being exposed to the elements or immunized from disease, they will not win out against erroneous ones. Therefore, it is only by employing the method of discussion, criticism and reasoning that we can really foster correct ideas and overcome wrong ones, and that we can really settle issues (18). . . .

We must undoubtedly criticize wrong ideas of every description. It certainly would not be right to refrain from criticism, look on while wrong ideas spread unchecked and allow them to monopolize the field. Mistakes must be criticized and poisonous weeds fought wherever they crop up. However, such criticism should not be dogmatic, and the metaphysical method should not be used, but efforts should be made to apply the dialectical method. What is needed is scientific analysis and convincing argument. Dogmatic criticism settles nothing. We are against poisonous weeds of any kind, but we must carefully distinguish between what is really a poisonous weed and what is really a fragrant flower. Together with the masses of the people, we must learn to differentiate carefully between the two and to use correct methods to fight the poisonous weeds.

At the same time as we criticize dogmatism, we must direct our attention to criticizing revisionism. Revisionism, or Right opportunism, is a bourgeois trend of thought that is even more dangerous than dogmatism. The revisionists, the Right opportunists, pay lip-service to Marxism; they too attack "dogmatism". But what they are really attacking is the quintessence of Marxism. They oppose or distort materialism and dialectics, oppose or try to weaken the people's democratic dictatorship and the leading rôle of the Communist Party, and oppose or try to weaken socialist transformation and socialist construction (19). . . .

Finally, Mao Tse-tung discussed the slogan: "Long-term co-existence and mutual supervision". He said:

The idea of long-term co-existence had been there for a long time. . . . Why should the bourgeois and the petty bourgeois democratic parties be allowed to exist side by side with the party of the working class over a long period of time? Because we have no reason for not adopting the policy of long-term co-existence with all those political parties which are truly devoted to the task of uniting the people for the cause of socialism and which enjoy the trust of the people. . . . It is the desire as well as the policy of the Communist Party to exist side by side with the various democratic parties for a long time to come. . . . Mutual supervision among the various parties is also a long-established fact, in the sense that they have long been advising and criticizing each other. Mutual supervision is obviously not a one-sided matter; it means that the Communist Party should exercise supervision over the democratic parties, and vice versa. Why should the democratic parties be allowed to exercise supervision over the Communist Party? Because a party as much as an individual has great need to hear opinions different from its own. We all know that supervision over the Communist Party is mainly exercised by the working people and the Party membership. But the existence of the democratic parties is also to our benefit (20). . . .

The views set out above are based on China's specific historical conditions. Conditions vary in different socialist countries and with different Communist Parties. Therefore, we do not maintain that other countries and Parties should or must follow the Chinese way (21). . . .

Democracy among the people, and the Party subjected, as in a true democracy, to the criticism of the people: this appeal for cricitism, for freedom of expression, for the blossoming of the "Hundred Flowers", launched by Mao, was heard throughout China. A massive ground-swell surged against the Party, challenging its methods, its bureaucracy, its inadequacies and its injustices. The Party apparatus, Liu Shao-ch'i at its head, took fright. The people were clearly not ready and had to be held in check. Mao, who believed in democracy, was a hothead compromising the revolution. The blossoming of the Hundred Flowers was violently interrupted, all China once again subjected to rigorous control by the Party's cadres. The Party discreetly sealed Mao's lips, and gradually steered him away from responsibility for domestic policies towards questions of foreign policy. Mao's fight grew in size and became world-wide.

G

9 Mao Tse-tung and the United States

Communist victory on the mainland was not yet finally secured – the people's army had only just seized Shanghai – but Mao Tse-tung was already briefly defining new China's international position:

We are willing to discuss with any foreign government the establishment of diplomatic relations on the basis of the principles of equality, mutual benefit and mutual respect for territorial integrity and sovereignty, provided it is willing to sever relations with Chinese reactionaries, stops conspiring with them or helping them and adopts an attitude of genuine and not hypocritical, friendship towards People's China. The Chinese people wish to have friendly co-operation with the people of all countries and to resume and expand international trade in order to develop production and promote economic prosperity (1).

Nevertheless, this positive statement was accompanied by several provisos:

China must be independent, China must be liberated, China's affairs must be decided and run by the Chinese people themselves, and no further interference, not even the slightest, will be tolerated from any imperialist country (2). . . .

We proclaim to the whole world that what we oppose is exclusively the imperialist system and its plots against the Chinese people (1). . . .

And Mao Tse-tung concluded, in typically Chinese fashion, by invoking the classics: "Chu Hsi, philosopher of the dynasty . . . wrote: 'Deal with a man as he deals with you.' This is just what we do; we deal with the imperialists and their running dogs as they deal with us. That is all there is to it! (3)."

The problem of international relations was most crucial where the United States was concerned.

Mao's position with regard to the United States was elaborated in detail only after the Second World War, and basically as a result of the support given to Chiang Kai-shek by Washington. Until 1945, it seems that Mao had referred to America only occasionally, and his statements were relatively moderate. Moreover, they reflected a schematic, crude and dogmatic knowledge of the United States. Generally speaking, the United States was to Mao part of "Western imperialism". However, he had for some time criticized them far less than the British.

It is worth noting that in July 1923, Mao, in his article on "The Peking *Coup d'Etat* and the Merchants", had already said that "America is actually the most murderous of hangmen" and invited his readers to reflect how it had "created the greatest effort to obstruct the policy of prohibiting the export of cotton which the merchants demanded". He exhorted the latter to "see the error of superstitiously believing in America". The same year, still on the conflict over the export of cotton and the duty on cigarettes, he referred to "the false show of friendship by foreigners (especially Englishmen and Americans) which is merely a pretence of 'amity' in order that they may squeeze out more of the fat and blood of the Chinese people (4)".

In his account of the interviews he had with Mao in 1936, Edgar Snow did not assess the Chinese leader's position on the

United States. But in June 1937, in a letter to "Comrade Browder", the American Communist leader, Mao wrote:

We have heard from several American comrades and from other quarters that the American Communist Party and the great mass of the American people are profoundly concerned about China's Anti-Japanese struggle, and they have already aided us in several ways. This gives us the feeling that our struggle is not an isolated one, that we are receiving heroic assistance from abroad; at the same time, we have the feeling, that when we obtain victory, this victory will be of great assistance to the struggle of American people for liberation (5). . . .

At the start of the Second World War, Mao gave his approval – with certain reservations – to Roosevelt:

We are [he said] in agreement with President Roosevelt's proclamation regarding the defence of democracy. We are on the other hand resolutely opposed to the policy of concessions to the fascist states in the West practised by Chamberlain. Up to this day, Chamberlain has also displayed a cowardly attitude towards Japan. I hope that the popular masses of England and America will arise and act positively to admonish their governments and make them adopt a new policy of resistance to wars of aggression – for the good of China and also for the good of England and America themselves (6).

Once war had begun in Europe, Mao became more inflexible:

In all the neutral countries, such as America, for instance, the members of the Communist Party should reveal to the people the imperialist policy of the bourgeois government, which calls itself neutral, but in reality aids the war and seeks to enrich itself in war (7). . . .

The United States' entry into the war against Japan alongside China helped to muzzle any expression of feeling about the United States between 1941 and 1945.

On 16 August 1945, Mao commented on the communiqué from the "Yalta Conference":

The Soviet Union, the United States and Britain declared in the Crimea, "establish conditions of internal peace" and "form interim governmental authorities broadly representative of all democratic elements in the population and pledged to the earliest possible establishment through free elections of governments responsive to the will of the people". That is exactly what the Communist Party of China has persistently advocated – the formation of a "coalition government" (8). . . .

It may therefore be said that, until spring 1945, there was nothing to prevent the development of at least normal relations between the United States and a people's China led by Mao.

The latter's modification in attitude towards the United States must be seen in the light and context of the Chinese civil war.

It was the attitude of the United States ambassador to China, Patrick Hurley, and the line taken by American policy after the death of Roosevelt which provoked the first violent reactions by the Chinese Communists.

Mao Tse-tung is regarded by experts (9) as the author of two anonymous articles appearing in the Party newspaper *Chieh-fang Jih-pao* on 13 and 30 July 1945. It says in them that "it becomes more and more obvious" that Hurley's policy "is creating a danger for both the Chinese and American peoples" and that this danger (which is "that of civil war in China") "can be surmounted only by taking into account the over-all interests of China and America for a long period". The author recalls that Roosevelt had refused to apply "the policy of helping one side in China against the other", of supporting the Kuomintang unilaterally against the Communist Party, and that when Ambassador Hurley arrived in November 1944 as Roosevelt's personal representative in China, "he adopted a favourable attitude towards the plans proposed by the Communist Party for the abolition of the Kuomintang's one-party dictatorship and the establishment of a democratic coalition government".

Now, the article went on, Hurley, in a statement made in

Washington on 2 April 1945, praised the Kuomintang government and pilloried the Communist Party.

What is more, he even bluntly declared that the United States would collaborate only with Chiang Kai-shek, not with the Chinese Communist Party:

> This is however an erroneous and dangerous opinion, contrary to Roosevelt's policy.... The danger of the U.S. policy ... as represented by Hurley consists of its encouragement of the reactionary trend of the Kuomintang government and the increased danger of civil war in China. If this peril is not eliminated, the inevitable result will be not only a long period of misfortune for the people of China: by the same token, the American government with its own hands will place a crushing burden on its own back. That is to say, it will fall hopelessly into the deep, stinking cesspool of Chinese reaction; it will place itself in opposition to the hundreds of millions of awakened or awakening Chinese people. ... On the question of China's future, a large part of American public opinion as well as quite a few politicians and military men have clearly perceived that the irresistible forces of the Chinese people who demand independence, freedom, democracy and unity ... will burst forth and supplant both foreign oppression and feudal oppression. They feel acutely worried about such a dangerous policy towards China as Hurley's and demand that it be changed. Whether or when the policy of the United States will be changed, we cannot say at present. But one thing is certain. If such a policy as Hurley's, a policy that aids and abets antipopular forces in China, in opposition to the Chinese people whose number is so immense, is to continue, it will place a crushing burden on the government and the people of the United States and plunge them into endless woes and troubles. ...

The sensitivity of the Chinese Communists was further exacerbated by an article published in *Reader's Digest* in June 1945, in which it was openly stated that Washington's policy consisted of placing China under America's *leadership* and that the path taken by Chiang Kai-shek was "the path of American democracy".

The Communist newspaper, again in the article attributed to Mao, now claimed that this meant "that the 'path of American democracy' was simply the path of feudal Fascism disguised as democracy" and that since Chiang's path must lead to giving America the *leadership* of China, it followed that "the 'path of American democracy' in China would also lead quite naturally to making China an American colony. . . . Of course, added the writer of the article, "the people of China do not wish to follow the path of a colony which the American imperialists want to impose on it".

Mao Tse-tung was hard put to conceal a certain anxiety. In a telegram to the American Communist Party on 29 July 1945 he said that the "reactionary U.S. capitalist groups . . . are doing their utmost to extend their influence in China too; they are supporting . . . the reactionary clique inside the Kuomintang . . . and are thereby confronting the Chinese people with the grave danger of civil war and jeopardizing the interests of the peoples of our two great countries, China and the United States both during and after the war" (10). He noted, with apparent relief, shortly after the Potsdam Conference, that since "at present the Soviet Union, the United States and Great Britain all disapprove of civil war in China", it will still be possible to avoid it (11). After the Chungking negotiations in October 1945, Mao was satisfied with the understanding which he had encountered : "I also met many foreigners, including Americans, who sympathize with us. The broad masses of the people in foreign countries are dissatisfied with the reactionary forces in China and sympathize with the Chinese people's forces. . . . We have many friends in all parts of the country and of the entire world . . . (12)"

But this time, Mao Tse-tung did not have many illusions left and his warnings were firmer : on 13 August 1945, before the Japanese surrender, he had declared :

U.S. imperialism wants to help Chiang Kai-shek wage civil war and turn China into a U.S. dependency. . . . We must not believe the "nice words" of the imperialists nor be intimidated by their bluster. . . . "If you Americans, sated with bread and sleep, want to curse people and back Chiang Kai-shek, that's your business and I won't interfere. What we have now is millet plus rifles, what you have is bread plus cannon. If you like to back Chiang Kai-shek, back him, back him as long as you want. But remember one thing. To whom does China belong? China definitely does not belong to Chiang Kai-shek, China belongs to the Chinese people. The day will surely come when you will find it impossible to back him any longer." Comrades! These Americans were trying to scare people. Imperialists are masters at this sort of stuff, and many people in the colonial countries do get scared. The imperialists think that all people in the colonial countries can be scared, but they do not realize that in China there are people who are not afraid of that sort of stuff (13). . . .

In the summer and autumn of 1946 Mao gave his final warnings. In August 1946 he told Anna Louise Strong : "If the American people stay the hands of the American reactionaries who are helping Chiang Kai-shek fight the civil war, there is hope for peace (14)." On 29 September 1946, he told A. T. Steele, another American journalist :

I doubt very much that the policy of the U.S. government is one of "mediation". Judging by the large amounts of aid the United States is giving Chiang Kai-shek to enable him to wage a civil war on an unprecedented scale, the policy of the U.S. government is to use the so-called mediation as a smoke-screen for strengthening Chiang Kai-shek in every way and suppressing the democratic forces in China through Chiang Kai-shek's policy of slaughter so as to reduce China virtually to a U.S. colony. The continuation of this policy will certainly arouse the firm resistance of all patriotic people throughout China. . . .

If the U.S. government abandons its present policy of aiding Chiang Kai-shek, withdraws its forces now stationed in China and carries out the agreement reached at the Moscow Conference of the Foreign Ministers of the Soviet Union, the United States and Britain, the Chinese civil war is sure to end at an early date. Otherwise it may turn into a long war. This would of course bring suffering to the Chinese people, but on the other hand, the Chinese people would certainly unite, fight for survival and decide their own fate. Whatever the difficulties and hardships, the Chinese people will certainly fulfil their task of achieving independence, peace and democracy. No forces of suppression, domestic or foreign, can prevent the fulfilment of this task (15). . . .

In autumn 1946, the final illusions vanished. On 1 October 1946, Mao revealed that broad strata of the Chinese people now realized that "Marshall's mediation is a fraud", "that the Kuomintang and the United States government are working in collusion, and have started civil war (16)". . . .

Mao violently denounced the treaties of "national betrayal" which Chiang Kai-shek signed with the United States, by which, he said, "U.S. monopoly capital and Chiang's bureaucrat-comprador capital have become tightly intertwined and control the economic life of the whole country", and whose aim was "to turn China into a U.S. colony (17)". These treaties were the Sino-American Treaty of friendship, trade and navigation on 4 November 1946, the Sino-American agreement on air transport and the Sino-American bi-lateral agreement on aid. Mao also attacked all agreements which gave the United States exorbitant privileges in China : the right to station land, sea and air forces in China, to set up military bases, to prospect for mines and to enjoy a monopoly in certain trades.

He explained :

To maintain his dictatorship and carry on the civil war, Chiang Kai-shek has not hesitated to sell out our country's sovereign rights to foreign imperialism, to collude with the U.S. armed forces so that they should remain in Tsingtao and elsewhere and to procure advisers from the United States to take part in directing the civil war and training troops to slaughter his own fellow-countrymen. Aircraft, tanks, guns and ammunition for the civil war are shipped from the United States in great quantities. Funds for the civil war are borrowed from the United States on a large scale. In return for its favours, Chiang Kai-shek has presented U.S. imperialism with military bases and the rights of air flight and navigation and concluded with it a commercial treaty of enslavement – acts of treason many times worse than those of Yüan Shih-k'ai (18).

At the beginning of 1947, a key theme about the United States emerged in Mao's "intellectual universe" which he kept putting forward because it had considerable shock effect in mobilizing Chinese nationalism against the U.S.A. "U.S. imperialism and its running dog Chiang Kai-shek, he said, have replaced Japanese imperialism and its running dog Wang Ching-wei, and adopted the policies of turning China into a U.S. colony, launching a civil war and strengthening the fascist dictatorship (19). . . ." This was what might be called the Chinese version of the theme; but it was now that the Chinese Communist Party, showing complete solidarity with the Soviet Union, adopted the "Kominform version" of the schema, which Mao formulated thus:

After the victorious conclusion of the anti-fascist Second World War, U.S. imperialism and its lackeys in various countries stepped into the shoes of German and Japanese imperialism and their lackeys and formed a reactionary camp against the Soviet Union, against the People's Democracies in Europe, against the workers' movements in the capitalist countries, against the national movements in the colonies and semi-colonies and against the liberation of the Chinese people. At such a time the Chinese reactionaries headed by Chiang Kai-shek acted as the running dog for U.S. imperialism, just as Wang Ching-wei had done for Japanese imperialism, sold out China to the United States and unleashed a war against the Chinese people to check the advances of their liberation (20).

As a result, "intervention by the United States in China's domestic affairs" and her "participation in Chinese civil war" were denounced with increasing vigour:

The U.S. military personnel have recommended to Chiang Kai-shek one kind of strategy and tactics after another for destroying the People's Liberation Army; they have trained Chiang Kai-shek's troops and supplied them with military equipment. But none of these efforts can save the Chiang Kai-shek bandit gang from defeat (21). . . .

The war to turn China into a U.S. colony, a war in which the United States of America supplies the money and guns and Chiang Kai-shek the men to fight for the United States and slaughter the Chinese people has been an important component of the U.S. imperialist policy of world-wide aggression since World War II (22). . . .

U.S. naval, ground and air forces did participate in the war in China. There were U.S. naval bases in Tsingtao, Shanghai and Taiwan. U.S. troops were stationed in Peiping, Tientsin, Tangshan, Chinwangtao, Tsingtao, Shanghai and Nanking. The U.S. air force controlled all of China's air space and took aerial photographs of all China's strategic areas for military maps. At the town of Anping near Peiping, at Chiutai near Changchun, at Tangshan and in the Eastern Shantung Peninsula, U.S. troops and other military personnel clashed with the People's Liberation Army and on several occasions were captured. Chennault's air fleet took an extensive part in the civil war. Besides transporting troops for Chiang Kai-shek, the U.S. air force bombed and sank the cruiser *Chungking* which had mutinied against the Kuomintang. All these were acts of direct participation in the war, although they fell short of an open declaration of war and were not large in scale, and although the principal method of U.S. aggression was the large-scale supply of money, munitions and advisers to help Chiang Kai-shek fight the civil war.

The use of this method by the United States was determined by the objective situation in China and the rest of the world, and not by any lack of desire on the part of the Truman-Marshall group, the ruling clique of U.S. imperialism, to launch direct aggression against China. Moreover, at the outset of its help to Chiang Kai-shek in fighting the civil war, a crude farce was staged in which the United States appeared as mediator in the conflict between the Kuomintang and the Communist Party; this was an attempt to soften up the Communist Party of China, deceive the Chinese people and thus gain control of all China without fighting. The peace negotiations failed, the deception fell through and the curtain rose on the war (23). . . .

Although the Kuomintang was corrupt and incompetent, "demoralized and unpopular", the United States nevertheless supplied it with money and guns and made it fight. . . . The United States refrained from dispatching large forces to attack China, not because the U.S. government didn't want to, but because it had worries. First worry : the Chinese people would oppose it, and the U.S. government was afraid of getting hopelessly bogged down in a quagmire. Second worry : the American people would oppose it, and so the U.S. government dared not order mobilization. Third worry : the people of the Soviet Union, of Europe and of the rest of the world would oppose it, and the U.S. government would face universal condemnation (24). . . .

About this time, in 1949, Mao Tse-tung denounced U.S. foreign policy in these words :

During the anti-fascist Second World War in which the Soviet Union was the main force, three big imperialist powers were knocked out, while two others were weakened. In the whole world only one big imperialist power, the United States of America, remained uninjured. But the United States faced a grave domestic crisis. It wanted to enslave the whole world (25). . . .
The U.S. policy of aggression has several targets. The three main targets are Europe, Asia and the Americas. China, the centre of gravity in Asia, is a large country with a population of 475 million; by seizing China, the United States would possess all of Asia. With its Asian front consolidated, U.S. imperialism could concentrate its forces on attacking Europe. U.S. imperialism considers its front in the Americas relatively secure (26). . . .
The latest war of aggression against the Chinese people, which has gone on for three years, has been waged to all appearances by Chiang Kai-shek but in reality by the United States (27). . . .

The history of Sino-American relations

At this point, Mao turned to a retrospective analysis of a century of Chinese history to give his new struggle a rational basis, to place it in a light which could only gratify Chinese nationalism, and revive many grievances and frustrations. This was when the famous *White Paper* on Sino-American relations from 1844 to 1949 was published in Washington. This is the Maoist version of the history:

The history of the aggression against China by U.S. imperialism, from 1840 when it helped the British in the Opium War to the time it was thrown out of China by the Chinese people, should be written into a concise textbook for the education of Chinese youth. The United States was one of the first countries to force China to cede extraterritoriality – witness the Treaty of Wanghia of 1944, the first treaty ever signed between China and the United States, a treaty to which the White Paper refers. In this very treaty, the United States compelled China to accept American missionary activity, in addition to imposing such terms as the opening of five ports for trade. For a very long period, U.S. imperialism laid greater stress than other imperialist countries on activities in the sphere of spiritual aggression, extending from religious to "philanthropic" and cultural undertakings. . . . Many well-known educational institutions in China, such as Yenching University, Peking Union Medical College, the Huei Wen Academies, St. John's University, the University of Nanking, Soochow University, Hangchow Christian College, Hsiangya Medical School, West China Union University and Lingnan University, were established by Americans. It was in this field that Leighton Stuart made a name for himself; that was how he became U.S. ambassador to China. Acheson and his like know what they are talking about, and there is a background for his statement that "our friendship for that country has always been intensified by the religious, philanthropic and cultural ties which have united the two peoples". It was all for the sake of "intensifying friendship", we are told, that the United States worked so hard and deliberately at running these undertakings for 105 years after the signing of the Treaty of 1844.

Participation in the Eight-Power Allied Expedition to defeat China in 1900, the extortion of the "Boxer indemnity" and the later use of this fund "for the education of Chinese students" for purposes of spiritual aggression – this too counts as an expression of "friendship". . . .

"Aid to China during and since the close of the War", totalling over 4,500 million U.S. dollars according to the White Paper, but over 5,914 million U.S. dollars according to our computation, was given to help Chiang Kai-shek slaughter several million Chinese – this counts as yet another expression of "friendship".

All the "friendship" shown to China by U.S. imperialism over the past 109 years (since 1840 when the United States collaborated with Britain in the Opium War), and especially the great act of "friendship" in helping Chiang Kai-shek slaughter several million Chinese in the last few years – all this had one purpose, namely, it "consistently maintained and still maintains those fundamental principles of our foreign policy toward China which include the doctrine of the Open Door, respect for the administrative and territorial integrity of China, and opposition to any foreign domination of China".

Several million Chinese were killed for no other purpose than first, to maintain the Open Door, second, to respect the administrative and territorial integrity of China and, third, to oppose any foreign domination of China.

Today, the only doors still open to Acheson and his like are in small strips of land, such as Canton and Taiwan, and only in these places is the first of these sacred principles "still maintained". In other places, in Shanghai for instance, the door was open after liberation, but now someone is using U.S. warships and their big guns to enforce the far from sacred principle of the Blockaded Door.

Whether non-interference in China's domestic affairs also counts as a principle, Acheson didn't say; probably it does not. Such is the logic of the U.S. mandarins. Anyone who reads Acheson's letter of Transmittal to the end will attest to its superior logic (28).

In four famous articles, Mao Tse-tung now commented on this 1054-page *White Paper* on Sino-American relations published by the American Secretary for State, Dean Acheson.

Why this *White Paper*? he first asked:

The White Paper is a counter-revolutionary document which openly demonstrates U.S. imperialist intervention in China. In this respect, imperialism has departed from its normal practice. The great, victorious Chinese revolution has compelled one section or faction of the U.S. imperialist clique to reply to attacks from another by publishing certain authentic data on its own actions against the Chinese people and drawing reactionary conclusions from the data, because otherwise it could not get by. . . . Opposed by the people on the one hand and by another faction in their own camp on the other, the newly arrived, upstart and neurotic U.S. imperialist group – Truman, Marshall, Acheson, Leighton Stuart and others – have considered it necessary and practicable to reveal publicly some (but not all) of their counter-revolutionary doings in order to argue with opponents in their own camp as to which kind of counter-revolutionary tactic is the more clever. In this way they have tried to convince their opponents so that they can go on applying what they regard as the cleverer counter-revolutionary tactics. Two factions of counter-revolutionaries have been competing with each other. One said, "Ours is the best method." The other said, "Ours is the best." When the dispute was at its hottest, one faction suddenly laid its cards on the table and revealed many of its treasured tricks of the past – and there you have the White Paper.

And so the White Paper has become material for the education of the Chinese people. For many years, a number of Chinese (at one time a great number) only half-believed what we Communists said on many questions, mainly on the nature of imperialism and of socialism, and thought, "It may not be so." This situation has undergone a change since 5 August 1949. For Acheson gave them a lesson and he spoke in his capacity as U.S. Secretary of State. In the case of certain data and conclusions, what he said coincides with what we Communists and other progressives have been saying. Once this happened, people could not but believe us, and many had their eyes opened – "So that's the way things really were!" (29)

The publication of the U.S. White Paper and Acheson's letter of Transmittal is worthy of celebration, because it is a bucket of cold water and a loss of face for those who believe that everything American is good and hope that China will model herself on the United States (30). . . .

Let those Chinese who are short-sighted, muddle-headed liberals or democratic individualists listen. Acheson is giving you a lesson; he is a good teacher for you. He has made a clean sweep of your fancied U.S. humanity, justice and virtue. Isn't that so? Can you find a trace of humanity, justice or virtue in the White Paper or in Acheson's Letter of Transmittal?

True, the United States has science and technology. But unfortunately they are in the grip of capitalists, not in the hands of the people, and are used to exploit and oppress the people at home and to perpetrate aggression and to slaughter people abroad. There is also "democracy" in the United States. But unfortunately it is only another name for the dictatorship of the bourgeoisie by itself. The United States has plenty of money. But unfortunately it is willing to give money only to the Chiang Kai-shek reactionaries, who are rotten to the core. The United States, it is said, is and will be quite willing to give money to its fifth column in China, but is unwilling to give it to the ordinary run of liberals or democratic individualists, who are much too bookish and do not know how to appreciate favours, and naturally it is even more unwilling to give money to the Communists. Money may be given, but only conditionally. What is the condition? Follow the United States. The Americans have sprinkled some relief flour in Peiping, Tientsin and Shanghai to see who will stoop to pick it up. Like Chiang Tai Kung fishing, they have cast the line for the fish who want to be caught. But he who swallows food handed out in contempt will get a bellyache.

We Chinese have backbone. . . . What matter if we have to face some difficulties? Let them blockade us! Let them blockade us for eight or ten years! By that time all of China's problems will have been solved. Will the Chinese cower before difficulties when they are not afraid even of death? Lao Tzu said, "The people fear not death, why threaten them with it?" U.S. imperialism and its running dogs, the Chiang Kai-shek reactionaries, have not only "threatened" us with death, but actually put many of us to death. . . . They have killed millions of Chinese in the last three years with U.S. carbines, machine-guns, mortars, bazookas, howitzers, tanks and bombs dropped from aeroplanes. This situation is now coming to an end. They have been defeated. . . . We have already begun to breathe more easily than in the past three years. We have come triumphantly through the ordeal of the last three years, why can't we overcome these few difficulties of today? Why can't we live without the United States? (31).

"Prepare for the struggle"

Mao Tse-tung now once again addressed the "liberal intellectuals" "who have illusions about the United States" :

They are unwilling to draw a distinction between the U.S. imperialists, who are in power, and the American people, who are not. They are easily duped by the honeyed words of the U.S. imperialists as though these imperialists would deal with People's China on the basis of equality and mutual benefit without a stern, long struggle. . . .
The slogan "Prepare for struggle", is addressed to those who still cherish certain illusions about the relations between China and the imperialist countries, especially between China and the United States (32). . . .

Mao noted, as Dean Acheson said, that the United States "could not pull out lock, stock and barrel" from China because this "would have represented an abandonment of international responsibilities and of the traditional policy of friendship of the United States for China", and he replied :

So that's how things stand; the "international responsibilities" of the United States and its "traditional policy of friendship for China" are nothing but intervention against China. Intervention is called assuming international responsibilities and showing friendship for China; as to non-intervention it simply won't do (33).

Mao Tse-tung warned his readers that the struggle would now unquestionably change in character, and that the United States, held in check politically and militarily, would now resort to propaganda and subversion :

Acheson openly declares that the Chinese democratic individualists will be "encouraged" to throw off the so-called "foreign yoke". That is to say, he calls for the overthrow of Marxism-Leninism and the people's democratic dictatorship led by the Communist Party of China. For this "ism" and this system, it is alleged, are "foreign", with no roots in China, imposed on the Chinese by the German, Karl Marx (who died sixty-six years ago), and the Russians, Lenin (who died twenty-five years ago), and Stalin (who is still alive); this "ism" and this system, moreover, are downright bad, because they advocate the class struggle, the overthrow of imperialism, etc.; hence they must be got rid of (34). . . .

There are still some intellectuals and other people in China who have muddled ideas and illusions about the United States. Therefore we should explain things to them, win them over, educate them and unite with them so they will come over to the side of the people and not fall into the snares set by imperialism. But the prestige of U.S. imperialism among the Chinese people is completely bankrupt, and the White Paper is a record of its bankruptcy (35).

America seen by Mao

The light which Mao now shed on Sino-American relations was naturally dominated by the way in which he saw America. Now his vision of this country is extraordinarily schematic. He developed it in a reply to the following phrase in Dean Acheson's letter to President Truman: "The inherent strength of our system is the responsiveness of the Government to an informed and critical public opinion. It is precisely this informed and critical public opinion which totalitarian governments, whether Rightist or Communist, cannot endure and do not tolerate."

As to what Acheson calls a "Rightist totalitarian government" . . . the U.S. and British governments belong to the type in which the bourgeoisie, and this class alone, exercises dictatorship over the people. Contrary in all respects to the people's government, this type of government practises so-called democracy for the bourgeoisie but is dictatorial towards the people. The governments of Hitler, Mussolini, Tojo, Franco and Chiang Kai-shek discarded the veil of democracy for the bourgeoisie or never used it because the class struggle in their countries was extremely intense and they found it advantageous to discard, or not to use, this veil lest the people too should make use of it. The U.S. government still has a veil of democracy, but it has been cut down to a tiny patch by the U.S. reactionaries and become very faded, and is not what it used to be in the days of Washington, Jefferson and Lincoln. The reason is that the class struggle has become more intense. When the class struggle becomes still more intense, the veil of U.S. democracy will inevitably be flung to the four winds (36). . . .

In considering public opinion, the Achesons have mixed up the public opinion of the reactionaries with that of the people. Towards the public opinion of the people, the Achesons have no "responsiveness" whatsoever and are blind and deaf. For years they have turned a deaf ear to the opposition voiced by the people of the United States, China and the rest of the world to the reactionary foreign policy of the U.S. government. What does Acheson mean by "informed and critical public opinion"? Nothing but the numerous instruments of propaganda, such as the newspapers, news agencies, periodicals and broadcasting stations which are controlled by the two reactionary parties in the United States, the Republicans and the Democrats, and which specialize in the manufacture of lies and in threats against the people. Of these things Acheson says rightly that the Communists "cannot endure and do not tolerate" them (nor do the people). That is why we have closed down the imperialist offices of information, stopped the imperialist news agencies from distributing their dispatches to the Chinese press and forbidden them the freedom to go on poisoning the souls of the Chinese people on Chinese soil.

To say that a government led by the Communist Party is a "totalitarian government" is also half true. It is a government that exercises dictatorship over domestic and foreign reactionaries and does not give them any freedom to carry on their counter-revolutionary activities. Becoming angry, the reactionaries rail: "Totalitarian government!" Indeed, this is absolutely true so far as the power of the people's government to suppress the reactionaries is concerned. This power is now written into our programme; it will also be written into our constitution. Like food and clothing, this power is something a victorious people cannot do without even for a moment. It is an excellent thing, a protective talisman, an heirloom, which should under no circumstances be discarded before the thorough and total abolition of imperialism abroad and of classes within the country. The more the reactionaries rail "totalitarian government", the more obviously is it a treasure. But Acheson's remark is also half false. For the masses of the people, a government of the people's democratic dictatorship led by the Communist Party is not dictatorial or autocratic but democratic.

It is the people's own government (37). . . .

However, there was no definitive breach between the Chinese people and the American people :

Certain ties do exist between the Chinese people and the American people. Through their joint efforts, these ties may develop in the future to the point of the "closest friendship". But the obstacles placed by the Chinese and U.S. reactionaries were and still are a great hindrance to these ties. Moreover, because the reactionaries of both countries have told many lies to their peoples and played many filthy tricks, that is, spread much bad propaganda and done many bad deeds, the ties between the two peoples are far from close. What Acheson calls the "ties of closest friendship" are those between the reactionaries of both countries, not between the peoples. Here Acheson is neither objective nor frank, he confuses the relations between the two peoples with those between the reactionaries. For the peoples of the two countries the victory of the Chinese revolution and the defeat of the Chinese and U.S. reactionaries are the most joyful events that have ever happened, and the present period is the happiest of their lives (38). . . .

IO "Imperialism is a Paper Tiger"

In the speech which he made on 21 September 1949 at the opening of the Chinese People's Political Consultative Conference, Mao expressed the pride of new China, liberated from the war and from the foreign presence, as well as her intention to fill the eminent position on the world scene which she considered hers :

We have a common feeling that our work will be written down in the history of mankind, and that it will clearly demonstrate the fact that the Chinese, who comprise one quarter of humanity, have from now on stood up. The Chinese have always been a great, courageous and industrious people. It was only in modern times that they fell behind, and this was entirely the result of the oppression and exploitation of foreign imperialism and the domestic reactionary government . . .

We proclaim the establishment of the People's Republic of China. Our nation will from now on enter the large family of peace-loving and freedom-loving nations of the world. It will work bravely and industriously to create its own civilization and happiness, and will at the same time, promote world peace and freedom. Our nation will never again be an insulted nation. We have stood up. Our revolution has gained the sympathy and acclamation of the broad masses throughout the entire world. We have friends everywhere the world over.

Our revolutionary work is not yet concluded. . . . The imperialists and the domestic reactionaries will certainly not take their defeat lying down. . . . Daily, hourly, they will try to restore their rule in China. . . . We must not relax our vigilance. . . . Our national defence will be consolidated and no imperialist will be allowed to invade our territory again. . . .

The Chinese people have had extremely abundant experience in overcoming difficulties. If we and our predecessors could come through the long period of extreme difficulties and defeat the powerful domestic and foreign reactionaries, why can we not build up a prosperous and flourishing country after our victory? . . . Following an upsurge of economic construction, an upsurge in cultural construction will inevitably arise. The era in which the Chinese were regarded as uncivilized is now over. We will emerge in the world as a nation with a high culture. . . . Through the Chinese people's indomitable energies, we will steadily reach our goal (1). . . .

The foreign policy of the Chinese People's Republic has many facets in common with that of previous regimes, both imperial and republican. There is beyond doubt a continuity in Chinese policy, in so far as it is determined by geographical position, historic rights or those acquired by the Han people, international dangers and domestic structure. But since 1949, certain new facets have gathered increasing importance. They are related to the revolutionary character of the new regime, its leaders' consciousness – Mao Tse-tung's in particular – of having un-rivalled "experience" of what has become a major problem of our time, the emancipation of the peasantry in poor countries, and their consciousness of the efficacy of "ideological weapons" in promoting Chinese policy to the world scale.

As has been seen, the success of Communism in China is largely due to the fusion between nationalism and Marxism within the Chinese Communist Party, thanks to the "Sinifica-tion of Marxism" achieved by Mao Tse-tung. The People's Republic's foreign policy is governed by two factors:

i) Chinese nationalism means to restore China's lawful and historic rights over all that foreign imperialism wrested from her throughout a century, and also to restore China's power so that she cannot again be humiliated.

ii) Chinese socialism means definitively breaking the power of the "reactionary" propertied classes (landlords, big bourgeoisie, militarists, etc.). Now the latter were and still are backed by the United States which has become, since Japan's defeat, the most threatening of the "imperialist" powers against China.

Nationalism and aspiration to political and economic democracy in China are thus linked : Peking is fighting the U.S.A., firstly because she threatens China's safety and is unwilling to give China back what belongs to her (Taiwan, seat in U.N.O.); but also because she backs the "reactionary" regime which the revolution drove from the mainland and which could return only with foreign support.

Since its birth in October 1949, the Chinese People's Republic has thus inherited from the Communist Party :

– a conviction of the Western imperialism's basic hostility towards it (especially true of the United States);

– extreme distrust of, even avowed antagonism towards Japan;

– the conviction that she must rely on the Soviet Union to assert herself in the world.

This distrust, this certainty that bitter fighting still lay in store were expressed in summer 1949 in the following statement by Mao Tse-tung :

The imperialists and their running dogs, the Chinese reactionaries, will not resign themselves to defeat in this land of China. They will continue to gang up against the Chinese people in every possible way. For example, they will smuggle their agents into China to sow dissension and make trouble. That is certain; they will never neglect these activities. To take another example, they will incite the Chinese reactionaries, and even throw in their own forces, to blockade China's ports. They will do this as long as it is possible. Furthermore, if they still hanker after adventures, they will send some of their troops to invade and harass China's frontiers; this, too, is not impossible. All this we must take fully into account (2).

While certain leaders, such as Liu Shao-ch'i in his speech of 16 November 1949, had already offered a Chinese model of a united front and armed struggle to the Third World, President Mao Tse-tung and Chou En-lai concluded a Sino-Soviet treaty "of friendship, alliance and mutual aid" on 14 February 1950 in Moscow aimed basically at Japan or any power which allied itself with her. This alliance gave Mao great confidence. Five years later, on 14 February 1955, he also said :

With the co-operation between our two great countries, China and the Soviet Union, I am convinced that the aggressive plans of imperialism will be smashed.

It is plain for all to see that with the great co-operation between China and the Soviet Union, there are no imperialist plans for aggression which cannot be smashed. They will undoubtedly all be smashed. Should the imperialists start a war of aggression, we will, together with the people of the whole world, certainly wipe them off the face of the earth (3).

Peking's foreign policy was now dominated for a long time by three major preoccupations :

i) The recognition of the new regime by the powers of the whole world, and by corollary, entry to the U.N.O. as the only legitimate government in China.

ii) Obtaining the return of Formosa to China, and the elimination of the Kuomintang regime.

iii) Making sure that the peace treaty with Japan keeps her disarmed, deprive her of all means of re-adopting an aggressive policy, and that no foreign power may use the Nippon archipelago for ends hostile to China.

These objectives were well on the way to being attained in 1950 when the Korean War broke out on 25 June 1950, which Peking considered had been triggered off by the Americans and South Koreans. An objective analysis of this war's causes makes it clear that neither Moscow nor Peking had anything to gain from starting it, but that it was basically the result of initiatives by North Korea (4).

Be that as it may, the military reversal achieved by General MacArthur in 1950 and the prospect of a reunified Korea under American protectorate, in close proximity to the industrial complex in Manchuria, led China, after a series of warnings repeatedly ignored by the West, to intervene in Korea on 24 October 1950. The Common Statement of Democratic Parties in China, published on 4 November 1950, gave details of the reasons for this intervention. Mao Tse-tung may have had a hand in its compilation. The statement denounced American intervention in Korea as the prelude to general aggression against China, the aim of the Americans in Korea, especially in approaching the Yalu, being to set up a base for an invasion of Chinese territory. China had to avert the threat by helping Korea. "By helping your neighbour, you protect yourself." A few days later, Peking stressed that "American imperialism was harbouring designs to annex Korea, and after that, our North-Eastern and Northern provinces. . . . The Chinese people will not tolerate a repetition of what happened in 1905 . . . this is why we must be on the same front as the Korean people so as to resist American aggression to the end".

The MacArthur offensive halted, and the American forces once thrown back to the 38th Parallel, the People's Republic of China put forward its proposals for a negotiated settlement on the basis of Peking's immediate entry into the U.N.O., the handing back of Formosa, the unification of Korea and the evacuation of the country by foreign troops, and the signing of a general, collective treaty with Japan. Washington openly rejected this "package deal". In spite of French and British reservations, the U.S.A. had the "Chinese aggression" condemned by the U.N.O on 1 February 1951, at the same time provoking a breach in relations between China and the U.N.O. which still exists and the protracted isolation of Peking. For most of the Western world, the Kuomintang regime, having sought refuge in Formosa, continued to "represent China".

After months of fighting and manoeuvring, during which she managed to force the U.S.S.R. to reckon with her basic interests (5), China, shortly after Stalin's death, agreed to sign* the Korean armistice at Pan Mun Jom on 27 July 1953. Although the United States had integrated Japan into her defence system by the 1951 treaty, this was the beginning of a period of detente which the U.S.S.R. prolonged by joining in discussions with the three Western powers about an eventual Indo-Chinese settlement. In January 1954, in Berlin, the "Big Four" decided to hold a conference in Geneva to which the Big Fifth, China, was invited for the first time. This was the People's Republic of China's entry into the ranks of the Great Powers. She played an important part in the restoration of peace in Indo-China, in June–July 1954.

For China, the chief advantage of the Geneva agreements was to ensure the independence of the Indo-Chinese states – by leaving a barely dangerous French presence there – and banning the installation of foreign, that is, American military bases in that area.

Ever since 1952, the People's Republic of China had endeavoured to establish normal relations with uncommitted or neutral countries in Asia, especially India, Indonesia and Burma. On the other hand she was trying to establish trade relations with England, France and Western Germany in order to beat the economic blockade to which the United States was subjecting her.

In April 1954, China implemented her policy of friendly

---

*On 7 February 1953, Mao stated in this respect: "We are for peace. But so long as U.S. imperialism refuses to give up its arrogant and unreasonable demands and its scheme to extend aggression, the only course for the Chinese people is to remain determined to go on fighting side by side with the Korean people. Not that we are warlike. We are willing to stop the war at once and leave the remaining questions for later settlement. But U.S. imperialism is not willing to do so. All right then, let the fighting go on. However many years U.S. imperialism wants to fight, we are ready to fight right up to the moment when it is willing to stop, right up to the moment of complete victory for the Chinese and Korean peoples."

relations with Nehru's India. New Delhi and Peking together proclaimed the Five Principles of peaceful co-existence, and a few months later at the Afro-Asian Conference in Bandung in February 1955, China suddenly emerged as one of the two leaders of the Third World, perhaps even the stronger.

From now on the Chinese regime felt more confident. After summer 1955 the collectivization of the countryside, until then only tentative, made very rapid strides.

But, in 1956 the horizon darkened.

First of all, destalinization, hurriedly carried out by Khrushchev, without a word to Peking, dismayed and offended the Chinese leaders. The Chinese Communist Party, in an article published in the *People's Daily* on 5 April 1956, "On the Historical Experience of the Dictatorship of the Proletariat" (6), drew a more balanced picture of Stalin's achievements and mistakes than that which Khrushchev had outlined in his famous report to the Soviet Twentieth Party Congress.

In his opening speech to the Chinese Communist Party Eighth Congress on 15 September 1956, Mao Tse-tung emphasized China's desire for peace :

Our country and all the other Socialist countries want peace; so do the peoples of all the countries of the world. The only ones who crave war and do not want peace are certain monopoly capitalist groups in a handful of imperialist countries which depend on aggression for their profits. . . .

To achieve a lasting world peace, we must further develop our friendship and co-operation with the fraternal countries in the socialist camp and strengthen our solidarity with all peace-loving countries. We must endeavour to establish normal diplomatic relations on the basis of mutual respect for territorial integrity and sovereignty, and equality and mutual benefit, with all countries willing to live together with us in peace. We must give active support to the national independence and liberation movement in countries in Asia, Africa and Latin America, as well as to the peace movement and to just struggles in all countries in the world (7).

However, additional signs convinced Peking that the danger from outside was far from negligible. The American foothold in South Vietnam and Saigon's refusal to implement the clauses in the Geneva agreements about elections in June 1956, the Anglo-French landings at Suez and above all the Hungarian revolt in October–November 1956, were regarded in China as indications that the "imperialists" had not halted all their activities against the socialist camp and against certain neutrals.

Mao Tse-tung and war

World tension had revived. However, Mao Tse-tung referred to it optimistically in his famous speech of 27 February 1957 :

People all over the world are now discussing whether or not a third world war will break out. On this question, too, we must be mentally prepared and do some analysis. We stand firmly for peace and against war. But if the imperialists insist on unleashing another war, we should not be afraid of it. Our attitude on this question is the same as our attitude towards any disturbance : first, we are against it; second, we are not afraid of it. The First World War was followed by the birth of the Soviet Union with a population of 200 million. The Second World War was followed by the emergence of the socialist camp with a combined population of 900 million. If the imperialists insist on launching a third world war, it is certain that several hundred million more will turn to socialism, and then there will not be much room left on earth for the imperialists; it is also likely that the whole structure of imperialism will utterly collapse.

In given conditions, each of the two opposing aspects of a contradiction invariably transforms itself into its opposite as a result of the struggle between them. Here, the conditions are essential. Without the given conditions, neither of the two contradictory aspects can transform itself into its opposite. Of all the classes in the world the proletariat is the one which is most eager to change its position, and next comes the semi-proletariat, for the former possesses nothing at all while the latter is hardly better off. The present situation in which the United States controls a majority in the United Nations and dominates many parts of the world is a temporary one, which will eventually be changed. China's position as a poor country denied her rights in international affairs will also be changed – the poor country will change into a rich one, the country denied its rights into one enjoying its rights – a transformation of things into their opposites. . . .

To strengthen our solidarity with the Soviet Union, to strengthen our solidarity with all the socialist countries – this is our fundamental policy, this is where our basic interest lies. Then there are the Asian and African countries and all the peace-loving countries and peoples – we must strengthen and develop our solidarity with them. United with these two forces, we shall not stand alone. As for the imperialist countries, do business with them and prevent any possible war, but under no circumstances should we harbour any unrealistic notions about them (8).

In the summer of 1957, both for domestic reasons (rivalries within the Party ranks) and international reasons (Soviet space triumphs), Peking began to adopt "tougher" positions in its foreign policy, and to preach more active and open resistance to American policy as interpreted by two brothers, Messrs. John Foster Dulles (State Department) and Allen Dulles (C.I.A.).

Khrushchev's rise to the supreme leadership in Moscow had temporarily given a new impetus to Sino-Soviet collaboration: in October 1957, an agreement was signed, organizing technical collaboration between the two countries with a view to the manufacture of a Chinese atomic bomb.

In November 1957, the Conference of 64 Communist Parties in Moscow was characterized by apparent Sino-Soviet unity, especially against "imperialism". The Chinese were by now adopting an energetic and militant attitude. On 6 November 1957, in his speech to the Supreme Soviet of the U.S.S.R. on the 40th anniversary of the October Revolution, Mao Tse-tung declared:

In addition to staking their fate on oppressing the people at home and in the colonial and semi-colonial countries, the imperialists pin their hopes on war. But what can they expect from war? . . . If the imperialist "heroes" are bent on starting a third world war, the only result will be to hasten the complete destruction of the world capitalist system (9).

On 18 November 1957, addressing the Conference of Communist Parties, Mao Tse-tung was far more explicit.

It is my opinion that the international situation has now reached a new turning point. There are two winds in the world today, the East wind and West wind. There is a Chinese saying, "Either the East wind prevails over the West wind or the West wind prevails over the East wind." It is characteristic of the situation today, I believe, that the East wind is prevailing over the West wind. That is to say, the forces of socialism are overwhelmingly superior to the forces of imperialism (10).

On the previous day, 17 November, Mao had described this superiority during an address to some Chinese students:

The world now has a total population of 2,700 million; the socialist countries account for nearly 1,000 million, the independent, formerly colonial countries account for more than 700 million, and the countries now struggling for independence or for complete independence and the capitalist countries with tendencies towards neutralism have 600 million. The population of the imperialist camp is only about 400 million and, what is more, is internally divided (11).

Mao recalled what he had said in 1945: "At all events, we must not let ourselves be intimidated by the frightening visage of reactionaries", and he went on, in his 18 November 1957 speech:

· When Chiang Kai-shek attacked us in 1946, many of our comrades and the people of the whole country were deeply worried about whether the war could be won. I myself was also worried about this. But of one thing we were confident . . . I said that all the reputedly powerful reactionaries were merely paper tigers. The reason was that they were divorced from the people. Was not Hitler a paper tiger? Was Hitler not overthrown? I also said that the Russian tsar, the Chinese emperor and Japanese imperialism were all paper tigers. As we know, they were all overthrown. U.S. imperialism is not yet overthrown and it has the atom bomb. I believe that it also will be overthrown. It is a paper tiger too. Chiang Kai-shek was very powerful; he had more than four million regular troops. We were then in Yenan. What was the population of Yenan? Seven thousand. How many troops did we have? We had 900,000 guerillas, all cut off from one another in scores of base areas by Chiang Kai-shek. But we said Chiang Kai-shek was only a paper tiger and we would certainly defeat him. For the struggle against the enemy, we developed over a long period the concept that strategically we should despise all our enemies, but that tactically we should take them all seriously. This also means that with respect to the whole we should despise the enemy but that with respect to each and every concrete question we must take them seriously. If with respect to the whole we do not depise the enemy, we shall be committing the error of opportunism. Marx and Engels were only two persons. Yet in those early days they declared that capitalism would be overthrown throughout the world. But in dealing with concrete problems and particular enemies we shall be committing the error of adventurism unless we take them seriously. In war, battles can only be fought one by one and the enemy forces can only be destroyed one by one. Factories can only be built one by one. The peasants can only plough the land plot by plot. The same is true of eating a meal. Strategically, we take the eating of a meal lightly: we know we can finish it. But in the actual process of eating, we do it mouthful by mouthful. It is impossible to swallow an entire banquet in one gulp. This is known as a piecemeal solution. In military parlance, it is called smashing the enemy forces one by one (12).

Mao now replied to those who contended that such limited "wars of liberation" would end by provoking a general war which, because of the certain involvement of the U.S.S.R. and the United States, would inevitably be a full-scale nuclear war. He said:

I discussed this matter with a foreign statesman. He believed that if an atomic war took place, the entire human race would be wiped out. I replied that at the worst half the human race would perish, but that the other half would survive, whereas imperialism would be totally and radically eliminated and the entire world would become socialist. In a few years, there would once again be 2,700 million inhabitants on the earth and the rise in population would continue. We Chinese have not yet finished our construction and we desire peace. However, if imperialism insists on fighting a war, we will have no alternative but to take the firm resolution to fight to the finish before going ahead with our construction. If you are afraid of war day in day out, what will you do if war eventually comes? First I said that the East wind is prevailing over the West wind, and war will not break out, and now I have added these explanations about the situation in case war should break out. Both possibilities have thus been taken into account (13).

It was not the first time that Mao Tse-tung had tackled the problem of the war in its more general aspects. His most significant statements dated back to the years 1936–1938:

War is the highest form of struggle for resolving contradictions, when they have developed to a certain stage, between classes, nations, states, or political groups ... (14).

"War is the continuation of politics." In this sense war is politics and war itself is a political action; since ancient times there has never been a war that did not have a political character ...

But war has its own particular characteristics and cannot be equated with politics in general. "War is the continuation of politics by other ... means." When politics develops to a certain stage beyond which it cannot proceed by the usual means, war breaks out to sweep the obstacles from the way ... When the obstacle is removed, our political aim will be attained, and the war concluded. But if the obstacle is not completely swept away, the war will have to continue till the aim is fully accomplished ... It can therefore be said that politics is war without bloodshed while war is politics with bloodshed. ...

History shows that wars are divided into two kinds, just and unjust. All wars that are progressive are just and all wars that impede progress are unjust. We Communists oppose all unjust wars that impede progress, but we do not oppose progressive, just wars. Not only do we Communists not oppose just wars, we actively participate in them . . .

Revolutions and revolutionary wars are inevitable in class society, and without them it is impossible to accomplish any leap in social development and to overthrow the reactionary ruling classes and therefore impossible for the people to win political power (15).

This is why Mao Tse-tung did not believe that the world had seen the last of wars :

War, this monster of mutual slaughter among men, will be finally eliminated by the progress of human society, and in the not too distant future too. But there is only one way to eliminate it and that is to oppose war with war, to oppose counter-revolutionary war with revolutionary war, to oppose national counter-revolutionary war with national revolutionary war, and to oppose counter-revolutionary class war with revolutionary class war. . . . All counter-revolutionary wars are unjust, all revolutionary wars are just. Mankind's era of wars will be brought to an end by our own efforts . . . When human society advances to the point where classes and states are eliminated, there will be no more wars, counter-revolutionary or revolutionary, unjust or just; that will be the era of perpetual peace for mankind. . . .

We are advocates of the abolition of war, we do not want war; but war can only be abolished through war, and in order to get rid of the gun, it is necessary to take up a gun (16).

Could there, however, be limited revolutionary wars in the nuclear age which did not threaten East-West balance, and which did not therefore lure the world dangerously towards an atomic catastrophe of an apocalyptic nature? This was the opinion of Moscow in 1957 where the Soviet leaders were moving resolutely towards a policy of peaceful co-existence with the West, to which they attached, without saying so, far

H

more importance than to the emancipation, and especially the violent emancipation of the Asiatic or African peoples whom they considered unripe for independence. The re-creation of areas of influence through armed action seemed to them likely to provoke a general conflict in which the atomic bomb would inevitably be used. Mao Tse-tung, who considered that this was shameless blackmail exerted by the atomic powers against oppressed peoples, now recalled in spectacular fashion the remarks which he had made to the American journalist, Anna Louise Strong in 1946 :

The United States and the Soviet Union are separated by a vast zone which includes many capitalist, colonial and semi-colonial countries in Europe, Asia and Africa. Before the U.S. reactionaries have subjugated these countries, an attack on the Soviet Union is out of the question. In the Pacific the United States now controls areas larger than all the former British spheres of influence there put together; it controls Japan, that part of China under Kuomintang rule, half of Korea, and the South Pacific. It has long controlled Central and South America. It seeks also to control the whole of the British Empire and Western Europe. Using various pretexts, the United States is making large-scale military arrangements and setting up military bases in many countries. The U.S. reactionaries say that the military bases they have set up and are preparing to set up all over the world are aimed against the Soviet Union. True, these military bases are directed against the Soviet Union. At present, however, it is not the Soviet Union but the countries in which these military bases are located that are the first to suffer U.S. aggression. I believe it won't be long before these countries come to realize who is really oppressing them, the Soviet Union or the United States. The day will come when the U.S. reactionaries find themselves opposed by the people of the whole world. . . .

The fact that the U.S. reactionaries are now trumpeting so loudly about a U.S.-Soviet war and creating a foul atmosphere, so soon after the end of World War II, compels us to take a look at their real aims. It turns out that under the cover of anti-Soviet slogans they are frantically attacking the workers and democratic circles in the United States and turning all the countries which are the targets of U.S. external expansion into U.S. dependencies. I think the American people and the peoples of all countries menaced by U.S. aggression should unite and struggle against the attacks of the U.S. reactionaries and their running dogs in these countries. Only by victory in this struggle can a third world war be avoided; otherwise it is unavoidable (17).

Anna Louise Strong then asked: "But suppose the United States uses the atom bomb?" Mao replied:

The atom bomb is a paper tiger which the U.S. reactionaries use to scare people. It looks terrible, but in fact it isn't. Of course, the atom bomb is a weapon of mass slaughter, but the outcome of a war is decided by the people, not by one or two new types of weapon.

All reactionaries are paper tigers. In appearance, the reactionaries are terrifying, but in reality they are not so powerful. From a long-term point of view, it is not the reactionaries but the people who are really powerful. . . .

The U.S. reactionaries, are all paper tigers too. Speaking of U.S. imperialism, people seem to feel that it is terrifically strong. Chinese reactionaries are using the "strength" of the United States to frighten the Chinese people. But it will be proved that the U.S. reactionaries, like all the reactionaries in history, do not have much strength. In the United States there are others who are really strong – the American people.

Take the case of China. We have only millet plus rifles to rely on, but history will finally prove that our millet plus rifles are more powerful than Chiang Kai-shek's aeroplanes plus tanks. Although the Chinese people still face many difficulties and will long suffer hardships from the joint attacks of U.S. imperialism and the Chinese reactionaries, the day will come when these reactionaries are defeated and we are victorious. The reason is simply this: the reactionaries represent reaction, we represent progress (18).

China did not therefore take the view that peaceful co-existence and nuclear balance meant that the socialist powers should abandon those peoples struggling for their independence and liberation to their fate; on the contrary she thought that it was her duty to back them, even by taking risks. In 1958, Moscow and Peking were faced with new crises, in Indonesia, Laos, Iraq and the Lebanon. While the U.S.S.R. generally adopted prudent attitudes, China on the contrary assured "struggling" peoples of her sympathy and solidarity—especially the Arab peoples—in July 1958.

Moscow was by now concerned with China's domestic evolution, with the speeding up of the revolution which began with the "Great Leap Forward" in industry decreed in May 1958 and the beginning of experiments with people's communes.

But the Kremlin was also concerned with affairs in the Near East, where Syro-Jordanian tension, the Iraqi *coup d'état*, the Lebanese crisis and the American landing in the Lebanon in July 1958, were creating an explosive situation. On 28 July 1958, Khrushchev suggested a five power summit conference (U.S.S.R., U.S.A., Britain, France and India) to discuss the Near East problems. A few days later, on his return from a secret visit to Peking, he withdrew the suggestion. Mao Tse-tung had vetoed it : China could not accept a five power conference that excluded her. Moscow now decided on a direct approach to Washington. Three weeks later, to make it quite clear to Nikita Khrushchev that he could not come to a private understanding with the White House, Peking created sudden tension in the Straits of Formosa (August-September). At the time, Mao Tse-tung made a few comments which, given the context, were not lacking in boldness :

To achieve their ends of aggression and enslavement of the peoples of all countries, the U.S. imperialists have been creating tension in all parts of the world. They calculate that they will always benefit from tense situations, but the fact is that the tension created by the United States has led to the opposite of what they desire. It serves to mobilize the people of the world against the U.S. aggressors.

If the U.S. monopoly groups persist in their policies of

aggression and war, the day is bound to arrive when the people of the whole world will hang them by the neck. The same fate awaits the accomplices of the United States. . . .

China's territory of Taiwan, the Lebanon, and all the other military bases of the United States on foreign territory are so many nooses around the neck of U.S. imperialism. The nooses have been fashioned by the Americans themselves, and by nobody else, and it is they themselves who put these nooses round their own necks, handing the ends of the ropes to the Chinese people, the peoples of the Arab countries and all the peoples of the world who love peace and oppose aggression. The longer the U.S. aggressors remain in those places, the tighter the nooses round their necks become (19).

On 29 September 1958, Mao Tse-tung further added, in an interview with the Hsinhua News Agency :

Imperialism will not last long, because it consistently commits all sorts of evil. It persists in grooming and supporting reactionaries in all countries who are against the people. It forcibly occupies many colonies and semi-colonies, and it has set up many military bases. It threatens the peace with atomic warfare. Thus, imperialism has forced more than 90 per cent of the people of the world to rise against it or prepare to fight it. But imperialism is still alive and kicking, still riding roughshod over Asia, Africa and Latin America. In the West the imperialists are still oppressing the people of their own countries. This situation must change. It is the task of the people of the whole world to put an end to the aggression and oppression perpetrated by imperialism, and especially by U.S. imperialism (20).

However, Mao Tse-tung's domestic policy, especially his efforts towards "people's communes", provoked serious opposition in the higher spheres of the Chinese Communist Party. In a minority since the Sixth Plenary Session of the Eighth Party Central Committee, Mao announced, on 10 December 1958, that he would not be a candidate for the chairmanship of the republic in 1959. From now on he would devote himself essentially to Party affairs – he retained the presidency of the

Central Committee – and to foreign affairs. His centre of interest in this field was the Third World, with its thousands of millions of proletarians.

Mao Tse-tung and the fight by "proletarian peoples"

The Chinese people, whom Li Ta-chao regarded in 1919 as the greatest of the proletarian peoples, had liberated themselves from foreign domination, and as Mao wrote in 1949 to an Algerian leader, it was natural that they should consider with sympathy and even with fervent hope "the struggles for liberation of all oppressed peoples". From now on, Peking pointed out to everyone that the contradictions of the contemporary world were found mainly in Asia, Africa and Latin America, where "wars of liberation and revolutions were striking the most direct blows against imperialism".

Viewed from Peking, the Third World did not firstly raise a problem of economic development or financial aid. It raised a political problem : that of wresting power from landed feudal systems and from the bourgeoisie linked with foreigners. Mao had been clear on this point: "Dependence on American imperialism is the common feature of the reactionary in all countries since World War II (21)."

To Mao and his friends, the peoples of Asia, Africa and Latin America were, for the most part, faced with the same problem as that which the Chinese Communist Party had had to face during its twenty-two years of struggle, from 1927 to 1949, and China was therefore, to such peoples, an interesting model for study and observation.

Everything depends, said Mao, on seizing power :

All revolutionary struggles in the world are aimed at seizing political power and consolidating it (22).

The seizure of power by armed force, the settlement of the issue by war, is the central task and the highest form of revolution. The Marxist-Leninist principle of revolution holds good universally, for China and for all other countries.

Now power, said Mao, can only be seized by force:

"Whoever has an army has power." . . . Every Communist must grasp the truth, "Political power grows out of the barrel of a gun." . . . All things grow out of the barrel of a gun. . . . Whoever wants to seize and retain state power must have a strong army. . . . The guns of the Russian Communist Party created socialism. We shall create a democratic republic. Experience in the class struggle in the era of imperialism teaches us that it is only by the power of the gun that the working class and the labouring masses can defeat the armed bourgeoisie and landlords; in this sense we may say that only with guns can the whole world be transformed (23).

What Mao was implicitly and even explicitly recommending to the peoples of the Third World was guerilla warfare, revolutionary war, whose development in China was described earlier in Chapters 4 and 5:

What is guerilla warfare? It is the indispensable and therefore the best form of struggle for the people's armed forces to employ over a long period in a backward country, a large semi-colonial country, in order to inflict defeats on the armed enemy and build up their own bases. So far both our political line and our Party building have been closely linked with this form of struggle. It is impossible to have a good understanding of our political line and, consequently, of our Party building in isolation from armed struggle, from guerilla warfare. . . . We have learned that without armed struggle neither the proletariat nor the people, nor the Communist Party would have any standing at all in China and that it would be impossible for the revolution to triumph. In these years the development, consolidation and bolshevization of our Party have proceeded in the midst of revolutionary wars; without armed struggle the Communist Party would assuredly not be what it is today. Comrades throughout the Party must never forget this experience for which we have paid in blood (24).

This armed struggle was, by definition, a just war:

Only wars of national liberation and wars of popular liberation, as well as wars undertaken by socialist countries to support these two kinds of liberation movements, are just wars (25).

The present circumstances, Mao emphasized, were favourable to such movements in many countries:

The reactionary policy of U.S. imperialism is rousing increasing discontent among the broad masses of the people in all countries. The level of political consciousness of the people in all countries is rising every day. The people's democratic struggle is mounting in all capitalist countries, the strength of the Communist Parties in many countries has greatly increased, and it will be impossible for the reactionaries to reduce them to submission. . . . We can defeat the Chinese and foreign reactionaries, no matter how rampant they are (26).

But, in fact, is U.S. imperialism after World War II as powerful as Chiang Kai-shek and the reactionaries of other countries imagine? . . . The strength of the United States of America is only superficial and transient. Irreconcilable domestic and international contradictions, like a volcano, menace U.S. imperialism every day. U.S. imperialism is sitting on this volcano. This situation has driven the U.S. imperialists to draw up a plan for enslaving the world, to run amuck like wild beasts in Europe, Asia and other parts of the world, to muster the reactionary forces in all countries, the human dregs cast off by their peoples, to form an imperialist and anti-democratic camp against all the democratic forces headed by the Soviet Union, and to prepare for war in the hope that in the future, at a distant time, some day, they can start a third world war to defeat the democratic forces. This is a preposterous plan. The democratic forces of the world must defeat this plan and certainly can defeat it.

The strength of the world anti-imperialist camp has surpassed that of the imperialist camp. It is we, not the enemy, who are in the superior position. The anti-imperialist camp headed by the Soviet Union has already been formed. . . . In the European capitalist countries the people's anti-imperialist forces are developing, with those in France and Italy taking the lead. Within the United States, there are people's democratic forces which are getting stronger every day. The peoples of Latin

America are not slaves obedient to U.S. imperialism. In the whole of Asia a great national liberation movement has arisen. All the forces of the anti-imperialist camp are uniting and forging ahead.

The Communist and Workers' Parties of nine European countries have established their Information Bureau and issued a call to the people of the world to rise against the imperialist plan of enslavement. This call to battle has inspired the oppressed people of the world, charted the course of their struggle and strengthened their confidence in victory. It has thrown world reaction into panic and confusion. All the anti-imperialist forces in the countries of the East, too, should unite together, oppose oppression by imperialism and by their domestic reactionaries and make the goal of their struggle the emancipation of the more than 1,000 million people of the East. We certainly should grasp our own destiny in our own hands. We should rid our ranks of all impotent thinking. All views that over-estimate the strength of the enemy and underestimate the strength of the people are wrong. If everyone makes strenuous efforts, we, together with all the democratic forces of the world, can surely defeat the imperialist plan of enslavement, prevent the outbreak of a third world war, overthrow all reactionary regimes and win lasting peace for mankind (27).

There would be many difficulties and harsh ordeals lying in store for liberation movements. Whatever the circumstances, Mao recommended patience and faith in ultimate victory.

In a speech in memory of the martyrs of the Chinese revolution on 17 June 1945, he had said :

All reactionaries try to stamp out revolution by mass murder, thinking that the greater their massacre, the weaker the revolution. But contrary to this reactionary wishful thinking, the fact is that the more the reactionaries resort to massacre, the greater the strength of the revolution and the nearer the reactionaries approach their doom. This is an inexorable law (28).

A few months later he added :

The principle of the reactionary forces in dealing with the democratic forces of the people is definitely to destroy all they can and to prepare to destroy later whatever they cannot destroy now. Face to face with this situation, the democratic forces of the people should likewise apply the same principle to the reactionary forces (29).

The main thing was not to be discouraged and to see things clearly, Mao once again repeated :

Make trouble, fail, make trouble again, fail again . . . till their doom; that is the logic of the imperialists and all reactionaries the world over in dealing wtih the people's cause, and they will never go against this logic. This is a Marxist law. When we say "imperialism is ferocious", we mean that its nature will never change, that the imperialists will never lay down their butcher knives, that they will never become Buddhas, till their doom.

Fight, fail, fight again, fail again . . . till victory; that is the logic of the people, and they too will never go against this logic. This is another Marxist law. The Russian people's revolution followed this law, and so has the Chinese people's revolution (30).

The reactionary forces and we both have difficulties. But the difficulties of the reactionary forces are insurmountable because they are forces on the verge of death and have no future. Our difficulties can be overcome because we are new and rising forces and have a bright future (31).

In his "Statement Supporting the People of the Congo against Aggression" on 28 November 1964, Mao Tse-tung declared :

Peoples of the world, unite and defeat the U.S. aggressors and all their running dogs! People of the world, be courageous, dare to fight, defy difficulties and advance wave upon wave. Then the whole world will belong to the people. Monsters of all kinds shall be destroyed.

After thirty-four years of revolution, what was this but a resurgence in China of Li Li-san's line of "adventurism", of "Leftist" opportunism?

From Vietnam to Alabama

For more than a quarter of a century, Mao Tse-tung and the Chinese Communist Party applied, among others, the following basic principle: "We should support whatever the enemy opposes and oppose whatever he supports (32)."

In applying this principle, Mao Tse-tung has made statements, sent messages and given encouragement in a certain number of concrete situations. Four such statements are worth repeating.

On 8 May 1960, he told some South American visitors:

The Chinese people, just like the Latin American people, had for long suffered from imperialist oppression and exploitation. . . . The Chinese people are fully confident that they can build their country well and therefore they need time, peace and friends. The Cuban people, the people of Latin America and the people of the whole world, he said, are all friends of the Chinese people; and imperialism and its lackeys are our common enemy, but they are a tiny minority. The winning of world peace, he said, depends primarily on the struggles of the peoples of the various countries. . . . The people are the decisive factor. Reliance on the unity and struggle of the people is bound to bring about the defeat of imperialism and its lackeys and achieve lasting world peace (33).

On 9 May 1960 he told some visitors from the Near East:

The biggest imperialism in the world today is U.S. imperialism. It has its lackeys in many countries. Those backed by imperialism are precisely those discarded by the broad masses of the people. Chiang Kai-shek, Syngman Rhee, Kishi, Batista, Said, Menderes and their ilk have either been overthrown or will be overthrown by the people. The risings of the people in these countries against the lackeys of U.S. imperialism and other imperialism are also a fight against the reactionary rule of imperialism itself. . . . The days of imperialism are numbered. The imperialists have committed all manner of evils and all the oppressed peoples of the whole world will never forgive them (34).

His "Statement Opposing Aggression against South Vietnam and the Slaughter of Its People by the U.S.–Ngo Dinh Diem Clique" was made on 29 August 1963 at a reception for a delegation of the South Vietnamese National Liberation Front:

Recently the reactionary Ngo Dinh Diem clique in south Vietnam has been intensifying its sanguinary suppression of Buddhists, students, intellectuals and the masses of the people. The Chinese people are deeply indignant at the monstrous crimes of the Ngo Dinh Diem clique and strongly condemn them. . . .

U.S. imperialism and its lackey Ngo Dinh Diem have been following the policy of turning southern Vietnam into a U.S. colony, unleashing counter-revolutionary war and reinforcing their fascist dictatorship. This has compelled the people of various strata in southern Vietnam to unite on a broad scale and wage a resolute struggle against them.

U.S. imperialism and the Diem clique now find themselves besieged by all the people of southern Vietnam against whom they have set themselves. No matter what inhuman weapons U.S. imperialism may use or what ruthless means of suppression the Diem clique may employ, that regime cannot escape its fate of total isolation and collapse, and U.S. imperialism will finally have to get out of southern Vietnam.

Ngo Dinh Diem is a faithful lackey of U.S. imperialism. However, once a lackey has outlived his usefulness and becomes an encumbrance to the U.S. imperialist policy of aggression, the U.S. imperialists do not hesitate to replace him with another. The fate of Syngman Rhee in South Korea provides a precedent. A flunkey who allows himself to be led by the nose by U.S. imperialism will only end up in the same grave as his master.

U.S. imperialism has violated the agreements reached at the first Geneva Conference by obstructing the reunification of Vietnam, conducting open armed aggression against southern Vietnam and engaging in so-called special warfare over a period of years. It has also violated the agreements of the second Geneva Conference by its flagrant intervention in Laos in an attempt to rekindle the civil war there. Apart from those who are deliberately deceiving the people and those who are utterly naive, no one will assert that a treaty can make U.S. imperialism lay down its butcher's knife and suddenly become a Buddha, or for that matter behave itself even a little better.

The oppressed peoples and nations must not pin their hopes for liberation on the "sensibleness" of imperialism and it lackeys. They will only triumph by strengthening their unity and persevering in their struggle. This is what the people of southern Vietnam are doing.

In their just patriotic struggle against U.S. imperialism and the Diem clique the people of southern Vietnam have won major victories both politically and militarily. We the Chinese people firmly support their struggle.

I am convinced that through struggle they will attain the goal of liberating the southern part of Vietnam and contribute to the peaceful reunification of their fatherland.

It is my hope that the working class, the revolutionary people and progressives throughout the world will all stand by the people of southern Vietnam and, in response to President Ho Chi Minh's call, support the struggle of the heroic people of southern Vietnam and oppose aggression and oppression by the counter-revolutionary U.S.–Diem clique, and thus help the people there save themselves from slaughter and achieve complete liberation (35).

Finally, on 8 August 1963, during "some talks with African friends", Mao made a "Statement Calling on the People of the world to Unite to Oppose Racial Discrimination by U.S. Imperialism and Support the American Negroes in their Struggle against Racial Discrimination". Here are a few significant passages from it :

On behalf of the Chinese people, I wish to take this opportunity to express our resolute support for the American Negroes in their struggle against racial discrimination and for freedom and equal rights.

There are more than 19 million Negroes in the United States, or about 11 per cent of the total population. They are enslaved, oppressed and discriminated against – such is their position in society. The overwhelming majority of the Negroes are deprived of their right to vote. In general, it is only the most back-breaking and despised jobs that are open to them. Their average wages are no more than a third or a half those of the white people. The ratio of unemployment among them is highest. In many states they are forbidden to go to the same school, eat at the same table, or travel in the same section of a bus or train as the white people. Negroes are frequently and arbitrarily arrested, beaten up and murdered by the U.S. authorities at various levels and by members of the Ku Klux Klan and other racists. About half of the American Negroes are concentrated in eleven states in the south of the United States, where the discrimination and persecution they suffer are especially shocking.

The American Negroes are awakening and their resistance is becoming stronger and stronger. In recent years there has been a continuous expansion in the mass struggle of the American Negroes against racial discrimination and for freedom and equal rights.

This year, the struggle of the American Negroes started early in April in Birmingham, Alabama. Unarmed, bare-handed Negro people were subjected to wholesale arrests and the most barbarous suppression merely because they were holding meetings and parades against racial discrimination. . . . Aroused to indignation and defying brutal suppression, these Negro masses carried on their struggle even more courageously and quickly won the support of Negroes and all sections of the people throughout the United States. A gigantic and vigorous nation-wide struggle is going on in nearly every state and city of the United States; and the struggle is mounting. . . .

The speedy development of the struggle of the American Negroes is a manifestation of the sharpening of the struggle and national struggle within the United States; it has been causing increasing anxiety to U.S. ruling circles. The Kennedy Administration has resorted to cunning two-faced tactics. On the one hand, it continues to connive at and take part in the discrimination against Negroes and their persecution; it even sends troops to suppress them. On the other hand, in its attempt to lull the fighting will of the Negro people and deceive the masses throughout the country, the Kennedy Administration is parading as an advocate of the "defence of human rights" and "the protection of the civil rights of Negroes," is calling upon the Negro people to exercise "restraint" and is proposing the "civil rights legislation" to Congress. But more and more Negroes are seeing through these tactics of the Kennedy Administration. The fascist atrocities committed by the U.S. imperialists against the Negro people have laid bare the true nature of the so-called democracy and freedom of the United States and revealed the inner link between the reactionary policies pursued by the U.S. government at home and its policies of aggression abroad.

I call on the workers, peasants, revolutionary intellectuals, enlightened elements of the bourgeoisie and other enlightened persons of all colours in the world, whether white, black, yellow or brown, to unite to oppose the racial discrimination practised by U.S. imperialism and support the American Negroes in their struggle against racial discrimination. In the final analysis, a national struggle is a question of class struggle. In the United States, it is only the reactionary ruling circles among the whites who oppress the Negro people. They can in no way represent the workers, farmers, revolutionary intellectuals and other enlightened persons who comprise the overwhelming majority of the white people. At present, it is the handful of imperialists headed by the United States, and their supporters, the reactionaries in different countries, who are inflicting oppression, aggression and intimidation on the overwhelming majority of the nations and peoples of the world. We are in the majority and they are in the minority. At most, they make up less than 10 per cent of the 3,000 million population of the world. I am firmly convinced that, with the support of more than 90 per cent of the people of the world, the American Negroes will be victorious in their just struggle. The evil system of colonialism and imperialism grew up along with the enslavement of Negroes

240 / WHAT MAO *REALLY* SAID

and the trade in Negroes, and it will surely come to its end with the thorough emancipation of the black people (36).

It was because the leaders of the Chinese Communist Party were, on the whole, profoundly aware of the solidarity uniting China with the Third World (analogous or comparable experience, common enemy and therefore need for mutual support, etc.), that Peking adopted, especially after 1957, an active policy towards Asia, Africa and Latin America when, because of Sputnik, "the East wind seemed to be prevailing over the West wind". In so doing, China not only inevitably entered into composition with the U.S.S.R., but also created new risks which, because of the 1950 treaty of alliance, the U.S.S.R. could be the first to run. The Kremlin could no longer remain indifferent.

I I Mao Tse-tung and "Khrushchevism"

The problem of the "liberation of proletarian peoples" was unquestionably at the very root of the quarrel which brought China into open conflict with the U.S.S.R. Peking – because of the way in which the problem was raised there, in concrete form in 1954–5, after the Geneva and Bandung conferences – upset the traditional schemas of a Marxism which had remained essentially European or White in its doctrine. Which human groups in the world, after decolonization, were now to be called the "proletariat", the "bourgeoisie", the "aristocracy", etc.?

The theatre of social struggle had, according to Peking, now spread to the entire world: the vast majority of the world proletariat was now *in fact* yellow, brown or black. Yet a White power, the United States, with 6 per cent of the earth's population, owned more than 40 per cent of the world's wealth. However, the social struggle ought not, at least in principle or theory, to acquire a racialist character. In so doing, it could only degenerate and lose its direction. It was the establishment of socialism which, according to the schema, should liberate the proletariat. In this way all proletarians throughout the world ought to fight for socialism, whatever the colour of their skin.

The path of socialism was, however, long and tortuous. It passed through many intermediate stages, and required objective conditions which varied from one country to another, so that in a period of history like the second half of the twentieth century, in which imperialism still owned vast spaces and powerful forces, the development of the revolution could only be extremely unequal.

According to the Chinese, as they put it round about 1948–50, the token of success was the existence of a "socialist camp" with the Soviet Union at its head, increasing, after World War II and the Communist victory in China, from 200 million to 900 million inhabitants. This was the solid basis, from now on regarded as invincible because of the Soviet Communist Party's long experience and the U.S.S.R.'s technical and scientific progress, for the development of the world proletarian struggle.

This idea was expressed by Mao Tse-tung on several occasions during these years, and especially in the following article published in the *Kominform Review* in November 1948:

The October Revolution has opened up wide possibilities for the emancipation of the peoples of the world and opened up the realistic paths towards it; it has created a new front of revolutions against world imperialism, extending from the proletarians of the West, through the Russian revolution, to the oppressed peoples of the East. This front of revolutions has been created and developed under the brilliant guidance of Lenin and, after Lenin's death, of Stalin.

In the more than one hundred years since the birth of Marxism, it was only through the example of the Russian Bolsheviks in leading the October Revolution, in leading socialist construction and in defeating fascist aggression, that revolutionary parties of a new type were formed and developed in the world. With the birth of revolutionary parties of this type, the face of the world revolution has changed. The change has been so great that transformations utterly inconceivable to people of the older generation, have come into being amid fire and thunder. The Communist Party of China is a party built and developed on the model of the Communist Party of the Soviet Union. With the birth of the Communist Party of China, the face of the Chinese revolution took on an altogether new aspect. Is this fact not clear enough? ...

If the October Revolution opened up wide possibilities for the emancipation of the working class and the oppressed peoples of the world and realistic paths towards it, then the victory of the anti-fascist Second World War has opened up still wider possibilities for the emancipation of the working class and the oppressed peoples of the world and has opened up still more realistic paths to it. It will be a very great mistake to under-estimate the significance of the victory of World War II.

Since the victory of World War II, U.S. imperialism and its running dogs in various countries have taken the place of fascist Germany, Italy and Japan and are frantically preparing a new world war and menacing the whole world. ... This enemy still has strength; therefore all the revolutionary forces of each country must unite, and the revolutionary forces of all countries must likewise unite, must form an anti-imperialist united front headed by the Soviet Union and follow correct policies; otherwise victory will be impossible (1).

Mao reaffirmed, in what was perhaps a slightly less categorical form, this pre-eminence of the Soviet Union and its Communist Party in a conversation which he had with some Chinese students in Moscow on 17 November 1957:

The forces of imperialism have a head, which is America; our socialist camp must have a head too, and that head is the Soviet Union. If we do not have a head, our forces are liable to disintegrate ... The fact that the representatives of the Communist parties and workers have come on this occasion to Moscow to take part in the celebration of the Fortieth Anniversary of the great October Revolution is an event of great scope, which demonstrates the unity of the socialist states, the Soviet Union at their head, with the Communist Party of the Soviet Union as its centre (2). ...

Thus, in 1957, Moscow remained the centre of the socialist camp to Mao Tse-tung, and there was still no question of competition from China, of a challenge to the pre-eminence of the

Soviet Union Communist Party. The Chinese Communist Party continued to regard the unity of the socialist camp and close co-operation between the Soviet and Chinese Communist parties as a basic condition for world victory.

Yet relations had not always been excellent or easy between the Russian Communists and the Chinese Communists. Mistakes by the Komintern and Stalin in 1924–7 had not been forgotten, nor the support later given, in 1930–4, by Moscow to the "Leftist" lines of Li Li-san and Wang Ming. In 1950–51, the Kremlin had tried to negotiate with Washington, over Korea, without considering Chinese interests. But Peking had forgiven Stalin. In 1963, Peking stated: "When Stalin did something wrong, he was capable of criticizing himself." He "had given bad counsel with regard to the Chinese revolution. After the victory of the Chinese revolution, he admitted his errors (3)".

Yet it was precisely because of Stalin that Moscow and Peking began to drift apart. The Chinese Communist Party was quite explicit. In September 1963, it wrote: "The differences of principle in the international Communist movement began with the Twentieth Congress of the Soviet Union Communist Party (C.P.S.U.) in 1956" which "was the first step along the road of revisionism taken by the leadership of the C.P.S.U." From the very outset "we held that a number of views advanced at the Twentieth Congress concerning the contemporary international struggles and the international Communist movement were wrong, were violations of Marxism-Leninism. In particular the complete repudiation of Stalin on the pretext of 'combating the personality cult' and the peaceful transition to socialism by the so-called 'parliamentary route' are gross errors of principle (4)." The Chinese Communist Party added: "Comrade Khrushchev completely negated Stalin at the Twentieth Congress of the C.P.S.U. He failed to consult the fraternal Parties in advance on this question of principle which involves the whole international communist movement, and afterwards tried to impose a *fait accompli* on them (5)."

Mao Tse-tung's position on this problem was clarified in an important article which appeared in Peking in September 1963:

In April 1956, less than 2 months after the 20th Congress, in conversations both with Comrade Mikoyan, member of the Praesidium of the Central Committee of the C.P.S.U., and with the Soviet Ambassador to China, Comrade Mao Tse-tung expressed our views on the question of Stalin. He emphasized that Stalin's "merits outweighed his faults" and that it was necessary to "make a concrete analysis" and "an all-round evaluation" of Stalin.

On 23 October 1956, on receiving the Soviet Ambassador to China, Comrade Mao Tse-tung pointed out, "Stalin deserves to be criticized, but we do not agree with the method of criticism, and there are some other matters we do not agree with".

On 30 November 1956, on receiving the Soviet Ambassador to China, Comrade Mao Tse-tung again pointed out that the basic policy and line during the period when Stalin was in power were correct and that methods that are used against enemies must not be used against one's comrades (6).

And the Chinese Communist Party stated: "Stalin's merits and mistakes are matters of historical, objective reality. A comparison of the two shows that his merits outweighed his faults. He was primarily correct, and his faults were secondary (7)."

These passages were published in 1963, but on 5 April 1956, in an article entitled "On the Historical Experience of the Dictatorship of the Proletariat", quite clearly expressing Mao's views, he had passed a long judgment on Stalin which was considerably less severe and one-sided than Khrushchev's.

This starting-point was regarded as very important by the Chinese Communist Party. In 1963 again, it stated: "The facts have shown ever more clearly that the C.P.S.U. leadership's revision of the Marxist-Leninist theories on imperialism, war and peace, proletarian revolution and the dictatorship of the proletariat, revolution in the colonies and semi-colonies, the proletarian party, etc., is inseparably connected with their complete negation of Stalin (8). . . ."

It was in fact because of the socialist camp's foreign policy that the two Communist powers first diverged. In October and November 1956, the Chinese Communist Party stood out for a very firm attitude to what it called "the Hungarian counter-revolution", and it supported the Poles against what it termed "the mistaken methods of great power chauvinism". But in 1957, as a result of the experience "gained" during the Hungarian and Suez crises, while Moscow thought it a good idea to make friendly advances to the United States, Peking on the contrary estimated that the American danger was growing and that it had to be opposed. In May 1957, the South Vietnamese president, Ngo Dinh Diem, visiting the United States, announced that "the United States frontier now reaches to the 17th Parallel". In return for an increase in American aid, he made his country a link in the chain of military bases which the Pentagon was constructing round China. China asked for help from the U.S.S.R. to arm herself with atomic weapons. On 15 October 1957, two weeks after the success of Sputnik, an "agreement on new techniques of national defence" was signed between China and the U.S.S.R., the latter undertaking to supply Peking with samples of atomic bombs and technical data about their manufacture.

At the Conference of Communist Parties in Moscow in November 1957, the Chinese Communist Party and its allies contrived to insert, in its final statement, the theories of imperialism, war and peace, revolution in colonial and semi-colonial countries which it thought consistent with pure Marxist-Leninist doctrine. It was especially emphasized in the statement that "American imperialism was the enemy of the peoples of the entire world".

We saw how, in 1958, after the Middle East crisis, Peking discouraged Mosow from taking the road to the Five Power Conference (without China) and how, by provoking another crisis in the Straits of Formosa, China killed off the Kremlin's attempts at direct agreement with Washington. From now on, tension between the two capitals grew progressively. The U.S.S.R. first tried to insist, in return for atomic techniques which she was handing over to China, that the latter should be integrated within the Soviet strategic dispositions: Peking in 1963 mentioned that "the leadership of the C.P.S.U. put forward unreasonable demands designed to bring China under Soviet military control" which "were rightly and firmly rejected by the Chinese Government" (9). Mao Tse-tung now stated that "in ten years' time China would have her own atomic bombs (10)".

Khrushchev began to attack Mao, still with innuendoes, declaring that "socialist construction in China was going beyond the appropriate stages", that it was "egalitarian Communism", and that the people's communes were "in effect reactionary". In December 1958, Mao Tse-tung announced that he would be giving up the leadership of the State in 1959, retaining only that of the Party. In April 1959, Liu Shao-ch'i became President of the Republic. On 20 June 1959, however, the Soviet government annulled the 1957 agreement on atomic techniques and refused to supply China with the samples of bombs and the technical data needed for the manufacture of the latter in China.

No statement, no Chinese reaction was visible from abroad. In fact, at a meeting of the Central Committee held in August 1959 in Lu Shan, the Chinese Communist Party "expressed satisfaction at the announcement, by the U.S.S.R. and the United States, of an exchange of visits between the heads of their governments". However, the Chinese Minister of Defence, P'eng Te-huai, evidently a supporter of the preservation of the Soviet alliance at the cost of politico-miliary concessions, was now replaced by General Liu Piao, master of "the strategy of guerilla warfare" (11).

The support given by Moscow to India on the frontier problem with China, and then the Eisenhower-Khrushchev meeting at Camp David in the U.S.A. in September 1959 annoyed the Chinese Communist Party, even though the Soviet leader, on his return from America, went to Peking where he stated that he was convinced of the United States' desire for peace, and that she was determined to promote the development of co-existence which, he said, would be favourable to Communism; Communism would speedily prove its superiority as an economic system as things grew more relaxed. As a means of encouraging this relaxation, Khrushchev suggested that China should accept a temporary agreement on the basis of "peaceful co-existence between the two Chinas", Peking and Formosa. This was all that was needed to rouse the suspicion, distrust and irony of the Chinese to its peak. Nikita Khrushchev hit back, angrily attacking Chinese "adventurism", and warning his listeners against "testing by force the stability of the capitalist system (12)".

The "spirit of Camp David" did not last long. In April 1960, while Peking was publishing a series of articles, "Long Live Leninism!", undoubtedly inspired by Mao Tse-tung, the U-2 affair, an American photographic spy plane shot down over the U.S.S.R., gave Peking a new opportunity of denouncing "Khrushchevian illusions" about imperialism. The summit conference arranged for Paris collapsed. In July, no doubt to "intimidate" Peking, Khrushchev recalled all Soviet experts from China, "thus ripping up hundreds of contracts" and dealing the Chinese economy a very serious blow from which it took months and even years to recover. In September 1960, the Vietnamese Lao Dong Congress in Hanoi brought into the open a new divergence between Russians and Chinese over the attitude to adopt towards the people's uprising in South Vietnam. In November 1960, the Moscow Conference of 81 Communist and Workers' Parties was, according to a Chinese report, "from start to finish, a struggle between two lines within the international Communist movement". The Communist and Workers' Parties, however, unanimously reaffirmed their loyalty to the Peace statement and manifesto adopted in 1957. The Chinese Communist Party, as in 1957, had assigned Mao Tse-tung to Moscow, and once again he managed to give the final statement a consistent "Leninist" flavour, as the following passages from the statement testify:

The course of international events in the last few years has produced fresh evidence that American imperialism is the main bastion of world reaction, the international police force, the enemy of the peoples of the entire world.

. . . The most burning problem today is that of war and peace. The imperialists in the United States are endeavouring to recreate a hotbed of war in the Far East. Trampling on the Japanese people's national independence, and acting in contempt of their wishes and with the complicity of the reactionary ruling circles in Japan, they have imposed on this country a new military treaty with a view to aggression against the Soviet Union, the People's Republic of China and other peaceful states. The American invaders have occupied the island of Taiwan, which belongs to the People's Republic of China, as well as affairs of South Vietnam. They have made these countries hot-beds of dangerous military adventure and provocations (13)....

John F. Kennedy's rise to power did not materially affect the Chinese position, and Peking became increasingly resentful at the sight of the U.S.S.R. becoming involved in a barely coherent policy in which threats and shock tactics (Berlin wall, aid to Cuba) were mingled with friendly advances and summit meetings (Vienna, June 1961), though the Kremlin was unable to use all its trumps, in Laos for instance, in obtaining an acceptable settlement to the Vietnamese conflict. The Soviet Communist Party's adoption of a new programme in 1961 persuaded Peking that the U.S.S.R., under Khrushchev's leadership, was embarking on a course which, according to the Chinese, had ceased to be a Leninist one. Mao Tse-tung sought more and more to weigh the consequences which this alteration in the character of the Soviet Communist Party would have on the socialist camp's policy and on the future of the world proletarian struggle.

But Mao Tse-tung was also studying China's domestic evolution. Now, as a result of the withdrawl of Russian experts and aid, of the undoubtedly excessive effort and of the confusion caused by the setting up of people's communes, by the policy of the Great Leap Forward, and also by natural disasters and the poor harvests which had resulted from it, a very serious brake had been put on China's economic development and socialist construction. During the phase of relative stability ushered in at the end of 1959, after the Lu Shan plenum, new "bourgeois" and "capitalist" tendencies were re-appearing, especially in the countryside. The landlords had practically been eliminated, but the rich and middle peasants were re-emerging and acquiring influential posts in the co-operatives and communes. The condition of the proletariat had of course improved, but once again it was in danger of being subjugated, this time within the socialist regime and system.

At the plenum of the Eighth Central Committee in September 1962, Mao Tse-tung drew attention to this key phenomenon. Even in a socialist regime, he recalled, "the class struggle must never be forgotten". He recommended the Party organizations to rely principally on the poor peasants in the countryside, and suggested to the Party, which agreed, to launch a vast campaign for socialist education throughout the countryside.

During this time, relations with the Soviet Union worsened. Nikita Khrushchev stepped up attacks or "insinuations" against his Chinese ally. In 1962, after contributing to a peaceful and acceptable solution to the Laotian conflict, the U.S.S.R., no doubt to intimidate or to "contain" China, improved her relations with Nehru's India, supplying her with arms and planes, granting her considerable economic aid, and taking her side in the Himalayan frontier problem. In October-November 1962, while Moscow, which had stuck its neck out in the West Indies by supporting Cuba, had to give way to the vigorous American reaction, Peking made a powerful military demonstration in the Himalayas which flung the Indian army back from the positions which it had established in the contested territories. The collapse of Nehru's army ended Indian neutrality. From now on, weighed down with military burdens and feeding problems, New Delhi depended more and more on foreign aid, American first, then Soviet, and drew further and further away from China. A strong current of hostility to Peking grew up within the ranks of Indian nationalism itself. Thus, reverting to Stalinist tactics, Peking was aiming its blows against "intermediary forces".

At the beginning of 1963, the Russians began to attack the Chinese Communist Party openly for the first time. For a few weeks, the latter did not react. But a new attack, the C.P.S.U.

Central Committee's 30 March 1963 letter, gave Peking no choice but open explanation. It came in the form of the famous twenty-five point 14 June 1963 letter in which the Chinese Communist Party recapitulated, in remarkably clear terms, its position on most of the problems under discussion. It is not certain if this letter is *by* Mao Tse-tung, but it seems that it broadly reflects his ideas, and certain passages even seem to be in his style.

After recalling that the 1957 and 1960 Declarations defined "the international Communist movement's general line at the present stage", the Chinese letter pointed out :

This general line proceeds from the actual world situation taken as a whole and from a class analysis of the fundamental contradictions in the contemporary world, and is directed against the counter-revolutionary global strategy of U.S. imperialism.

This general line is one of forming a broad united front, with the socialist camp and the international proletariat as its nucleus, to oppose the imperialists and reactionaries headed by the United States; it is a line of boldly arousing the masses, expanding the revolutionary forces, winning over the middle forces and isolating the reactionary forces.

This general line is one of resolute revolutionary struggle by the people of all countries and of carrying the proletarian world revolution forward to the end; it is the line that most effectively combats imperialism and defends world peace.

If the general line of the international communist movement is one-sidedly reduced to "peaceful co-existence", "peaceful competition" and "peaceful transition", this is to violate the revolutionary principles of the 1957 Declaration and the 1960 Statement, to discard the historical mission of proletarian world revolution, and to depart from the revolutionary teachings of Marxism-Leninism (14). . . .

What are the fundamental contradictions in the contemporary world? Marxist-Leninists consistently hold that they are :

– the contradiction between the socialist camp and the imperialist camp;

– the contradiction between the proletariat and the bourgeoisie in the capitalist countries;

— the contradiction between the oppressed nations and imperialism; and

— the contradictions among imperialist countries and among monopoly capitalist groups.

The contradiction between the socialist camp and the imperialist camp is a contradiction between two fundamentally different social systems, socialism and capitalism. It is undoubtedly very sharp. But Marxist-Leninists must not regard the contradictions in the world as consisting solely and simply of the contradiction between the socialist camp and the imperialist camp. . . .

These contradictions and the struggles to which they give rise are interrelated and influence each other. Nobody can obliterate any of these fundamental contradictions or subjectively substitute one for all the rest.

It is inevitable that these contradictions will give rise to popular revolutions, which alone can resolve them (15). . . .

For this very reason, the imperialists and reactionaries invariably try in a thousand and one ways to influence the domestic and foreign policies of the countries in the socialist camp, to undermine the camp and break up the unity of the socialist countries and particularly the unity of China and the Soviet Union. They invariably try to infiltrate and subvert the socialist countries and even entertain the extravagant hope of destroying the socialist camp (16). . . .

Taking advantage of the situation after World War II, the U.S. imperialists stepped into the shoes of the German, Italian and Japanese fascists, and have been trying to erect a huge world empire such as has never been known before. The strategic objectives of U.S. imperialism have been to grab and dominate the intermediate zone lying between the United States and the socialist camp, put down the revolutions of the oppressed peoples and nations, proceed to destroy the socialist countries, and thus to subject all the peoples and countries of the world, including its allies, to domination and enslavement by U.S. monopoly capital (17). . . .

To make no distinction between enemies, friends and ourselves and to entrust the fate of the people and of mankind to collaboration with U.S. imperialism is to lead people astray (18). . . .

The various types of contradictions in the contemporary world are concentrated in the vast areas of Asia, Africa and Latin America; these are the most vulnerable areas under imperialist rule and the storm-centres of world revolution dealing direct blows at imperialism. . . .

The national democratic revolution in these areas is an important component of the contemporary proletarian world revolution (19). . . .

It is necessary for the socialist countries to engage in negotiations of one kind or another with the imperialist countries. . . . But necessary compromises between the socialist countries and the imperialist countries do not require the oppressed peoples and nations to follow suit and compromise with imperialism and its lackeys. No one should ever demand in the name of peaceful co-existence that the oppressed peoples and nations should give up their revolutionary struggles (20). . . .

The Chinese Communist Party also stated :

In recent years, certain persons have been spreading the argument that a single spark from a war of national liberation or from a revolutionary people's war will lead to a world conflagration destroying the whole of mankind. What are the facts? Contrary to what these persons say, the wars of national liberation and the revolutionary people's wars that have occurred since World War II have not led to world war. The victory of these revolutionary wars has directly weakened the forces of imperialism and greatly strengthened the forces which prevent the imperialists from launching a world war and which defend world peace (21).

But one of the most important points in this letter, and probably that in which Mao Tse-tung had most hand is Point 17, because it broadly conditioned the view which Peking now took of the Soviet Union :

For a very long historical period after the proletariat takes power, class struggle continues as an objective law independent of man's will, differing only in form from what it was before the taking of power.

After the October Revolution, Lenin pointed out a number of times that :

a. The overthrown exploiters always try in a thousand and one ways to recover the "paradise" they have been deprived of.
b. New elements of capitalism are constantly and spontaneously generated in the petty-bourgeois atmosphere.
c. Political degenerates and new bourgeois elements may emerge in the ranks of the working class and among government functionaries as a result of bourgeois influence and the pervasive, corrupting atmosphere of the petty bourgeoisie.
d. The external conditions for the continuance of class struggle within a socialist country are encirclement by international capitalism, the imperialists' threat of armed intervention and their subversive activities to accomplish peaceful disintegration.

Life has confirmed these conclusions of Lenin's.

Four decades or even longer periods after socialist industrialization and agricultural collectivization, it will be impossible to say that any socialist country will be free from those elements which Lenin repeatedly denounced, such as bourgeois hangers-on, parasites, speculators, swindlers, idlers, hooligans and embezzlers of state funds; or to say that a socialist country will no longer need to perform or be able to relinquish the task laid down by Lenin of conquering "this contagion, this plague, this ulcer that socialism has inherited from capitalism."

In a socialist country, it takes a very long historical period gradually to settle the question of who will win – socialism or capitalism. The struggle between the road of socialism and the road of capitalism runs through this whole historical period. This struggle rises and falls in a wave-like manner, at times becoming very fierce, and the forms of the struggle are many and varied.

The 1957 Declaration rightly states that "the conquest of power by the working class is only the beginning of the revolution, not its conclusion".

To deny the existence of class struggle in the period of the dictatorship of the proletariat and the necessity of thoroughly completing the socialist revolution on the economic, political and ideological fronts is wrong, does not correspond to objective reality and violates Marxism-Leninism (22). . . .

This passage was part of a letter dated 14 June 1963. It is very significant that a month beforehand, on 9 May 1963, Mao Tse-tung, in a note on the Party's activity in Chekiang, wrote the following, which sheds light on all his activities in the ensuing years :

Class struggle, the struggle for production and scientific experiment are the three great revolutionary movements for building a mighty socialist country. These movements are a sure guarantee that Communists will be free from bureaucracy and immune against revisionism and dogmatism, and will for ever remain invincible. They are a reliable guarantee that the proletariat will be able to unite with the broad working masses and realize a democratic dictatorship. If, in the absence of these movements, the landlords, rich peasants, counter-revolutionaries, bad elements and ogres of all kinds were allowed to crawl out, while our cadres were to shut their eyes to all this and in many cases fail even to differentiate between the enemy and ourselves but were to collaborate with the enemy and become corrupted and demoralized, if our cadres were thus dragged into the enemy camp or the enemy were able to sneak into our ranks, and if many of our workers, peasants and intellectuals were left defenceless against both the soft and the hard tactics of the enemy, then it would not take long, perhaps only several years or a decade, or several decades at most, before a counter-revolutionary restoration on a national scale inevitably occurred, the Marxist-Leninist Party would undoubtedly become a revisionist party or a fascist party, and *the whole of China would change its colour* (23).

An extraordinary text when one considers that it was written nearly fourteen years after the seizure of power by the Party and the proletariat, but which perfectly explains certain attitudes by Peking towards the Soviets, and whose contents published in Peking on 14 July 1964 and entitled "On Khrushchev's Phoney Communism and Its Historical Lessons for the World", were very strikingly expressed. Here are its most significant passages :

The line Khrushchev pursues is a revisionist line through and through. Guided by this line, not only have the old bourgeois elements run wild but new bourgeois elements have appeared in large numbers among the leading cadres of the Soviet Party and government, the chiefs of state enterprises and collective farms, and the higher intellectuals in the fields of culture, art, science and technology. . . .

But since Khrushchev took over, usurping the leadership of the Party and the state step by step, the new bourgeois elements have gradually risen to the ruling position in the Party and government and in the economic, cultural and other departments, and formed a privileged stratum in Soviet society.

This privileged stratum is the principal component of the bourgeoisie in the Soviet Union today and the main social basis of the revisionist Khrushchev clique. The revisionist Khrushchev clique are the political representatives of the Soviet bourgeoisie, and particularly of its privileged stratum. . . .

Through this series of changes by Khrushchev the Soviet privileged stratum has gained control of the Party, the government and other important organizations.

The members of this privileged stratum have converted the function of serving the masses into the privilege of dominating them. They are abusing their powers over the means of production and of livelihood for the private benefit of their small clique.

The members of this privileged stratum appropriate the fruits of the Soviet people's labour and pocket incomes that are dozens or even a hundred times those of the average Soviet worker and peasant. They not only secure high incomes in the form of high salaries, high awards, high royalties and a great variety of personal subsidies, but also use their privileged position to appropriate public property by graft and bribery. Completely divorced from the working people of the Soviet Union, they live the parasitical and decadent life of the bourgeoisie.

The members of this privileged stratum have become utterly degenerate ideologically, have completely departed from the revolutionary traditions of the Bolshevik Party and discarded the lofty ideals of the Soviet working class. They are opposed to Marxism-Leninism and socialism. They betray the revolution and forbid others to make revolution. Their sole concern is to consolidate their economic position and political rule. All their activities revolve around the private interests of their own privileged stratum (24). . . .

The Khrushchev clique are spreading the tale that "there are no longer antagonistic classes and class struggle in the Soviet Union" in order to cover up the facts about their own ruthless class struggle against the Soviet people.

The Soviet privileged stratum represented by the revisionist Khrushchev clique constitutes only a few per cent of the Soviet population. Among the Soviet cadres its numbers are also small. It stands diametrically opposed to the Soviet people, who constitute more than 90 per cent of the total population, and to the great majority of the Soviet cadres and Communists. The contradiction between the Soviet people and this privileged stratum is now the principal contradiction inside the Soviet Union, and it is an irreconcilable and antagonistic class contradiction (25). . . .

A communist society with bourgeois ideas running rampant is inconceivable. Yet Khrushchev is zealously reviving bourgeois ideology in the Soviet Union and serving as a missionary for the decadent American culture. By propagating material incentive, he is turning all human relations into money relations and encouraging individualism and selfishness. Because of him, manual labour is again considered sordid and love of pleasure at the expense of other people's labour is again considered honourable. Certainly, the social ethics and atmosphere promoted by Khrushchev are far removed from communism, as far as can be. . . .

Khrushchev is altering the character of Soviet state power and changing the dictatorship of the proletariat back into an instrument whereby a handful of privileged bourgeois elements exercise dictatorship over the mass of the Soviet workers, peasants and intellectuals. . . .

The revisionist Khrushchev clique are leading the Soviet Union away from the path of socialism and on to the path of capitalism. . . .

Khrushchev has ulterior motives when he puts up the signboard of communism. He is using it to fool the Soviet people and cover up his effort to restore capitalism. He is using it to deceive the international proletariat and the revolutionary people the world over and betray proletarian internationalism. Under

I

this signboard, the Khrushchev clique has itself abandoned proletarian internationalism and is seeking a partnership with U.S. imperialism for the partition of the world; moreover, it wants the fraternal socialist countries to serve its own private interests and not to oppose imperialism or to support the revolutions of the oppressed peoples and nations, and it wants them to accept its political, economic and military control and be its virtual dependencies and colonies. Furthermore, the Khrushchev clique wants all the oppressed peoples and nations to serve its private interests and abandon their revolutionary struggles, so as not to disturb its sweet dream of partnership with imperialism for the division of the world (26). . . .

Khrushchev's "communism" is in essence a variant of bourgeois socialism (27). . . .

In this long letter by the Chinese Communist Party Central Committee, a single passage has so far been explicitly attributed to the Chairman of the Committee, Mao Tse-tung. Here it is:

Socialist society covers a very long historical period. Classes and class struggle continue to exist in this society, and the struggle still goes on between the road of socialism and the road of capitalism. The socialist revolution on the economic front (in the ownership of the means of production) is insufficient by itself and cannot be consolidated. There must also be a thorough socialist revolution on the political and ideological fronts. Here a very long period of time is needed to decide "who will win" in the struggle between socialism and capitalism. Several decades won't do it; success requires anywhere from one to several centuries. On the question of duration, it is better to prepare for a longer rather than a shorter period of time. On the question of effort, it is better to regard the task as difficult rather than easy. It will be more advantageous and less harmful to think and act in this way. Anyone who fails to see this or to appreciate it fully will make tremendous mistakes. During the historical period of socialism it is necessary to maintain the dictatorship of the proletariat and carry the socialist revolution through to the end if the restoration of capitalism is to be prevented, socialist construction carried forward and the conditions created for the transition to communism (28).

We do not intend here to retrace the Sino-Soviet conflict already dealt with so fully by eminent experts. But it was necessary to see it in its ideological framework, at least to try and bring out what was fundamental to Mao Tse-tung. It will be noticed that apart from certain very rare passages, officially attributed to Peking by Mao, the latter did not personally take issue with the U.S.S.R. as he had with the United States. In this conflict, he remained "in the second line", as Peking used to say.

The U.S.S.R.'s progressive evolution towards what will perhaps emerge as a new Finnish or Scandinavian type of socialism, that is, a "social democracy", may have gradually robbed her of her capacity to understand fully the problems of the peoples of Asia, Africa and Latin America still directly at grips with imperialism. Now, according to Peking, the danger from abroad was still on the increase. The war in Vietnam was intensifying. After the overthrow of Ngo Dinh Diem, in circumstances foreshadowed by Mao, the military cliques which succeeded him carried on the war with American help, in conditions which more and more recalled the American intervention on Chiang Kai-shek's side in the Chinese civil war. In July 1964, de Gaulle, Sihanouk, U Thant and Moscow expressed the desire to see a negotiated settlement in Indochina on the basis of the Geneva agreements. China came out in favour of such an idea, but Washington, London and Saigon rejected it. In August 1964, activities by the American navy in the Gulf of Tonkin provoked some mysterious incidents not far off the Chinese coast, incidents which enabled President Johnson to assume full powers of action in Vietnam. Would China react?

On 15 October 1964, Khrushchev was divested of power by the Soviet Communist Party Central Committee. The following day, as if to mark the event with solemnity, the People's Republic of China exploded its first atom bomb.

In Saigon, the regime, in difficulties, was vacillating. In Washington, the Pentagon, realizing that the war was politically on the way to being lost, decided to extend it militarily. It had only one recourse : to bomb the North, held responsible for the war, and force it to end the Southern uprising.

Mao Tse-tung, who had known, ever since spring 1964, that the blueprint for bombing North Vietnam was in Johnson's drawer, did not seem to think that the Americans would go that far. The conversation which he had with Edgar Snow in Peking on 9 January 1965 suggested that Mao still believed that the Americans would eventually tire of the war and agree to negotiate round a green baize table in Geneva. Mao stipulated one of the conditions for such a negotiation. . . . The Vietnamese problem could, he said, be solved by a conference provided that Washington gave up its plan to make South Vietnam into an American protectorate (29).

China, after Khrushchev's fall, had made suggestions for restoring the unity of the socialist camp. Mao had appealed for unity and had evoked Sino-Soviet friendship. A large Chinese delegation, with Chou En-lai, Ho Long, Kang Cheng, etc., went to Moscow in early November. But the gulf could not be bridged. Meanwhile, on 27 November 1964, in a special statement, the U.S.S.R. promised Hanoi her active support in the event of an American attack.

A few weeks later, a major turning-point was reached. On 7 February 1965, when Mr. Kosygin was in Hanoi, and while France and the U.S.S.R. were trying to convince Washington of the chance of peace moves in Vietnam, the White House gave orders for a systematic air offensive against North Vietnam.

This was the first attack made by the West against a member of the socialist camp. Peking immediately expressed its indignation and its support for Hanoi and waited. Now the U.S.S.R. which alone had means of dissuasion, reacted to the U.S. offensive only with verbal threats and promises of support and arms. She did not even attempt to take the question to the United Nations or to call for an international conference. The United Nations remained as passive and indifferent as the League of Nations when the Japanese army had attacked China in Manchuria in September 1931. Was the United States trying to create a new Manchukuo in South Vietnam? Was she, like

Japan thirty years earlier, trying to break down China's ramparts?

China could only draw the inevitable logical conclusions from this set of facts. Peking, it is known from a direct Chinese source, was now convinced that Moscow would not budge over Vietnam; consequently, the U.S. action had to go on, and sooner or later, as in Korea in 1950, China would no doubt be forced to intervene. But it looks certain that in April 1965 the Chinese general staff concluded that eventually an armed confrontation between China and the United States was *inevitable* and that China had to be got ready to face up to it.

12 The Cultural Revolution

In facing up to it, what strategy was to be adopted? Confronted by a potential enemy with overwhelming naval and air supremacy, and thereby able to inflict untold destruction on China, who, thanks to his fleet and bases, could even land sizeable forces on Chinese soil and secure bridgeheads, there was only one possible strategy, that of "protracted war": first to prevent the enemy from obtaining a *decision* and therefore avoid presenting him with important objectives; then to lure him into a war of attrition from which he would bleed and emerge relatively weaker than China, a war from which he would be unable to disengage, but which would finally make him let go. The Americans could of course destroy a thousand towns and ten thousand villages, they could defeat brigades and divisions and undertake "encirclement and suppression campaigns", but they would never get the better of the Chinese *people*. To face up to the American *Drang nach Westen*, the Chinese strategists seemed to think that only a "people's war", "revolutionary war" was conceivable.

Once this decision to face up to it, to accept the idea of fighting, had been taken and it is reasonable to suppose that this was in April or May 1965 – indications of "the new course" soon appeared. The removal of visible signs of ranks in May indicated a return to the traditions of the People's Liberation Army. The re-publication in August 1965 of Mao's article on "Questions of Strategy in the Anti-Japanese Guerilla War", followed in early September by the publication of a long article by the Minister of Defence, Lin Piao, "Long Live the Victory of the People's War, Long Live the Revolutionary War!" testified to the new and decisive importance of the Minister of Defence (1). In substance it stated that, on the world scale, the bases of imperialism, North America and Europe, are like towns, and the Third World, Asia, Africa, Latin America, is like the country-side. With protracted war – as shown by the war against Japan – those who dominate the countryside also finish by encircling the towns and winning out. The road is long and hard. In the total absence of a continuous front, guerilla activity from sup-port bases is the rule, and "peasant" units must rely chiefly on themselves. A flexible, pragmatic strategy is needed, calling for stamina, a clear view of what is at stake, and a revolutionary frame of mind in which men, in short, are more important than arms and which makes use of a large number of tactics, advances and withdrawals, applying all the rules which Mao and his men learnt between the Tsingkiang Mountains and Yenan.

In such circumstances, an opponent must not, as far as is possible, be allowed the least respite. He must not be allowed to consolidate his positions at any point and all to him must seem doubtful and uncertain. Wherever he is involved, as in Vietnam, he must be completely ensnared. . . .

The consequences – on the level of China's domestic affairs – of the decision to "face up to it" were considerable. The enemy could not be under-estimated. In order to confront the U.S.A., forces had to be rallied, and economic development, education, cultural and artistic life, and international relations had to be subjected to firm and clear leadership for years, with no falter-ing. Mobilizing the Chinese people for a "protracted war" on such a scale was no small matter and formidable resistance was to be expected. It was also obvious, in autumn 1965, that the majority of the Party did not approve of theories of "forward military elements": an article which created a stir put the question bluntly: "We want to know if guns command the Party or if the Party controls the guns".

It was at this juncture that the army turned to Mao Tse-tung. Who could tell whose hands China might not soon fall into, if care were not taken? Into the weak hands of eventual or disguised "revisionists", previously afraid of confronting imperialism, or into the hands of true revolutionaries? The problem raised in 1962, when the campaign for "socialist education" was launched at Mao's request, once again loomed as large as ever. By autumn 1964, the campaign had intensified after the Party and the army had noted the large scale resurgence of "capitalist tendencies" in the countryside. Would "Khrushchevism" leave its mark on China? Would the latter begin to slide at her moment of greatest danger?

Mao Tse-tung gradually emerged from the southern retreat where he had gone to ponder on China's destiny and to carry out his rural investigation. It appears that his analyses squared with those of the military leaders. The slide towards revisionism had to be halted, China had to be mobilized to face up to the military threat. This renewal of friendly relations between Mao Tse-tung and the army meant that in late 1965, probably in November, the fifty-eight-year-old Minister of Defence, Lin Piao, emerged as Mao Tse-tung's probable successor, rather than the man who had previously been regarded as such, the Chairman of the Republic, Liu Shao-ch'i. From now on the struggle for power was inevitable.

For several months, Mao Tse-tung had taken something of a back seat and there was even talk of semi-disgrace. The Party, over which he still presided, nominally at least, had passed into the control of the Liu Shao-ch'i, Teng Hsiao-p'ing and Peng Ch'en group. In September-October 1965, when the Mao Tse-tung–Lin Piao alliance was concluded, it was decided to launch the attack on a cultural level. On 10 November, *Wen Hui Bao,* a Shanghai daily paper, published an article severely criticizing a new historical play: *The Destitution of Hai Juei.* This was the cue for the Mao–Lin Piao group's offensive against the Party leadership and in support of the great cultural revolution. Simultaneously, the army launched a campaign aimed at the recognition, everywhere and in everything, of "the primacy of politics", that is, Mao's thought.

The two camps prepared for battle. While the Party leaders were holding discussions in December, there was a military conference from 30 December to 17 January 1966 to examine the instructions which Mao had sent in December to Lin Piao about ideological work in the army and on "the need to step up war preparations and to be ready at any moment to smash imperialist aggression by the United States". In January 1966, Hsiao Hua, head of the army political department, attacked "bourgeois military conceptions", and it is probable that the chief of the general staff, Lo Jui-ching, was one of the supporters of these "conceptions", because he was dismissed. In early February, Mao Tse-tung's wife, Chiang Ch'ing, was given the task by Lin Piao of organizing talks "to discuss certain questions concerning the work in literature and art in the armed forces" in Shanghai (2). Some of Mao's unpublished and little known writings were commented on at them. One, an instruction by Mao dated 12 December 1963, ended: "Isn't it absurd that many Communists are enthusiastic about promoting feudal and capitalist art and not socialist art?" The "minutes" of these talks, revised three times by Mao himself (3), are regarded as one of the basic documents of the cultural revolution.

A "special group" of five persons, including Peng Ch'en and Kang Cheng, had been put in charge of the cultural revolution at the urgent request of the Party. On 12 February 1966, this group circularized "an outline report" on the "current academic discussion". In fact, as Peking recently revealed, in May–June 1967, "while feigning compliance, the outline actually opposes and stubbornly resists" (4) the cultural revolution. It was Peng Ch'en who had circularized this report on his own initiative, practically without consulting anyone else and "not even" having "obtained the approval of comrade Mao Tse-tung, Chairman of the Central Committee". Peng Ch'en had, according to current critics, covered up "the serious political nature of this struggle", and obscured the "sharp class struggle that is taking place on the cultural and ideological front", Peng Ch'en's aim being to "Channel the political struggle . . . into so-called pure academic discussion".

The Mao–Lin Piao group now launched its offensive on what was currently known in Peking as "Peng Ch'en's counter-revolutionary revisionist clique". The first sign of Lin Piao's rise and his whole-hearted identification with Mao was the editorial of the 18 April 1966 *Liberation Army Daily* (*Jiefangun Bao*), on the need for a great proletarian cultural revolution, whose main trends were briefly indicated: the destruction of old ideas, old customs, old habits, old culture and their replacement by new ideas, new customs, new habits and a new culture (5).

Mao Tse-tung intervened directly. On 16 May 1966, the Central Committee decided to cancel the 12 February Peng Ch'en instruction by an important circular. In this circular, the following passages were recently officially ascribed to Mao (6).

There are a number of these (representatives of the bourgeoisie) in the Central Committee and in the Party, government and other departments at the central as well as at the provincial, municipal and autonomous region level.

The whole Party must "hold high the great banner of the proletarian cultural revolution, thoroughly expose the reactionary bourgeois stand of those so-called 'academic authorities' who oppose the Party and socialism, thoroughly criticize and repudiate the reactionary bourgeois ideas in the sphere of academic work, education, journalism, literature and art and publishing, and seize the leadership in these cultural spheres. To achieve this it is necessary at the same time to criticize and repudiate those representatives of the bourgeoisie who have sneaked into the Party, the Government, the army and all spheres of culture, to clear them out or transfer them to other positions."

Those representatives of the bourgeoisie who have sneaked into the Party, the Government, the army and various cultural circles are a bunch of counter-revolutionary revisionists. Once conditions are ripe, they will seize political power and turn the dictatorship of the proletariat into a dictatorship of the bourgeoisie. Some of them we have already seen through, others we have not. Some are still trusted by us and are being trained as our successors, persons like Khrushchev, for example, who are still nestling beside us. Party committees at all levels must pay full attention to this matter (6).

On 1 June, the Maoists turned out in force in Peking. Mao appeared on the first big-character poster from Peking University, "thus issuing the order to launch an all-out counter-attack against the handful of Party persons in authority taking the capitalist road" (7). Peng Ch'en, regarded as the head of the group against Mao, protector of the "revisionists" and third member of the "Liu clique" was arrested, and after his fall, the whole of the ruling cultural team in Peking was purged. The Party's central propaganda apparatus fell into the hands of the Mao–Lin Piao group. This was followed by violent action from revolutionary students in various universities, but especially in Peking, against intellectuals and teachers regarded as "reactionaries" or "traditionalists".

Some influential groups – within the Party itself – were however very hostile to the new orientation which the Mao–Lin Piao coalition was giving the country, no doubt for rather different reasons. Foreign policy was probably only one of the aspects, perhaps not the most important, of the conflict.

In fact, Mao and the army wanted politics to take precedence over technique everywhere in the future. "To be Red was more use than to be an expert", which amounted to openly subordinating all teachers, artists, technicians and experts to the Reds, that is, mainly to soldiers turned politician, often lacking in culture. The Party, its intellectuals, its experts, its bureaucrats and its youth, too, were not in agreement.

Giving the economy a new direction in order to mobilize it raised other problems. The Communist Party in China was to some extent rooted in the countryside; regional or local "fiefs" had been set up, where many arrangements existed. There was a certain amount of anxiety at the emergence of new tensions, new "leaps forward" likely to threaten a long awaited and now greatly appreciated calm. All that some local leaders in the Party or administration could do was instinctively to join forces with that section of the Party which was resisting Mao and Lin Piao.

However, the army had been testing out the ground. It had carefully prepared itself for the trial of strength. It turned to the "masses", to the "revolutionary Left" and to those even more easily inflammable, the youth. It found its allies in the proletarian youth from the schools and universities. Methodically established, the new youth organization, the "Red Guards", was, according to the *Liberation Army Daily* 18 April, editorial, encouraged by the army to "carry through the Revolution" with it, the whole of China being offered to it as a "testing bench". "In this way we shall learn to carry through the revolution," Mao had said.

It remained for him to wrest the leadership of the Party apparatus from the "Liu clique". In early July, the new voice of the Chinese press hinted at the imminence of a large-scale offensive by Mao, hailed as "the great guide of the Chinese people". Mao was in fact swimming in the Yangtze, proving his vitality.

This was the new "Northern Expedition". This time, there was a show of resistance in Peking, where a vain attempt was made hastily to manipulate the Party apparatus. The Central Committee met in plenary session in Peking under the effective chairmanship of Mao Tse-tung who, on 5 August, launched the slogan "Fire on the Headquarters Staff". On the 8th, the Central Committee approved a long sixteen-point resolution which defined the objectives of the cultural revolution. This resolution, which had been edited under Mao's "personal supervision" and which bore his mark, stated, among other things (8) :

i). The great proletarian cultural revolution now unfolding is a great revolution that touches people to their very souls and constitutes a new stage in the development of the socialist revolution in our country, a stage which is both broader and deeper. . . .

Although the bourgeoisie has been overthrown, it is still trying to use the old ideas, culture, customs and habits of the exploiting classes to corrupt the masses, capture their minds and endeavour to stage a come-back. The proletariat must do the exact opposite : it must meet head-on every challenge of the bourgeoisie in the ideological field and use the new ideas, culture, customs and habits of the proletariat to change the mental outlook of the whole of society. At present, our objective is to struggle against and overthrow those persons in authority who are taking the capitalist road, to criticize and repudiate the reactionary bourgeois academic "authorities" and the ideology of the bourgeoisie and all other exploiting classes, and to transform education, literature and art and all other parts of the superstructure not in correspondence with the socialist economic base, so as to facilitate the consolidation and development of the socialist system.

ii). The masses of the workers, peasants, soldiers, revolutionary intellectuals and revolutionary cadres form the main force in this great cultural revolution. . . .

Since the cultural revolution is a revolution, it inevitably meets with resistance. This resistance comes chiefly from those in authority who have wormed their way into the Party and are taking the capitalist road. It also comes from the force of habits from the old society. At present, this resistance is still fairly strong and stubborn. But after all, the great proletarian cultural revolution is an irresistible general trend. There is abundant evidence that such resistance will be quickly broken down once the masses become fully aroused.

Because the resistance is fairly strong, there will be reversals and even repeated reversals in this struggle. There is no harm in this. It tempers the proletariat and other working people, and especially the younger generation, teaches them lessons and gives them experience, and helps them to understand that the revolutionary road zigzags and does not run smoothly.

iii). The outcome of this great cultural revolution will be determined by whether or not the Party leadership dares boldly to arouse the masses. . . .

What the Central Committee of the Party demands of the Party Committees at all levels is that they persevere in giving correct leadership, put daring above everything else, boldly arouse the masses, change the state of weakness and incompetence where it exists, encourage those comrades who have made mistakes but are willing to correct them to cast off their mental burdens and join in the struggle, and dismiss from their leading posts all those in authority who are taking the capitalist road, and so make possible the recapture of the leadership for the proletarian revolutionaries.

iv). In the great proletarian cultural revolution, the only method is for the masses to liberate themselves, and any method of doing things in their stead must not be used.

Trust the masses, rely on them and respect their initiative. Cast out fear. Don't be afraid of disturbances. Chairman Mao has often told us that revolution cannot be so very refined, so gentle, so temperate, kind, courteous, restrained and magnanimous. Let the masses educate themselves in this great revolutionary movement and learn to distinguish between right and wrong and between correct and incorrect ways of doing things. . . .

v). Party leadership should be good at discovering the Left and developing and strengthening the ranks of the Left; it should firmly rely on the revolutionary Left. During the movement this is the only way to isolate the most reactionary Rightists thoroughly, win over the middle and unite with the great majority so that by the end of the movement we shall achieve the unity of more than 95 per cent of the cadres and more than 95 per cent of the masses.

Concentrate all forces to strike at the handful of ultra-reactionary bourgeois Rightists and counter-revolutionary revisionists. . . .

vi). A strict distinction must be made between the two different types of contradictions: those among the people and those between ourselves and the enemy; nor must contradictions between ourselves and the enemy be regarded as contradictions among the people.

It is normal for the masses to hold different views. Contention between different views is unavoidable, necessary and beneficial. In the course of normal and full debate, the masses will affirm what is right, correct what is wrong and gradually reach unanimity.

The method to be used in debates is to present the facts, reason things out, and persuade through reasoning. Any method of forcing a minority holding different views to submit is impermissible. The minority should be protected, because sometimes the truth is with the minority. Even if the minority is wrong, they should still be allowed to argue their case and reserve their views.

When there is a debate, it should be conducted by reasoning, not by coercion or force.

In the course of debate, every revolutionary should be good at thinking things out for himself and should develop the communist spirit of daring to think, daring to speak and daring to act. On the premise that they have the same general orientation, revolutionary comrades should, for the sake of strengthening unity, avoid endless debate over side issues. . . .

x). In the great proletarian cultural revolution a most important task is to transform the old educational system and the old principles and methods of teaching.

In this great cultural revolution, the phenomenon of our schools being dominated by bourgeois intellectuals must be completely changed.

The period of schooling should be shortened. Courses should be fewer and better. The teaching material should be thoroughly transformed, in some cases beginning with simplifying complicated material. . . .

xiv). The aim of the great proletarian cultural revolution is to revolutionize people's ideology and as a consequence to achieve greater, faster, better and more economical results in all fields of work. If the masses are fully aroused and proper arrangements are made, it is possible to carry on both the cultural revolution and production without one hampering the other, while guaranteeing high quality in all our work.

The great proletarian cultural revolution is a powerful motive force for the development of the social productive forces in our country. Any idea of counterposing the great cultural revolution to the development of production is incorrect (8). . . .

On 18 August 1966, during a massive demonstration by a million people in front of the T'ien An Men Gate, Mao Tse-tung took his stand, Lin Piao was "crowned" heir apparent, number two in the new hierarchy – Liu Shao-ch'i slipped from second to eighth place. The Red Guards suddenly made a public appearance, and by openly accepting their red armband, Mao Tse-tung assumed their leadership, in a highly symbolic way.

The purge, after 1966, affected or threatened many persons in the Party and the government; but Chou En-lai retained control of the government and managed to preserve, though not without difficulty, the majority of the members of his team (Li Fu-chun, Li Hsien-nien, Chen Yi, Tan Chen-lin, Chen Yun and Hsien Fu-shih). On the other hand, the circle tightened increasingly round a few leaders in the ruling apparatus, and in particular round the man known as the "Chinese Khrushchev", the President of the Republic, Liu Shao-ch'i.

It was in November 1966, when it seemed that the "revolutionaries" and the Red Guards in fact wanted not only to raise Mao Tse-tung to the supreme power but also to name Lin Piao as his successor, that the crisis broke out in its full force.

But Liu Shao-ch'i declined to bow before the storm. He refused not only any public confession of the "errors" imputed to him, but even to recognise the majority of these "errors". Cut off in his palace in Peking, from which he could not even reply to the attacks on him, he waited . . .

His supporters, however, were still strong. Everywhere now, the "apparatuses" and "structures", shaken by the "contestation" of the Red Guards, closed their ranks. This consolidation and hardening process was further speeded up after 23 November when the Red Guards began their attacks, in particular against Liu Shao-ch'i. The latter emerged unmistakably as the leader of those who did not feel that the "great proletarian cultural revolution", especially led in this way, was a necessity. Because they had tried to launch the masses against the Party, Mao and more especially Lin Piao had stirred up the cadres against them, and had at any rate prompted some of them to join forces with Liu Shao-ch'i. To dispose of the latter, the "revolutionaries" now directed their attacks at the soldiers in the Liu group (Peng Te-huai, Lo Jui-ching and then Ho Lung) and against the Pan-Chinese Federation of Workers' Unions, one of the bastions of Liu's influence (late December 1966).

The counter-attack by Liu's supporters and Lin Piao's enemies and more generally by those whom the Red Guards exasperated, was an extremely violent one, especially in Northern and Eastern China. In Shanghai in January 1967, the "revolutionaries" were only saved by the courageous intervention of Left-wing workers' organisations in response to a special appeal from the "proletarian headquarters". But elsewhere the situation became so serious for the Red Guards that, on 21 January 1967, Mao Tse-tung had to give the Army the order to shed its neutrality and to intervene actively on behalf of the "Left-wing revolutionaries".

Yet the Army, like the government, posed its conditions. First of all, by request of the latter, Mao was obliged to recall that it was not enough to "make revolution" but that it was also necessary "to stimulate production" and to rehabilitate, through his wife Chiang-Ch'ing, six persons in Chou's group who had been vilified by the Red Guards. Afterwards the Army saw to it that the cultural revolution within its ranks was carried out under the leadership of a special commission free from Lin Piao's control, and that the authority of the military leaders, whatever their opinions, would not be challenged by the "contestants". Finally, Tao Chou, the Left-wing extremist (*ultra-Leftist*), whom Lin Piao had imposed as the head of the Party's Propaganda Department, was removed from office.

While this reaction by the "moderates" and "realists" forced Lin Piao into temporary retreat, Mao Tse-tung, faced with chaos the unleashing of which he had to some extent encouraged, tried to establish a basis for new unity. First of all, he set the conflict in the widest possible context: "Apart from deserts," he said, "wherever men live, you can always point out a Left, Centre and Right. In ten thousand years it will be the same (9)." On 13 January 1967, he launched an appeal for the creation of a "Grand Alliance" of revolutionaries, and then of a "triple Union" of the revolutionary masses, the Army and the ruling cadres. It was immediately obvious that the Red Guards, after this appeal, were no longer to be regarded as an autonomous force, but had to be integrated with the revolutionary masses. The brake imposed on the "cultural revolution" by the moderates was such that in March 1967, the government

(Council of State) seemed to have recovered all the functions of administration, economy and public order, Mao Tse-tung retaining, amid general respect and exaggerated praise, responsibility only for the "outline" and the theoretical and ideological aspects of the revolution.

A counter-offensive by Lin Piao and the extreme Left (April to August 1967), which had repercussions as far away as Hong Kong (where Tao Chou had friends), met with such resistance from the authorities in the Army, the Party and the administration in most of the provinces that the cultural revolution was practically halted. Everywhere, in the administration as well as in industry, the cadres refused to co-operate with the contestants, dubbed as "revolutionaries". The Army had already intervened in the countryside to calm the "rebels" and to make sure that the work of the spring on which the future crops depended, was well in hand. From then on, it intervened in the towns and in the industrial establishments to restore normal conditions and to encourage the cadres to resume their activities. Strikes were forbidden.

Thus Lin Piao was unable to alter fate and destroy the obstacles which lay between himself and power. Liu-Shao-ch'i and the powerful network of connections and alliances which he had established throughout China resisted the thrusts of the extreme Left and the waves of propaganda which Tao Chou's successor, Wang Li, continued to hurl against them. Even Mao's appeals for unity were no longer heeded and the revolutionary committees which he wished to see formed, on the "Triple Union" basis, in the provinces and municipalities, did not materialise. By the end of July 1967, resistance by Wu Han's provincial leaders convinced Mao and Lin Piao that they would have to come to terms with them if they did not wish to plunge China into a new civil war. As far as the Army was concerned, it would have no further truck with the Red Guards in the majority of the provinces. Its provincial leaders (who no doubt had allies in Peking) indicated on what conditions they would agree to rally to Mao and the "new line".

For some years Mao Tse-tung had been preparing an orderly

retreat. He had celebrated the tenth anniversary of his speech on "The Correct Handling of Contradictions Among the People" and had stressed that today there was no question of "non-antagonistic contradictions". The present wave of the cultural revolution was depicted as a grand "rectification" similar, though on a far broader scale, to that which had been carried out in Yenan in 1942 – hence the very widespread circulation of the texts of that period. He pointed out that :

The present great cultural revolution is only the first; there will inevitably be many more in the future. The issue of who will win in the revolution can only be settled over a long historical period. If things are not properly handled, it is possible for a capitalist restoration to take place at any time. It should not be thought by any Party member or any one of the people in our country that everything will be all right after one or two great cultural revolutions, or even three or four. We must be very much on the alert and never lose vigilance (10).

The object of the cultural revolution had been defined by the Central Committee's 8 August 1966 sixteen point resolution, but its charter and its deeper significance were to be found in the "Introductions to Talks at the Yenan Forum on Literature and Art" (2 and 23 May 1942), a long text by Mao Tse-tung, published and circularized again in 1966 *and* in 1967 (11) on the occasion of its 25th anniversary which was celebrated in style. The most significant passages from this key text are these :

In the world today all culture, literature and art belong to definite classes and are geared to definite political lines. There is in fact no such thing as art for art's sake, art that stands above class or art that is detached from or independent of politics. Proletarian literature and art are part of the whole proletarian revolutionary cause; they are, as Lenin said, "cogs and wheels" in the whole revolutionary machine. . . .
Our aim is to ensure that revolutionary literature and art follow the correct path of development and provide better help to other revolutionary work in facilitating the overthrow of our national enemy and the accomplishment of the task of national liberation.

In our struggle for the liberation of the Chinese people there are various fronts, among which there are the fronts of the pen and of the gun, the cultural and the military fronts. To defeat the enemy we must rely primarily on the army with guns. But this army alone is not enough; we must also have a cultural army, which is absolutely indispensable for uniting our own ranks and defeating the enemy. . . .

The purpose of our meeting today is precisely to ensure that literature and art fit well into the whole revolutionary machine as a component part, that they operate as powerful weapons for uniting and educating the people and for attacking and destroying the enemy, and that they help the people fight the emeny with one heart and one mind. What are the problems that must be solved to achieve this objective? I think they are the problems of the class stand of the writers and artists, their attitude, their audience, their work and their study. . . .

Since the audience for our literature and art consists of workers, peasants and soldiers and of their cadres, the problem arises of understanding them and knowing them well. . . . Our writers and artists have their literary and art work to do, but their primary task is to understand people and know them well. . . . Since many writers and artists stand aloof from the masses and lead empty lives, naturally they are unfamiliar with the language of the people. Accordingly their works are not only insipid in language but often contain nondescript expressions of their own coining which run counter to popular usage. Many comrades like to talk about "a mass style". But what does it really mean? It means that the thoughts and feelings of our writers and artists should be fused with those of the masses of workers, peasants and soldiers. To achieve this fusion, they should conscientiously learn the language of the masses. How can you talk of literary and artistic creation if you find the very language of the masses largely incomprehensible? . . . If you want the masses to understand you, if you want to be one with the masses, you must make up your mind to undergo a long and even painful process of tempering. . . .What I mean by tempering is a change of feelings, a change from one class to another. If our writers and artists who come from the intelligentsia want their works to be well received by the masses, they must change and remould their thinking and their feelings. Without such a change, without such remoulding, they can do nothing well and will be misfits. . . .

At present, however, some comrades are lacking in the basic concepts of Marxism. For instance, it is a basic Marxist concept that being determines consciousness, that the objective realities of class struggle and national struggle determine our thoughts and feelings. But some of our comrades turn this upside down and maintain that everything ought to start from "love". Now as for love, in a class society there can be only class love; but these comrades are seeking a love transcending classes, love in the abstract and also freedom in the abstract, truth in the abstract, human nature in the abstract, etc. This shows that they have been very deeply influenced by the bourgeoisie. They should thoroughly rid themselves of this influence and modestly study Marxism-Leninism. It is right for writers and artists to study literary and artistic creation, but the science of Marxism-Leninism must be studied by all revolutionaries, writers and artists not excepted. Writers and artists should study society, that is to say, should study the various classes in society, their mutual relations and respective conditions, their physionomy and their psychology. Only when we grasp all this clearly can we have a literature and art that is rich in content and correct in orientation.

These were the essentials of the 2 May 1942 introductory speech, but in his concluding speech on 23 May 1942, Mao added some further revealing comments :

What then is the crux of the matter? In my opinion, it consists fundamentally of the problems of working for the masses and knowing how to work for the masses. . . . Who, then, are the masses of the people? The broadest sections of the people, constituting more than 90 per cent of our total population, are the workers, peasants, soldiers and urban petty bourgeoisie, Therefore, our literature and art are first for the workers, the class that leads the revolution. Secondly, they are for the peasants, the most numerous and more steadfast of our allies in the revolution. Thirdly, they are for the armed workers and peasants, namely the Eighth Route and New Fourth Armies and the other armed units of the people, which are the main forces of the revolutionary war. Fourthly, they are for the labouring masses of the urban petty bourgeoisie and for the petty-bourgeois intellectuals, both of whom are also our allies in the revolution and capable of long-term co-operation with us. These four kinds of people constitute the overwhelming majority of the Chinese nation – the broadest masses of the people.

Our literature and our art should be for the four kinds of people we have enumerated. To serve them, we must take the class stand of the proletariat and not that of the petty bourgeoisie. Today, writers who cling to an individualist, petty-bourgeois stand cannot truly serve the masses of revolutionary workers, peasants and soldiers. Their interest is mainly focussed on the small number of petty-bourgeois intellectuals. . . .

Our literary and art workers must accomplish this task and shift their stand; they must gradually move their feet over to the side of the workers, peasants and soldiers, to the side of the proletariat, through the process of going into their very midst and into the thick of practical struggles and through the process of studying Marxism and society. Only in this way can we have a literature and art that are truly for the workers, peasants and soldiers, a truly proletarian literature and art. . . .

Since our literature and art are basically for the workers, peasants and soldiers, "popularization" means to popularize among the workers, peasants and soldiers, and "raising standards" means to advance from their present level. What should we popularize among them? . . . We must popularize only what is needed and can be readily accepted by the workers, peasants and soldiers themselves. Consequently, prior to the task of educating the workers, peasants and soldiers, there is the task of learning from them.

This is even more true of raising standards. There must be a basis from which to raise. Take a bucket of water, for instance; where is it to be raised from if not from the ground? From mid-air? From what basis, then, are literature and art to be raised? From the basis of what feudal classes? From the basis of the bourgeoisie? From the basis of the petty-bourgeois intellectuals? No, not from any of these; only from the basis of the masses of workers, peasants and soldiers. . . . Only by starting from the workers, peasants and soldiers can we have a correct under-standing of popularization and of the raising of standards and find the proper relationship between the two.

In the last analysis, what is the source of all literature and art? Works of literature and art, as ideological forms, are pro-ducts of the reflection in the human brain of the life of a given society. Revolutionary literature and art are the products of the reflection of the life of the people in the brains of revolu-tionary writers and artists. The life of the people is always a mine of the raw materials for literature and art, materials in their natural form, materials that are crude, but most vital, rich and fundamental; they make all literature and art seem pallid by comparison; they provide literature and art with an inexhaustible source, their only source. They are the only source, for there can be no other. Some may ask, is there not another source in books, in the literature and art of ancient times and of foreign countries? In fact, the literary and artistic works of the past are not a source but a stream; they were created by our predecessors and the foreigners out of the literary and artistic raw materials they found in the life of the people of their time and place. We must take over all the fine things in our literary and artistic heritage, critically assimilate whatever is beneficial, and use them as examples when we create works out of the literary and artistic raw materials in the life of the people of our own time and place. It makes a difference whether or not we have such examples, the difference between crudeness and refinement, between roughness and polish, between a low and high level, and between slower and faster work. Therefore we must on no account reject the legacies of the ancients and the foreigners or refuse to learn from them, even though they are the works of the feudal or bourgeois classes. But taking over legacies and using them as examples must never replace our own creative work; nothing can do that. Uncritical transplantation or copying from the ancients and the foreigners is the most sterile and harmful dogmatism in literature and art. China's revolutionary writers and artists, writers and artists of promise, must go among the masses; they must for a long period of time unreservedly and whole-heartedly go among the masses of workers, peasants and soldiers, go into the heat of the struggle, go to the only source, the broadest and richest source, in order to observe, experience, study and analyse all the different kinds of people, all the classes, all the masses, all the vivid patterns of life and struggle, all the raw materials of literature and art. Only then can they proceed to creative work . . .

Since integration into the new epoch of the masses is essential, it is necessary thoroughly to solve the problem of the relationship between the individual and the masses. This couplet from a poem by Lu Hsun should be our motto :

Fierce-browed, I coolly defy a thousand pointing fingers,
Head-bowed, like a willing ox I serve the children.

The "thousand pointing fingers" are our enemies, and we will never yield to them, no matter how ferocious. The "children" here symbolize the proletariat and the masses. All Communists, all revolutionaries, all revolutionary literary and art workers should learn from the example of Lu Hsun and be "oxen" for the proletariat and the masses, bending their backs to the task until their dying day. Intellectuals who want to integrate themselves with the masses, who want to serve the masses, must go through a process in which they and the masses come to know each other well. This process may, and certainly will, involve much pain and friction, but if you have the determination, you will be able to fulfil these requirements (12). . . .

Reverting to the present, Mao Tse-tung said :

The great proletarian cultural revolution in progress is a great revolution which affects man in the deepest part of him and has been invoked to solve the problem of each one's world conception (13).

The aim of the cultural revolution was therefore to revolutionize and remould the Chinese people, a titanic undertaking which was both a struggle against human nature and a race against time, because results had to be obtained *before* the new generations, those who had not experienced the "warlords" or the civil war or the Japanese invasion, were deterred by the huge task which remained to be completed by some "Khrushchevite" form of evolution. Although Mao briefly called on all

Chinese to "combat egoism and refute revisionism", it is however hard to make out from the incredible verbal outpourings of
Chinese propaganda today the kind of life which it is offering
the men and women of China, in short the finality which it is
giving to socialist existence. Sacrifice, yes, of course, but for
what precisely? What will the everyday life of the individual,
family and the people, and national life in the society of the
future, the life which is being sought through cultural revolutions and waves of industrialization, be like? Who can be sure
that it will be materially different from the "goulash Communism?" The great difference is that Mao does not want the
Russians to enjoy this Communism until the last Chinese
proletarian has achieved it. A matter of timing. To anyone who
suggests: "We can now rest a little!", Mao replies: "No, we
must struggle on. Plenty and justice are things of tomorrow."
There is nothing at present to indicate that Maoist philosophy is
not basically participating in the same "spiritually under-
developed universe" as that of the Russian Communists.

While the ideological aims of the cultural revolution were to
some extent clarified, political victory by its adherents was not
thereby achieved, quite the contrary.

Having had to bring in the Army to save the "Left-wing
revolutionaries", Mao had opened its way to the installation of
provincial military governments throughout China. The latter
were not, generally speaking, easy on the "revolutionaries". It
was to solve this fundamental contradiction that Mao first devoted himself to re-establishing a harmonious relationship between the military and the population. On 1 September 1967,
he issued the directive: "Back the Army. Love the people",
which meant that the population was to support the popular
army (against trouble-makers and other revolutionaries), but
that the latter was to "love the people", that is, avoid any
repression of the kind practised by the Kuomintang. During
September, Mao carried out a vast inspection of the Northern,
Central and Eastern provinces. From this he probably concluded that only new gestures of conciliation and appeasement
would allow the restoration of unity and an escape from the

impasse into which the cultural revolution was gradually sliding.

In any case it was not until Mao had agreed to rehabilitate the cadres (the vast majority of which were good, he said), and until he had given up promoting the cultural revolution in the more sensitive military districts (Sinkiang, Tibet, etc.), restored the governing role to the working-class, and advocated the return of the Red Guards to school and the officering of the "contestants" by the Army, workers and poor peasants, that Mao Tse-tung was able to win over the provincial politico-military cliques and achieve the installation (negotiated in each case) of the revolutionary committees in each province. These compromises, needless to say, were received with great bitterness by the Red Guards and the contestant youth.

The dual character of the 1966–68 cultural revolution now emerged more clearly. At first, one faction, more aware of international dangers than the others, sensing that Mao's succession was near, attempted to seize power while there was still time, while Mao could still endorse what it was doing. Mao Tse-tung was the man who restored China's independence, unity and power, who gave her a new *raison d'être,* a new explanation of the world, a new philosophy. By invoking Mao, by raising him on a pedestal, by steeping China in his thought, in order to substitute the latter for the teachings of Confucius or Lao Tse, this faction evidently hoped to secure Mao's heritage, and make use of his prestige to ensure its dominance. Who would have dared, after all that Mao has done for China, to come out against his teaching, or go against his advice? It would seem to have been an attempt by a group to seize power by means of an ideology, which was not the first time that this had happened in Chinese history.

For anyone who has come to know Mao's thought well and to appreciate the realism with which he has tackled some of the major problems of our time, the way in which the adherents of the cultural revolution have long been applying Mao's teachings has been a source of great perplexity. What was the meaning, in the new Chinese as well as the international context, of "concentrate the attack on the main enemy", "isolate the main enemy and don't attack intermediary forces for fear of being cut off", "handle contradictions correctly among the people", "see things as a whole" and "don't hold views about foreign countries which do not square with reality"?

Wasn't it in fact a new "Leftist" opportunist line of the Li Li-san type, disguised as Maoism, which was prevailing? We know that Mao emphasized how much damage it did the Chinese revolution. In fact, didn't one faction try to out-flank Liu Shao-chi'i's clique from the Left? Although Mao's line had always basically been more "Rightist" than Liu's, the present adherents of the former were accusing the latter's of be-ing reactionary, of having taken the road of capitalism, etc., because they were concerned with seizing power and because it was easier do so by "attacking from the Left". All this was "good war". It was enough simply to know that what Liu's group was often accused of was frequently the work of the Mao group.

But at this time, in 1967–68, the "apparatuses" and the "structures" had been tougher, more resistant than the "revolu-tionaries" had anticipated. After several months of chaos and disorder, they had on the whole absorbed the shock and managed to re-establish a semblance of order. But Mao did not therefore renounce his grandiose aim, "to revolutionise man, to change his world conception", and for him the real problem remained "knowing who, Maoists or revisionists, controlled the leadership of the Party and the State", and "how to pursue the revolution under the conditions of a dictatorship of the proletariat", through "the continual rejection of what is outworn and the absorption of what is new".

Ever since the beginning of 1967, the "realists" have been assessing the situation. The whole of China is Maoist and nothing great, valuable or durable can any longer be achieved there except in the name of Chairman Mao, "within the context of Mao Tse-tung's ideas". But along with the cadres, the Army, the working-class and the revolutionary masses, a new Order, a new Harmony, a new System must be built, of which Mao will simultaneously be the flag, soul and alibi, but in which the various forces at work will all be forced into mutually acceptable compromises. "Politics command. They are the soul of everything," Mao said. Mao remains China's supreme guide, and now that a system has been installed by which the "realists" hold the controls in such a way that the extreme Left could never, for a long time to come, renew its "contestation", Lin Piao has been accepted as a probable successor and Liu Shao-ch'i sacrificed on the altar of Chinese unity. The Twelfth Plenary Session of the Central Committee resulting from the Eighth Congress (13–31 October 1968) felt that sufficient conditions were reunited for the Ninth Congress of the Chinese Communist Party to be made ready. Liu Shao-ch'i, denounced as a "renegade" and "traitor to the working-class", has been excluded once and for all from the Party and stripped of all his functions. Henceforth it is up to the Party, now being reconstituted, to forge a new legality.

A man has arteries and veins, and the circulation of his blood is operated by his heart; he breathes through his lungs, blowing out carbonic acid and taking in fresh oxygen. This is what is known as rejecting the old and absorbing the new. In the same way, a proletarian party must do away with the old and adopt the new; only in this way can it be filled with vitality. Without rejection of waste and absorption of fresh blood, the party will lack vitality (14).

With regard to world conceptions, there are basically only two schools of thought in our age, the proletarian school and the bourgeois school. There is either the proletarian conception or the bourgeois conception (15).

Mao Tse-tung has once again ranged himself alongside Youth, the Future and Growth. Swamped by innumerable expressions of his ideas, China is trying to make out what her venerated Chairman really meant to say. In any case, it is the Maoists who, all together, hold sway in Peking today. But what will they do tomorrow, when Mao "has seen God"*?

*This is the expression which Mao Tse-tung himself used in the interview which he gave to Edgar Snow on 9 January 1965, *New Republic*, 27 January 1965, when referring to his death.

Conclusion: "The Foolish Old Man and the Two Mountains"

Mao Tse-tung's life, his revolutionary career and his achievements have developed in time by successive waves and in space like concentric waves. Let us quickly look at them in perspective.

Mao's career began in practice at the time and place when Chinese nationalism, humiliated and exacerbated, was "impregnated" with Marxism. Mao Tse-tung was the intimate disciple, only slightly younger, of the two men who introduced Marxism to China, Ch'en Tu-hsiu and Li Ta-chao. The 4 May 1919 Movement was the first expression of the new epoch.

After several years of practice, training and ordeals, it was proved by Chiang Kai-shek himself that in China's concrete conditions, the power of the various feudalisms could only be shaken and later overthrown, imperialism driven out of China and China's independence restored by armed struggle. But armed struggle was adopted, it must be emphasized, because it was *first of all* necessary to escape from repression, in short, to *survive*.

The struggle began in 1927 in the Tsingkiang Mountains; this is the cradle of revolutionary experience which Mao is proffering today. This experience was later developed over six years in Kiangsi from 1928–34 where the tactics and strategy of guerilla warfare were perfected. The struggle, at first waged against the enemy within, whose many "encirclement and suppression" campaigns had to be smashed, shifted ground and extended after 1937, when it was concentrated against an invader from without, Japan and her Chinese agents. This eight year war, from 1937–45, waged against Japan and co-ordinated from the austere capital of Yenan, actually ended four years later in 1949, with the complete rout of the enemy within on the Chinese mainland and the elimination of the Western footholds.

The Tsingkiang Mountains, Kiangsi, Yenan and then Peking. . . . What began at the initial base, in the "Soviet Republic of Workers, Peasants and Soldiers", continued in the "liberated zones" and the "base areas" of the North-West and spread to the whole of China : the socialist transformation of the country. But at each stage Mao stressed the need to educate the peasants, to "revolutionize" them, to liberate them from feudal and bourgeois exploitation. To Mao, China had to be governed and industrialized, *first of all* to make life acceptable to the untold masses of peasants, who made up three-quarters of the people of China and whose revolutionary potential he had perceived in 1927.

To succeed in this very, very long drawn-out undertaking, to shun threats from outside, Mao Tse-tung's China was relying on the alliance and firm support of the Soviet Union and her Communist Party. But the U.S.S.R.'s powers of dissuasion were considerably reduced after Stalin's death, and Russia grew increasingly more concerned with the demands of her own security and economic development than the fate and the emancipation of the disinherited peoples of the world. After 1957, Peking sensed that "encirclement and suppression" campaigns of a new kind were once again looming on the horizon : Korea (1951–3), Indonesia (1957–8), Vietnam (1958–?), Laos (1958–?), Tibet (1959). . . . This time the base area which the enemy was trying to approach and encircle before "suppressing" was not merely the Tsingkiang Mountains, Kiangsi or Yenan but the whole of China. In this case, the People's Republic of China was to become the gigantic Yenan of the new world. China was now the principal "base area" for waging "protracted war" on a world scale against the enemy, who had left his North American island to invade Asia, Latin America, Africa and even Europe from all sides.

China's emphasis, after 1965, on the Yenan period, the systematic, mass publication of Maoist texts of this period indicate that an influential section of the Chinese leadership now sees the world situation from this angle: "Problems of Strategy in Guerilla War Against Japan" (Yenan, May 1938), "On Protracted War" (Yenan, May 1938), "Talks at the Yenan Forum on Literature and Art" (Yenan, May 1942) and the "three most-read articles", that is, "In Memory of Norman Bethune" (Yenan, 21 December 1939), "Serve the People" (Yenan, 8 September 1944) and "The Foolish Old Man Who Removed the Mountains" (Yenan, 11 June 1945). It is hard not to be impressed by the resurgence of the work of the "Yenan Military and Political Anti-Japanese Institute" where tens of thousands of cadres who won the Communist Party its victory on the mainland, were trained.

The Yenan spirit. . . . In Mao's great life cycle and its example to new China, Yenan is without question a key point in the understanding of the present Chinese vision of the world. There was Yenan and the powerful North-West base (Shensi-Kansu-Ningsia), but there were also secondary bases in Kwangtung, Chekiang, Hunan, Kiangsu, etc. If China today is Yenan, then Vietnam, Cuba, Tanzania, Albania and Syria must be anti-imperialist "base areas". The "bases" in the Congo, Indonesia and Ghana have fallen into the hands of the Americans, but for how long? Retaliation by the world proletariat has now been carried out on the native soil of the United States, where "Black Power" has emerged in Watts, Chicago, Detroit, etc.

Thus, according to Peking, which is now a second Yenan, the whole world since February-March 1965 has become involved in a "protracted war". In its first phase this is basically a "guerilla war", waged on a number of local scenes, according to the concrete conditions of the terrain. It is to be hoped that this struggle will not degenerate into a world conflict and that the United States will halt its thrust into Asia in time. But if *armed* conflict with the United States should break out one day, which China will probably do everything in her power to delay so far as she is concerned, it will be a conflict in which "people in arms" (people's armies of liberation) would play an essential role. Against "conventional armies", even backed by the navy, air force and "special forces", people in arms would probably be able to occupy *space,* the countryside, mountains and forests in tropical areas . . . And if the Americans, in exasperation, should one day turn on the "holy of holies", the "nerve centre" of resistance against them everywhere – Peking wants to become this nerve centre – by exploiting its atomic superiority, China, because of her nuclear arms, will at least be able to retaliate. But as Peking points out, China will never be first to use these weapons of massive destruction.

In this long "struggle for Asia, Africa and Latin America" which China believes inevitable and already in existence, to obtain "control of the countryside", the peasants and the world countryside, Mao especially recommends patience, abnegation and work. It is particularly significant that since 1966 Mao's three most often prescribed articles for regular reading and intensive study in China are those which stress such virtues. Here are the almost complete texts of these three articles :

The Foolish Old Man Who Removed the Mountains

We should fire the whole people with the conviction that China belongs not to the reactionaries but the Chinese people. There is an ancient Chinese fable called "The Foolish Old Man Who Removed the Mountains". It tells of an old man who lived in northern China long, long ago and was known as the Foolish Old Man of North Mountain. His house faced south and beyond his doorway stood the two great peaks, Taihang and Wangwu, obstructing the way. He called his sons, and hoe in hand they began to dig up these mountains with great determination. Another greybeard, known as the Wise Old Man, saw them and said derisively: "How silly of you to do this! It is quite impossible for you few to dig up these two huge mountains." The Foolish Old Man replied, "When I die, my sons will carry on; when they die, there will be my grandsons, and then their sons and grandsons, and so on to infinity. High as they are, the mountains cannot grow any higher and with every bit they dig, they will be that much lower. Why can't we clear them away?" Having refuted the Wise Old Man's wrong view, he went on digging every day, unshaken in his conviction. God was moved by this, and he sent down two angels, who carried the mountains away on their backs. Today, two big mountains lie like a dead weight on the Chinese people. One is imperialism, the other is feudalism. The Chinese Communist Party has long made up its mind to dig them up. We must persevere and work unceasingly, and we, too, will touch God's heart. Our God is none other than the masses of the Chinese people. If they stand up and dig together with us, why can't these two mountains be cleared away? (1).

The Chinese people, the masses of the people, are a kind of obsession with Mao Tse-tung. Take for instance the article "Serve the People", written on 8 September 1944 in memory of a common soldier:

Our Communist Party and the Eighth Route and New Fourth Armies led by our Party are battalions of the revolution. These battalions of ours are wholly dedicated to the liberation of the people and work entirely in the people's interests. Comrade Chang Szu-teh was in the ranks of these battalions.

All men must die, but death can vary in its significance. The ancient Chinese writer Szuma Chien said, "Though death befalls all men alike, it may be heavier than Mount Tai or lighter than a feather." To die for the people is heavier than Mount Tai, but to work for the fascists and die for the exploiters and oppressors is lighter than a feather. Comrade Chang Szu-teh died for the people, and his death is indeed heavier than Mount Tai. . . .

We hail from all corners of the country and have joined together for a common revolutionary objective. And we need

K

the vast majority of the people with us on the road to this objective. Today, we already lead base areas with a population of 91 million, but this is not enough; to liberate the whole nation more are needed. In times of difficulty we must not lose sight of our achievements, must see the bright future and must pluck up our courage. The Chinese people are suffering; it is our duty to save them and we must exert ourselves in struggle. Wherever there is a struggle there is sacrifice, and death is a common occurrence. But we have the interests of the people and the sufferings of the great majority at heart, and when we die for the people it is a worthy death. Nevertheless, we should do our best to avoid unnecessary sacrifices. Our cadres must show concern for every soldier, and all people in the revolutionary ranks must care for each other and help each other (2) . . .

Knowing how to "avoid unnecessary sacrifices" naturally concerns the soldiers themselves, but still more the cadres who lead them. But generosity and devotion are personal qualities. And it was another death which gave Mao Tse-tung the chance to extol them :

In Memory of Norman Bethune.

Comrade Norman Bethune, a member of the Communist Party of Canada, was around fifty when he was sent by the Communist Parties of Canada and the United States to China; he made light of travelling thousands of miles to help us in our War of Resistance against Japan. He arrived in Yenan in the spring of last year, went to work in the Wutai Mountains, and to our great sorrow died a martyr at his post. What kind of spirit is this that makes a foreigner selflessly adopt the cause of the Chinese people's liberation as his own? It is the spirit of internationalism, the spirit of Communism, from which every Chinese Communist must learn. Leninism teaches that the world revolution can only succeed if the proletariat of the capitalist countries supports the struggle for liberation of the colonial and semi-colonial peoples and if the proletariat of the colonies and semi-colonies supports that of the proletariat of the capitalist countries. Comrade Bethune put this Leninist line into practice. We must unite with the proletariat of the capitalist countries, with the proletariat of Japan, Britain, the United States, Germany, Italy and all other capitalist countries, for this is the only way to overthrow imperialism, to liberate our nation and people and to liberate the other nations and peoples of the world. This is our internationalism, the internationalism with which we oppose both narrow nationalism and narrow patriotism.

Comrade Bethune's spirit, his utter devotion to others without any thought of self, was shown in his great sense of responsibility in his work and his great warm-heartedness towards all comrades and the people. Every Communist must learn from him. There are not a few people who are irresponsible in their work, preferring the light and shirking the heavy, passing the burdensome tasks on to others and choosing the easy ones for themselves. At every turn they think of themselves before others. When they make some small contribution, they swell with pride and brag about it for fear that others will not know. They feel no warmth towards comrades and the people but are cold, indifferent and apathetic. In truth such people are not Communists, or at least cannot be counted as devoted Communists. No one who returned from the front failed to express admiration for Bethune whenever his name was mentioned, and none remained unmoved by his spirit. In the Shansi-Chahar-Hopei border area, no soldier or civilian was unmoved who had been treated by Dr. Bethune or had seen how he worked. Every Communist must learn this true communist spirit from Comrade Bethune.

Comrade Bethune was a doctor, the art of healing was his profession and he was constantly perfecting his skill, which stood very high in the Eighth Route Army's medical service. His example is an excellent lesson for those people who wish to change their work the moment they see something different and for those who despise technical work as of no consequence or as promising no future.

Comrade Bethune and I met only once. Afterwards he wrote me many letters. But I was busy and I wrote him only one letter and do not even know if he ever received it. I am deeply grieved over his death. Now we are all commemorating him, which shows how profoundly his spirit inspires everyone. We must all learn the spirit of absolute selflessness from him. With this spirit everyone can be very useful to the people. A man's ability may be great or small, but if he has this spirit, he is already noble-minded and above vulgar interests, a man who is of value to the people (4).

There is barely anything to be added to this funeral oration in which Mao proffered the example of a North American Communist to the Chinese Communists. But at the end of this attempt to present, as objectively as possible, what in Mao's thought has real importance for the non-Chinese world today, the reader is probably expecting the author to express, in a few words, his own "view", his own "conclusion" about the great Chinese leader. Even if the author feels that this is rash, even impudent, can he evade the issue, remain "neutral"?

Whatever one's opinion of Mao Tse-tung, his character, his ideological choice and his methods, if one is familiar with his thought and his works, and if one is honest, it seems that one can draw only a single general conclusion: that he is a man who has given his entire life to China and the restoration of her dignity and independence, to the Chinese people, to the peasants of China and especially to the poorest of them.

What Mao has said and done over half a century is all the more important because one man in five in the world today is Chinese and there are more Chinese peasants than there are Whites in America and Western Europe. What China says is important to us and will be more and more so. By trying to take even the intellectual leadership of the "proletarian peoples" of Asia, Africa and Latin America, China will in fact be setting the world problems of extreme and mounting gravity.

In his analysis of the *concrete* conditions in which the Chinese people's struggle for independence, democracy and the full use of their productive forces has developed, in the masterly way in which he has, throughout the struggle, been able to check deviations to Left and Right, Mao Tse-tung has without doubt made a basic contribution not only to Marxism-Leninism but also to mankind's political and military experience. He explains better than Marx, better than Lenin, the basic conflicts of the second half of the 20th century.

However the fact remains that on many points, Mao has

merely formulated, in a new and sometimes "Marxistic" way, what eminent men in Asia, the Near East and Europe had said before him – sometimes centuries or even hundreds of centuries earlier. Thus Mao and his work must be seen in the long chain of those who throughout history have communicated their thoughts on the political and military arts. Mao's contribution is relative, and still more so because, in spite of its great diversity, it has not in practice touched on the profoundest questions which man, even proletarian man, asks, confronted with himself and the universe. In such circumstances, one could not claim to substitute it for what the Chinese people, its philosophers and thinkers have been discovering in this field for three thousand years or more, still less try and elevate "Mao Tse-tung's thought" as the intellectual sun of the contemporary world.

Mao Tse-tung's contribution is relative too because it is both Marxist and Chinese. Mao was able, in a remarkable way, to apply what he called "the universal truth of Marxism-Leninism" to the Chinese reality. But although the demands of a long, harsh struggle evidently did not leave him time to discover the "relativity" of Marxism as an explanation of the world, with its inability to grasp certain of its dimensions, the basic fact remains that Mao Tse-tung's experience is primarily, principally and deeply *Chinese*. Mao has only left China three times, and only to go to Moscow. What does he really know about European and American workers, or about Indian, Arab, African and Andean peasants? In 1928, in his article "Why Is It That Red Political Power Can Exist in China?", he was at great pains to point out that the conditions in which China's "armed struggle" developed were peculiar to her. And it was not without good reason that in his "Problems of Strategy in China's Revolutionary War" (5), Mao recalled the words of Lenin who, when criticizing Bela Kun, said : "He gives up the most essential thing in Marxism, *the concrete analysis of concrete conditions.*" North Koreans, Vietnamese, Africans and Cubans have already partly learnt the lesson that derives from this idea, while others realize that "Maoism" is a great moment in Chinese thought, just as Marxism is *one* of the currents, *one* of the moments in human thought.

From now on, Mao Tse-tung's works will take their place – one of first importance – among those which are required reading for anyone who wants to understand the "contradictions" of our age, and especially the great conflict which, in a now undivided world, is pitting rich against poor, "bloated towns against famished countryside", satisfied individuals against angry multitudes. No one can understand the policy and rôle of the People's Republic of China if he has not at least "dipped into Mao". Now the peoples of Europe today stand in need of clear-sightedness and world vision. To obey their traditions they must, like everyone else, and as Mao advised the Chinese intellectuals, "learn to think for themselves", learn to see China not through others' glasses or propaganda, but through their own eyes.

Bibliographical notes

CHAPTER 1

(1) For this discussion, see especially Stuart Schram, *The Political Thought of Mao Tse-tung*, Pall Mall Press, London, 1963.
(2) ibid., pp. 3-7 and Lucien Bianco, *Les origines de la révolution chinoise*, Gallimard, Paris, 1967, chap. II.
(3) Excellent photo of the village of Shaoshan in the 1968 calendar from *Ghozi, Shudian*, Peking.
(4) Edgar Snow, *Red Star Over China*, Gollancz, London, 1937, pp. 128-129.
(5) ibid., pp. 130-131.
(6) ibid., pp. 127-128.
(7) ibid., pp. 134-135.
(8) ibid., pp. 141-143.
(9) Schram, *The Political Thought of Mao Tse-tung*, pp. 8-9, 17.
(10) Snow, *Red Star Over China*, pp. 151-152.
(11) Schram stresses this aspect (cf. *The Political Thought of Mao Tse-tung*, pp. 11-14).
(12) Extracted from an article published in April 1917 in *Hsin Ch'ing-nien* entitled "A Study in Physical Education".

Translation in Schram, *The Political Thought of Mao Tse-tung,* pp. 98-99.

(13) Schram, *The Political Thought of Mao Tse-tung,* p. 13.

(14) Snow, *Red Star Over China,* p. 146.

(15) Schram, *The Political Thought of Mao Tse-tung,* who quotes Maurice Meisner, *Li Ta-chao and the Origins of Chinese Marxism,* Harvard University Press, 1966.

(16) Extracted from an article in Mao's review *Hsiang-chiang P'ing-lun,* Nos. 2, 3 and 4 (July and August 1919). Translation in Schram, *The Political Thought of Mao Tse-tung,* pp. 170-171, 105-106.

(17) Snow, *Red Star Over China,* p. 151.

(18) Schram, *Mao Tse-tung,* Penguin, London, 1966, p. 62.

(19) Schram, *The Political Thought of Mao Tse-tung,* p. 20.

(20) Hu Chiao-mu, *Thirty Years of the Communist Party of China,* Foreign Languages Press, Peking, 1951, pp. 5-6.

(21) Schram, *Mao Tse-tung,* Penguin, London, 1966, p. 69.

CHAPTER 2

(1) Hsin-hai, Chiang Kai-shek, *Asia's Man of Destiny,* Double-day, Doran and Co., Inc., New York, 1944, pp. 123-125.

(2) Extracted from the article "The Peking *Coup d'Etat* and the Merchants", published in *Hsiang-tao,* Nos. 31-32 (11 July 1923), pp. 233-234. Translation in Schram, *The Political Thought of Mao Tse-tung,* pp. 140-142.

(3) Extracted from the article "The Cigarette Tax" published in *Hsiang-tao,* No. 38 (29 August 1923), p. 288. Translation in Schram, *The Political Thought of Mao Tse-tung,* p. 143.

(4) From *Chung-kuo Kuomintang ti-erh-tz'u ch'üan-kuo tai-piao ta-hui hui-i chi-lu,* April 1926, published by the Central Executive Committee of the Kuomintang, p. 136. Translation in Schram, *Mao Tse-tung,* Penguin, 1966, pp. 85-86.

(5) Analysis of the Classes in Chinese Society, *Selected Works,* Vol. I, pp. 13-19.

(6) From *Chung-kuo Nung-min,* No. 5, 1926. Translation in Schram, *Mao Tse-tung,* p. 88.
(7) From *Chiang Chieh-shih Ch'üan-shu (The Complete Works of Chiang Kai-shek)* (n.p., 1927). Translation in Schram, *Mao Tse-tung,* pp. 92-93.

CHAPTER 3

(1) "Report on an Investigation of the Peasant Movement in Hunan", *Selected Works,* Vol. I, pp. 23-24, passim.
(2) ibid., p. 56.
(3) "On Correcting Mistaken Ideas in the Party", *Selected Works,* Vol. I, p. 115, note 1.

CHAPTER 4

(1) "The Struggle in the Tsingkiang Mountains", *Selected Works,* Vol. I, p. 74.
(2) "Why is it that Red Political Power Can Exist in China?", *Selected Works,* Vol. I, p. 64.
(3) ibid., pp. 65-67.
(4) ibid., p. 69.
(5) "The Struggle in the Tsingkiang Mountains", *Selected Works,* Vol. I, p. 73.
(6) ibid., p. 79.
(7) ibid., pp. 79-87, passim.
(8) ibid., pp. 90-92.
(9) "On Correcting Mistaken Ideas in the Party", *Selected Works,* Vol. I, p. 106.
(10) "The Struggle in the Tsingkiang Mountains", *Selected Works,* Vol. I, pp. 97-98.
(11) ibid., pp. 98-99.
(12) "A Single Spark Can Start a Prairie Fire", *Selected Works,* Vol. I, pp. 117-118.
(13) ibid., pp. 118-120.
(14) ibid., pp. 121-124.
(15) Schram, *Mao Tse-tung,* pp. 141, 148-149.

(16) "Problems of Strategy in China's Revolutionary War", *Selected Works,* Vol. I, p. 214.
(17) Snow, *Red Star Over China,* p. 180.

CHAPTER 5

(1) "Problems of Strategy in China's Revolutionary War", *Selected Works,* Vol. I, p. 213.
(2) ibid., p. 187.
(3) ibid., pp. 189-190.
(4) ibid., p. 185.
(5) ibid., pp. 200-205.
(6) ibid., pp. 210-215.
(7) ibid., pp. 216-218.
(8) ibid., pp. 221-223.
(9) ibid., pp. 223-224.
(10) ibid., p. 231.
(11) ibid., pp. 232-237.
(12) ibid., pp. 238-239.
(13) ibid., pp. 239-242.
(14) ibid., pp. 244-246.
(15) ibid., pp. 248-249.
(16) "Pay Attention to Economic Work", *Selected Works,* Vol. I, pp. 129-134.
(17) "On Economic Policy", *Selected Works,* Vol. I, pp. 142-145.
(18) "Be Concerned with the Well-being of the Masses, Pay Attention to Methods of Work", *Selected Works,* Vol. I, pp. 147-151.
(19) "Problems of Strategy in China's Revolutionary War", *Selected Works,* Vol. I, pp. 192-193.

CHAPTER 6

(1) See : *Peking Review,* 5 August 1966, No. 32.
(2) These two essays were published (along with two more) in a separate booklet : *Four Philosophical Essays,* Foreign Languages Press, Peking, 1966.
(3) "On Practice", *Selected Works,* Vol. I, pp. 295-299.

(4) ibid., pp. 299-301.

(5) ibid., pp. 301-302.

(6) ibid., p. 303.

(7) Lenin, "Conspectus of Hegel's Lectures on the History of Philosophy", *Collected Works,* Russ. ed., Moscow, 1958, Vol. XXXVIII, p. 249.

(8) "On Contradiction", *Selected Works,* Vol. I, p. 311.

(9) ibid., pp. 313-315.

(10) See Lenin, "Communism" (12 June 1920), in which the author criticizes Bela Kun, *Collected Works,* Russ. ed., Moscow, 1950, Vol. XXXI, p. 143.

(11) "On Contradiction", *Selected Works,* Vol. I, pp. 316-326.

(12) ibid., pp. 327-337.

(13) Lenin, "Conspectus of Hegel's *The Science of Logic*", *Collected Works,* Russ. ed., Moscow, 1958, Vol. XXXVIII pp. 97-98.

(14) Lenin, "On the Question of Dialectics", *Collected Works,* Russ. ed., Moscow, 1958, Vol. XXXVIII, p. 358.

(15) "On Contradiction", *Selected Works,* Vol. I, pp. 337-345.

(16) ibid., p. 346.

(17) Lenin, "What Is To Be Done?", *Collected Works,* Eng. ed., F.L.P.H., Moscow, 1961, Vol. V, p. 369.

(18) Lenin, *Materialism and Empiric-Criticism,* Eng. ed., F.L.P.H., Moscow, 1952, p. 141.

(19) Stalin, "The Foundations of Criticism", *Problems of Leninism,* Eng. ed., F.L.P.H., Moscow, 1954, p. 31.

(20) "On Practice", *Selected Works,* Vol. I, pp. 304-308.

(21) "Whence Do Correct Ideas Come From?", *Four Essays on Philosophy,* F.L.P., Peking, 1966, pp. 134-135.

(22) "On Practice", *Selected Works,* Vol. I, p. 308.

CHAPTER 7

(1) "On Protracted War", *Selected Works,* Vol. II, p. 128.

(2) ibid., pp. 133-134.

(3) ibid., p. 130.

(4) ibid., p. 145.

(5) ibid., p. 136.
(6) ibid., p. 137.
(7) ibid., p. 138.
(8) ibid., p. 139.
(9) ibid., p. 140.
(10) ibid., p. 172.
(11) ibid., p. 173.
(12) ibid., pp. 174-175.
(13) ibid., p. 141.
(14) "On New Democracy", *Selected Works,* Vol. II, p. 342.
(15) "The Chinese Revolution and the Chinese Communist Party", *Selected Works,* Vol. II, pp. 315-318.
(16) ibid., p. 324.
(17) ibid., pp. 324-325.
(18) ibid., p. 325.
(19) ibid., p. 329.
(20) ibid., pp. 326-327.
(21) ibid., p. 327.
(22) ibid., pp. 330-331.
(23) "On New Democracy", *Selected Works,* Vol. II, p. 350.
(24) ibid., pp. 357-358.
(25) ibid., p. 365.
(26) ibid., pp. 356, 369.
(27) ibid., pp. 366-367.
(28) ibid., p. 369.
(29) ibid., pp. 380-382.

CHAPTER 8

(1) "The Situation and Our Policy after the Victory in the War of Resistance Against Japan", *Selected Works,* Vol. IV, pp. 13-14.
(2) ibid., p. 15.
(3) ibid., pp. 18-19.
(4) ibid., pp. 19-20.

(5) "On the People's Democratic Dictatorship", *Selected Works,* Vol. IV, pp. 417-418.

(6) ibid., pp. 418-419.

(7) ibid., p. 419.

(8) ibid., pp. 420-422.

(9) ibid., pp. 422-423.

(10) cf. official statement by the Fourth Plenary Session of the Seventh Central Committee of the Communist Party, 6-10 February 1954.

(11) "On the Correct Handling of Contradictions Among the People", *Selected Readings,* pp. 350-352.

(12) ibid., pp. 353-354.

(13) ibid., p. 355.

(14) ibid., pp. 355-356.

(15) ibid., pp. 357, 358-359.

(16) ibid., pp. 360-361.

(17) ibid., pp. 374-376.

(18) ibid., pp. 376-377.

(19) ibid., p. 377.

(20) ibid., pp. 379-380.

(21) ibid., p. 379.

CHAPTER 9

(1) "Address to the Preparatory Committee of the New Political Consultative Conference", *Selected Works,* Vol. IV, p. 408.

(2) ibid., pp. 407-408.

(3) "On the People's Democratic Dictatorship", *Selected Works,* Vol. IV, p. 420.

(4) Extracted from accounts in the Chinese press in 1960 and also from the article "The Peking *Coup d'Etat* and the Merchants", published in *Hsiang-tao,* Nos. 31-32 (11 July 1923), pp. 233-234. Translation in Schram, *The Political Thought of Mao Tse-tung,* pp. 262, 142.

(5) Letter to Comrade Browder. Extracted from *Mao Tse-tung Lun-wen Chi,* Shanghai, 1937, pp. 156-157. Translation in Schram, *The Political Thought of Mao Tse-tung,* p. 291.

(6) Extracted from Mao's preface to Eng. ed. of "On Protracted War" dated 20 January 1939. Translation in Schram, *The Political Thought of Mao Tse-tung,* p. 270.

(7) Extracted from a lecture to the Party cadres in Yenan, 14 September 1939, reported in *Chieh-fang,* No. 85 (30 September 1939), pp. 1-6. Translation in Schram, *The Political Thought of Mao Tse-tung,* p. 275.

(8) "On a Statement by Chiang Kai-shek's Spokesman", *Selected Works,* Vol. IV, p. 44.

(9) such as Schram, *The Political Thought of Mao Tse-tung,* p. 276. The Chinese authenticate this text as Mao's.

(10) Telegram to Comrade William Z. Foster, *Selected Works,* Vol. III, p. 337.

(11) "On Peace Negotiations with the Kuomintang", *Selected Works,* Vol. IV, p. 48.

(12) "On the Chungking Negotiations", *Selected Works,* Vol. IV, p. 55.

(13) "The Situation and Our Policy After the Victory in the War of Resistance Against Japan", *Selected Works,* Vol. IV, pp. 20-21.

(14) Talks with the American Correspondent Anna Louise Strong, *Selected Works,* Vol. IV, p. 97.

(15) "The Truth About U.S. 'Meditation' and the Future of the Civil War in China", *Selected Works,* Vol. IV, p. 109.

(16) "A Three Months' Summary", *Selected Works,* Vol. IV, p. 117.

(17) "The Chiang Kai-shek Government is Besieged by the Whole People", *Selected Works,* Vol. IV, p. 138.

(18) "Manifesto of the Chinese People's Liberation Army", *Selected Works,* Vol. IV, p. 149.

(19) "Greet the New High Tide of the Chinese Revolution", *Selected Works,* Vol. IV, p. 120.

(20) "The Present Situation and Our Tasks", *Selected Works,* Vol. IV, pp. 158-159.

(21) ibid., p. 162.

(22) "Farewell, Leighton Stuart!", *Selected Works,* Vol. IV, p. 433.

(23) ibid., p. 434.

(24) ibid., p. 436-437.

(25) "On the People's Democratic Dictatorship", *Selected Works,* Vol. IV, p. 414.

(26) "Farewell, Leighton Stuart!", *Selected Works,* Vol. IV, pp. 433-434.

(27) "Cast Away Illusions, Prepare for Struggle", *Selected Works,* Vol. IV, p. 426.

(28) " 'Friendship' or Aggression?", *Selected Works,* Vol. IV, pp. 447-449.

(29) "Why it is Necessary to Discuss the White Paper", *Selected Works,* Vol. IV, pp. 442-443.

(30) "Cast Away Illusions, Prepare for Struggle", *Selected Works,* Vol. IV, p. 430.

(31) "Farewell, Leighton Stuart!", *Selected Works,* Vol. IV, pp. 437-438.

(32) "Cast Away Illusions, Prepare for Struggle", *Selected Works,* Vol. IV, pp. 427, 429-430.

(33) "Farewell, Leighton Stuart!", *Selected Works,* Vol. IV, p. 435.

(34) "Cast Away Illusions, Prepare for Struggle", *Selected Works,* Vol. IV, p. 430.

(35) "Farewell, Leighton Stuart!", *Selected Works,* Vol. IV, pp. 438-439.

(36) "Why it is Necessary to Discuss the White Paper", *Selected Works,* Vol. IV, p. 445.

(37) ibid., p. 444.

(38) ibid., pp. 443-444.

CHAPTER 10

(1) *On People's Democratic Dictatorship,* F.L.P., Peking, 1950, pp. 39-45.

(2) "Address to the Preparatory Committee of the New Political Consultative Conference", *Selected Works,* Vol. IV, p. 407.

(3) *Comrade Mao Tse-tung on "Imperialism and all Reactionaries are Paper Tigers"*, F.L.P., Peking, 1958, p. 29.

(4) cf. Philippe Devillers, "L'U.R.S.S., la Chine et les origines de la guerre de Corée", *revue Française de Science Politique,* December 1964, pp. 1179-1194.

(5) cf. Philippe Devillers, "Les Prémices du Conflit sino-soviétique", *Trois Continents,* Paris, 1967, No. 2, pp. 70-79.

(6) Published as a booklet under the same title in Peking, 1951, F.L.P., 35 pages.

(7) *Quotations from Mao Tse-tung,* Peking, 1966, pp. 65-66.

(8) "On the Correct Handling of Contradictions Among the People", *Selected Readings,* pp. 382-383, 386.

(9) *Comrade Mao Tse-tung on "Imperialism etc.,"* pp. 26-27.

(10) ibid., pp. 25-26.

(11) ibid., p. 26.

(12) ibid., pp. 24-25.

(13) Speech at the Moscow Meeting of Communist and Workers' Parties (18 November 1957), quoted in "Statement by the Spokesman of the Chinese Government", *Quotations from Mao Tse-tung,* pp. 66-67.

(14) "Problems of Strategy in China's Revolutionary War", *Selected Works,* Vol. I, p. 180.

(15) "On Protracted War", *Selected Works,* Vol. II, pp. 152-153, 150; "On Contradiction", *Selected Works,* Vol. I, p. 344.

(16) "Problems of Strategy in China's Revolutionary War", *Selected Works,* Vol. I, p. 182; "Problems of War and Strategy", *Selected Works,* Vol. II, p. 225.

(17) Talk with the American Correspondent Anna Louise Strong, *Selected Works,* Vol. IV, pp. 99-100.

(18) ibid., pp. 100-101.

(19) *Comrade Mao Tse-tung on "Imperialism etc.,"* p. 30.

(20) ibid., p. 30.

(21) "The Present Situation and our Tasks", *Selected Works,* Vol. IV, p. 162.

(22) *Peking Review,* 16 June 1967, No. 25.

(23) "Problems of War and Strategy", *Selected Works,* Vol. II, pp. 219, 223-224.

(24) Introducing *The Communist,* No. 1 (4 October 1939), *Selected Works,* Vol. II, pp. 291-292.

(25) Extract from a letter to the Party cadres in Yenan, 14 September 1939, reported in *Chieh-fang,* No. 85 (30 September 1939), pp. 1-6. Translation in Schram, *The Political Thought of Mao Tse-tung,* p. 272.

(26) "A Three Months' Summary", *Selected Works,* Vol. IV, p. 117.

(27) "The Present Situation and our Tasks", *Selected Works,* Vol. IV, pp. 172-173.

(28) *Comrade Mao Tse-tung on "Imperialism etc.",* p. 5.

(29) "Some Points in Appraisal of the Present International Situation", *Selected Works,* Vol. IV, pp. 87-88.

(30) "Cast Away Illusions, Prepare for Struggle", *Selected Works,* Vol. IV, p. 428.

(31) "Greet the New High Tide of the Chinese Revolution", *Selected Works,* Vol. IV, p. 125.

(32) "Interview with Three Correspondents", *Selected Works,* Vol. II, p. 272.

(33) *Chairman Mao's Important Talks with Guests from Asia, Africa and Latin America,* F.L.P., Peking, 1960, pp. 3-4.

(34) ibid., p. 4.

(35) *People of the World, Unite and Defeat the U.S. Aggressors and all their Lackeys,* F.L.P., Peking, 1964, pp. 5-7.

(36) *Statement Calling on the People of the World to Unite to Oppose Racial Discrimination by U.S. Imperialism and Support the American Negroes in their Struggle Against Racial Discrimination,* F.L.P., Peking, 1964, pp. 1-6.

CHAPTER 11

(1) "Revolutionary Forces of the World Unite, Fight Against Imperialist Aggression!", *Selected Works,* Vol. IV, pp. 283-285.

(2) Address to some Chinese Students studying in the Soviet Union on 17 November 1957.

(3) "On the Question of Stalin", *The Polemic of the General Line of the International Communist Movement,* F.L.P., Peking, 1965, p. 129.

(4) "The Origin and Development of the Differences between the Leadership of the C.P.S.U. and Ourselves", *The Polemic, etc.,* pp. 59-60.

(5) "On the Question of Stalin", *The Polemic, etc.,* p. 118.

(6) "The Origin and Development, etc.", *The Polemic, etc.,* p. 64.

(7) "On the Question of Stalin", *The Polemic, etc.,* p. 121.

(8) ibid., p. 131.

(9) "The Origin and Development, etc.", *The Polemic, etc.,* p. 77.

(10) *Peking Review,* 23 June 1967, No. 26.

(11) *Peking Review,* 18 and 25 August 1967, Nos. 34 and 35.

(12) "The Origin and Development, etc.", *The Polemic, etc.,* p. 78.

(13) Statement by the Conference of 81 Communist and Workers' Parties, Moscow, November 1960.

(14) "A Proposal Concerning the General Line of the International Communist Movement", *The Polemic, etc.,* Point 3, pp. 5-6.

(15) ibid., Point 4, p. 7.

(16) ibid., Point 6, p. 10.

(17) ibid., Point 7, p. 11.

(18) ibid., Point 7, pp. 12-13.

(19) ibid., Point 8, p. 13.

(20) ibid., Point 16, p. 32.

(21) ibid., Point 14, p. 29.

(22) ibid., Point 17, pp. 33-34.

(23) "Note on the Seven Well-Written Documents of the Chekiang Province Concerning Cadres' Participation in Physical Labour, On Khrushchev's Phoney Communism and its Historical Lessons for the World", *The Polemic, etc.,* pp. 476-477.

(24) "On Khrushchev's Phoney Communism, etc.", *The Polemic, etc.,* pp. 440-442.

(25) ibid., p. 443.

(26) ibid., pp. 461-463.

(27) ibid., p. 464.

(28) ibid., pp. 471-472.

(29) Edgar Snow, "La guerre sino-américaine", *Le Nouvel Observateur,* No. 89, 27 July 1966, p. 3.

CHAPTER 12

(1) *Peking Review,* 4 August 1967, No. 32.

(2) *Peking Review,* 2 June 1967, No. 23, p. 10.

(3) *Peking Review,* 2 June 1967, No. 23, p. 8.

(4) *Peking Review,* 19 May 1967, No. 21, pp. 6-7.

(5) *Peking Review,* 29 April 1966, No. 18, p. 5.

(6) *Peking Review,* 19 May 1967, No. 21, pp. 10-11.

(7) *Peking Review,* 2 June 1967, No. 23, p. 24.

(8) *Decision of the Central Committee of the Chinese Communist Party Concerning the Great Cultural Revolution,* F.L.P., Peking, 1966, pp. 1-12. passim. *Peking Review,* 5 August 1966, p. 12.

(9) *Hongqi/Renmin Ribao,* 27 April 1968, quoted by *Peking Review,* 5 May 1968, No. 19.

(10) *Peking Review,* 2 June 1967, No. 23, p. 19.

(11) *Peking Review,* 8 July 1966, No. 28, and 26 May 1967, No. 22.

(12) Talks at the Yenan Forum on Literature and Art, *Selected Works,* Vol. III, pp. 69-97, passim.

(13) *Peking Review,* 1968, No. 5.

(14) *Peking Review,* 25 October 1968, No. 43.

(15) *Peking Review,* 5 May 1968, No. 19.

CONCLUSION

(1) "The Foolish Old Man Who Removed the Mountains", *Selected Works,* Vol. III, pp. 321-322.

(2) "Serve the People", *Selected Works,* Vol. III, pp. 227-228.

(3) The article is dated 2 December 1939, at the beginning of World War II.

(4) "In Memory of Norman Bethune", *Selected Works,* Vol. II, pp. 337-338.
(5) See Lenin, "Communism", *Collected Works,* Russ. ed., Moscow, 1950, Vol. XXXI, p. 143, quoted in "Problems of Strategy in China's Revolutionary War", *Selected Works,* Vol. I, p. 251, note 10.

The poem *K'unlun* appears in: Mao Tse-tung, *Poems,* Peking, F.L.P. The translation by Michael Bullock and Jérôme Ch'én, appears in Jérôme Ch'én, *Mao and the Chinese Revolution,* with 37 poems by Mao Tse-tung, Oxford University Press, 1965.

References and sources

Mao Tse-tung's writings reproduced or quoted in this book are mainly taken from official Peking publications in English (Foreign Languages Press). The only other sources are a number of passages translated from the Chinese by Stuart Schram and published in his *The Political Thought of Mao Tse-tung,* Pall Mall Press, London, 1963, and in his *Mao Tse-tung,* Penguin, London, 1966.

In presenting the historical context to Mao Tse-tung's writings before 1935, the author mainly consulted the books of Edgar Snow, *Red Star Over China,* Gollancz, London, 1937; Stuart Schram, *The Political Thought of Mao Tse-tung,* Pall Mall Press, London, 1963, and *Mao Tse-tung,* Penguin, London, 1966; Lucien Bianco, *Les origines de la révolution chinoise,* Paris, Gallimard, 1967; Jacques Guillermaz, *La Chine populaire,* Paris, P.U.F., 1965; Roger Lévy, *La Chine,* P.U.F., 1964; and also Hu Chiao-mu's work: *Thirty Years of the Communist Party of China,* Foreign Languages Press, Peking, 1951.

Index

of the Proletariat", 245; retains
Party leadership only, 247;
attacks re-emergence of bourgeois tendencies in the countryside, 249–50; his "On Khrushchev's Phoney Communism and
Its Historical Lessons for the
World", 255–8; his "On Questions of Strategy in the Anti-
Japanese Guerrilla War", 263,
283; begins Cultural Revolution,
265; on the Cultural Revolution,
266–7, 268–71, 273–8; swims in
the Yangtze, 268; his "Introductions to Talks at the Yenan
Forum on Literature and Art",
275, 287; his "In Memory of
Norman Bethune", 287, 290–92;
his "Serve the People", 287,
289–90; his "The Foolish Old
Man Who Removed the Moun-
tains", 287, 288–90; importance
of his thought, 292–4
Mao Tse-tung's writings,
"Analysis of Classes in Chinese
Society", 42
"Chinese Revolution and the
Chinese Communist Party,
The", 160–66
"Cigarette Tax, The", 38, 39
"Foolish Old Man Who Re-
moved the Mountains, The",
287, 288–90
"Great Union of Popular Masses,
The", 32–4
"In Memory of Norman
Bethune", 287, 290–92
"Introductions to Talks at the
Yenan Forum on Literature
and Art", 275, 287
K'unlun, 19–20
"On Coalition Government",
174
"On Contradiction", 120, 154n

"On Correcting Mistaken Ideas
in the Party", 83–4
"On Khrushchev's Phoney Com-
munism and Its Historical
Lessons for the World", 255–8
"On New Democracy", 160,
166–71
"On Practice", 120, 154n
"On Protracted War", 156–9,
283
"On Questions of Strategy in
the Anti-Japanese Guerrilla
War", 263, 287
"On the Correct Handling of
Contradictions Among the
People", 185–93
"On the Historical Experience
of the Dictatorship of the
Proletariat", 245
"On the Problem of Agricultural
Co-operation", 184n
"Peking Coup d'Etat and the
Merchants, The", 38–9, 195
"Problems of Strategy in China's
Revolutionary War", 96–118,
289
"Report on an Investigation of
the Peasant Movement in
Hunan", 53–64
Selected Works, 12
"Serve the People", 287, 289–90
"Single Spark can Start a
Prairie Fire, A", 85–90
"Statement calling on the
People of the World to Unite
to Oppose Racial Discrimina-
tion by U.S. Imperialism and
Support the American Negroes
in Their Struggle against
Racial Discrimination", 237–
40
"Statement Opposing Aggression
against South Vietnam and
the Slaughter of Its People by